Murder and Intrigue on the Mexican Border

Number Forty-Three
Elma Dill Russell Spencer Series in the West and Southwest

Andrés Tijerina, General Editor

Murder and Intrigue on the Mexican Border

Governor Colquitt, President Wilson, and the Vergara Affair

John A. Adams Jr.

Texas A&M University Press   College Station

First edition

This paper meets the requirements of ANSI/NISO Z39.48–1992
(Permanence of Paper).
Binding materials have been chosen for durability.

Library of Congress Cataloging-in-Publication Data

Names: Adams, John A., Jr., 1951– author.
Title: Murder and intrigue on the Mexican border: Governor Colquitt, President Wilson, and the Vergara affair / John A. Adams Jr.
Description: First edition. | College Station: Texas A&M University Press, [2018] | Series: Elma Dill Russell Spencer series in the West and Southwest; number forty-two | Includes bibliographical references and index.
Identifiers: LCCN 2017054474 (print) | LCCN 2017057112 (ebook) | ISBN 9781623495855 (ebook) | ISBN 9781623495848 | ISBN 9781623495848(cloth :alk. paper)
Subjects: LCSH: Mexico—History—Revolution, 1910–1920—Causes. | Mexican-American Border Region—Politics and government—20th century. | United States—Relations—Mexico. | Mexico—Relations—United States. | Vergara, Clemente, –1914—Death and burial. | Colquitt, Oscar Branch, 1861–1940. | Wilson, Woodrow, 1856-1924.
Classification: LCC F1234 (ebook) | LCC F1234 .A186 2018 (print) | DDC 972/.1—dc23
LC record available at https://lccn.loc.gov/2017054474

Maps by Anne Boykin.

Front cover photo: Texas Rangers patrol the Rio Grande. From the author's collection.

Back cover photo: Post card of the memorial procession, May 11, 1914, Brooklyn, New York. A. Dell'Ebba Photo, N.Y.

A list of titles in this series is available at the end of the book.

In memory of

Ray M. Keck Jr.
and
Dr. Francisco M. Canseco

If given the choice between Righteousness and Peace, I choose Righteousness.

—Theodore Roosevelt

Contents

Preface

The idea for *Murder and Intrigue on the Mexican Border* dates back to over four decades ago in my reading of Walter P. Webb's *Texas Rangers: Century of Frontier Defense* (1935). Deep into the book was a brief story of Texas Ranger John J. Sanders, a tale dealing with the apparent kidnapping and murder of South Texas rancher Clemente Vergara during the violent early years of the Mexican Revolution along the Rio Grande border. Over the years I have referred often to Professor Webb and sorted through his extensive collection of documents and manuscript drafts and research items at the Dolph Briscoe Center for American History and the Benson Latin American Collection, both at the University of Texas at Austin.

On moving to Laredo in the late 1980s I rekindled a fascination with the history, lore, and dynamics of the Rio Grande border region and the impact of Mexico on the evolution and legacy of Texas and border events. I began my historical journey by reading about Mexico in general and the US southern border in particular as I conducted research for a book covering the turbulent period of the Mexican peso devaluation crisis in the mid-1990s, a crisis that affected the economies, monetary policies, and growth across Latin America for over a decade. As an international banking officer traveling in Mexico I had a front row seat when compiling *Mexican Banking and Investment in Transition* (1997), written during the early years of the North American Free Trade Agreement (NAFTA). My next book turned out to be a prophetic look at the dynamics of US-Mexico border relations, expansion of offshore manufacturing, commercial logistics, and immigration trends in *Bordering the Future: The Impact of Mexico on the United States* (2006). This was followed by the first comprehensive history of Laredo on its strategic location, economic development, and commercial significance in the evolution and growth of the second oldest continuously occupied city in Texas, *Conflict and Commerce on the Rio Grande: Laredo 1784–1954* (2008).

As my research into the border region expanded, I delved into the role and significance of the Rio Grande. I examined its twin border cities, looked at the development of bridging and transportation, and gained a better understanding of the role the thin and porous boundary has meant to generations—especially relying on Paul Horgan's *The Great River: The Rio Grande in American History*. In the process, I continually returned to the mystery of the sparsely researched circumstances regarding the Vergara affair of February–March 1914. To uncover the circumstances, fate, and resulting reaction to Clemente Vergara's death and public reaction to it, I began to research the early years of the Mexican Revolution and its impact on life along the border following the abrupt exit after the four-decade-long rule of President Porfirio Díaz in 1911. The revolution—*guerra civil*—that followed can be divided into four rather distinct periods:

> July 1911–February 1913: the departure of President Díaz followed by the rise and fall of Francisco I. Madero as president
>
> February 1913–August 1914: the dictatorship of General José Victoriano Huerta Márquez, first inauguration of President Woodrow Wilson, and US military intervention at Veracruz (April 1914)
>
> August 1914–August 1917: The fall of General Huerta, power struggle among the rebelling factions, the second US intervention in northern Mexico, and eruption of war in Europe
>
> August 1917–1920: Venustiano Carranza presidency and assassination, concerns with border security, and the eventual stability under Álvaro Obregón, who would be president from 1920 to 1924

Following the exile of Porfirio Díaz, the idealist Francisco I. Madero was subsequently ousted in a bloody coup d'état by General Huerta, which sparked a revolution that engulfed a decade of unrest across Mexico and violent intrigue and death on the US-Mexico border. Mexican revolutionary factions battled for the soul and future of Mexico—making the revolution the most important epic in the country's long history—an integral internal domestic event with international implications during the bloody decade. Historian John Mason Hart notes: "The violence that swept Mexico stemmed from central issues rather than diffuse minutia[e]." The Mexican provincial elites charged that the Mexican state had attempted to undergo "a socioeconomic transformation in collusion with foreign capital without broad domestic political participation." What is often overlooked is the near constant unrest, political intrigue, and violence along the US-Mexico border.

In researching events leading up to the Vergara incident, I located vast unexamined archival materials as well as data on the period surrounding the violence on the border that seemed to have been previously neglected, such as the records of the Texas Land Office in Austin. Another rich source comprised declassified confidential correspondence and intelligence reports of the British Foreign Ministry and the German command during 1913–14 between government officials in Mexico City, Berlin, London, and Washington. Period accounts, memoirs, and journals—as noted in this book's bibliography—helped place my narrative in the context of the period. These sources and documents along with the archival material in Mexico City helped bring clarity to the seemingly unimportant incident that came close to bringing the United States to the brink of war with Mexico weeks before the first of Woodrow Wilson's meddling and two military interventions in that country—the Veracruz invasion in April 1914. The latter shot down Wilson's lofty idealistic pronouncements—and forsaking a proclaimed policy of "watchful waiting"—that he would not embark on the adventurism of the Roosevelt and Taft era of "dollar diplomacy."

The events surrounding the Vergara affair take on growing significance as a part of a broader scope and tone when seen in the light of the Mexican Revolution. A number of dynamics impacted and shaped the US response to the Mexican Revolution. The status of President Wilson's chronic health problems and questions on how they influenced his decision-making process during his first year in the White House, often neglected, is covered. Thus, the attention afforded the Vergara affair was the most extension at the highest levels of the US government. The naïveté of the Wilson administration greatly affected the extraordinary response to a single individual incident, over any concern or response to the over five hundred Americans killed during the revolutionary decade.

Thus, a closer assessment of the Vergara mystery led me to assess the first year of the Wilson administration and to reinterpret the turbulent events on the border, as well as faraway decision-making and responses from foreign capitals, in a new and revealing framework. Webb's sources in *Texas Rangers* were primarily press reports and interviews conducted by Texas Rangers and the Texas Attorney General's Office in 1914. Otherwise, few have given attention to the Vergara case, although there is a tabloid article in the *Frontier Times* (1929) and Charles H. Harris and Louis R. Sadler do review the case in *The Texas Rangers and the Mexican Revolution* (2004). While a part of the narrative, this is not a study of the Texas Rangers or purely Texas politics. *Murder and Intrigue on the Mexican Border* reinterprets the turbulent 1914 border events and places Vergara in a revealing new frame.

Acknowledgments

Along the journey to assess the dynamic events on the Texas-Mexico border during the Mexican Revolution I have been assisted by a broad cross section of individuals who provided timely advice and counsel. Expert scholarly comments and review of early drafts of the manuscript was provided by Larry D. Hill, Henry C. Dethloff, Jerry Thompson, and J. Gilberto Quezado. In Laredo, I gained insight and clarification from Odie Arambula, Bill Green, David Perez, Jim Winch, Armengol Guerra III, and archivist Joe Moreno at the Laredo Public Library.

Assistance with primary Webb County documents, Vergara family ancestry, and legal documents: Martin Villarreal, Rosa Aldape, C. C. Gonzalez, Sylvia Killeby, Margie Ramirez Ibarra, and Maria Arriza. For years, Ceci and John Keck have been a source of reasoned counsel and an ongoing means to keep me humble.

Over the years of preparation of this manuscript, David Leon Cardwell of Laredo provided timely advice and was fully engaged in tracking down documents, cemetery data, searching county records, assisting in locating photographs, and details on legal land ownership deeds near Palafox. His search in Laredo, Nuevo Laredo, Mexico City, and San Antonio as well as a review of the Texas Land Office records on the status of lands along the Rio Grande proved critical to this project. I cannot thank David enough for years of friendship.

In Mexico, a number of individuals and archives gave freely of their time and resources to assist in locating rare revolutionary-era documents and data needed to complete the story. In Mexico City, Lic. Francisco Rodriquez Silva reviewed an early draft, making timely suggestions and referring me to source material in the capital. In Nuevo Laredo, longtime friend Lic. Luis Perez Benitez proved of great help in determining the availability of documents and individuals that could assist with information.

In Austin, I mined records at the Benson Latin American Collection assisted by Adán Benavides, Adrian Johnson, and José Montelongo. Additionally, the staffs of the Briscoe American Collection and Library and the Texas State Library and Archives located important collections. At the Cushing Archives and Evans Library at Texas A&M University I am indebted to Bill Page, Anton DuPlessis, Jenny Reibenspies, Pilar Baskett, and Jonathan Marner. A very special thanks to Jay Dew and Katie Duelm for shepherding me and this project along the way.

A great amount of gratitude goes to Sherry, who continues to tolerate these ongoing projects; for her never-ending love—I am a lucky guy!

Murder and Intrigue on the Mexican Border

Introduction

On the brisk cold morning of Friday, February 13, 1914, South Texas rancher Clemente Vergara left his ranch in Webb County near Palafox along with his nephew to investigate the theft of his horses pastured on a small unclaimed island in the Rio Grande. The border region was replete with bandits and *chiveras*—smugglers. While en route the two were confronted by a Federalist captain from the cross-border military garrison at the small village on the south bank of the river, Hidalgo, Mexico. The officer asked the rancher to come to the Mexican bank of the river to arrange payment for the horses. Texas Rangers stationed in the middle border region had cautioned Vergara not to cross the river, but no Ranger was present that morning. Angry at the loss of livestock, Vergara and his nephew crossed over. There on the Mexican bank Vergara was assaulted, pistol-whipped, and dragged to high ground while his nephew hid in the tall *carrizal* (reeds) bordering the riverbanks. Vergara's *huertista* captors —followers of President Victoriano Huerta—jailed him in Hidalgo where within a couple of days he was beaten, shot, and his body left hanging in a tree.

The seemingly random act of violence, kidnapping, and murder was in fact but one of hundreds of incidents along the tumultuous US-Mexico border during the Mexican Revolution, but the Vergara murder soon exploded into an international incident. Unlike other contretemps in the region that either went unnoticed, unreported, or—in cases of crime—unsolved during these explosive-violent times, the Vergara murder raised the rancher to near martyred status. Reporting in US newspapers centered on "an American" kidnapped from Texas soil and killed in Mexico in cold blood. The public response in Texas and the demands on government officials in Washington for justice reached all the way to President Woodrow Wilson. Soon the White House was involved and escalated the interests of the United States, bent on controlling the course of the Mexican Revolution and attempting to curb a Texas governor eager to deploy Texas Rangers to Mexico to retaliate. Wilson was also concerned with limiting interference from Europe and wished to eject General Huerta from the Mexican presidency and install a rebel Constitutionalist in power from a revolutionary force led by Venustiano Carranza, the former governor of Coahuila. The revolution that had toppled the regime of Porfirio Díaz was also a revolution against decades of socioeconomic inequities and extensive American and European landholdings and commercial investment interests—the latter totaling over $2.9 billion in foreign capital investment—that dominated the economy in Mexico.[1]

The murder of South Texas rancher Clemente Vergara and the outcry that followed would play a part in eventual US military intervention in Mexico. This episode has been largely overlooked and oftentimes overshadowed for decades by reported accounts that focused on other depredations, some just as critical, yet omitting the full ramifications of the Vergara incident. The cry of injustice soon escalated into increased demands from Texans, the state governor Oscar Branch Colquitt, and Americans with interventions in Mexico to protect American citizens and property—under the guise of bringing the perpetrators to justice.

This is a presentation to convey the larger political, social, and economic dynamics engulfing the border violence and the unprepared reaction during the first year of the Woodrow Wilson administration. The president's idealism was at odds with his skills in handling international affairs and perhaps at odds with his obsession to oust provisional president Victoriano Huerta. As the revolution spread across Mexico, scores of border confrontations, arms smuggling, and incidents, some involving murder, were swept under the carpet. Thus, this book endeavors to present the details and background and wider significance of the century-old mystery surrounding the death of Texas rancher Clemente Vergara in February 1914 as well as to clarify the attitudes and actions of the Wilson administration during this turbulent period of the Mexican Revolution.[2]

I
An Ugly Problem

I lie awake at night praying that the most terrible may be averted. No man can tell what will happen while we deal with a desperate brute like that traitor, Huerta. God save us from the worst!

—Woodrow Wilson
November 2, 1913

Díaz and Madero

President Porfirio Díaz had promised progress and stability yet slowly turned toward a progressively authoritarian regime that catered to foreign investors. By the Centennial Celebration of Mexico's independence, factions within factions, at both the local and national levels, vied for political and military control of the nation. Unlike the iron-fisted control by the President Porfirio Díaz government, successor central government officials in Mexico City were unable to either coerce or command the support of the many competing domestic factions. The vast majority of the population of fifteen million wanted change after the heavy-handed Díaz administration. And change did not diminish the hopes of those who harbored grand ideas for social change, landownership reform, and elite power and wealth.[1]

In the wake of the fall of Porfirio Díaz, an interim provisional government headed by Francisco León de la Barra approved by the congress was short-lived and collapsed as enthusiastic support and the presidency were bestowed on the primary leader of the Mexican Revolution, thirty-seven-year-old Francisco Ignacio Madero. His subsequent election to the presidency in late 1911 was undisputed. While reputedly a man of principle and kindness, Madero became overwhelmed by his nervousness and inability to delegate responsibility to capable subordinates. Charges of nepotism led to his losing trust with the people and provided a catalyst for hostile internal opposition. The president's brother, Gustavo, was considered by many to be the power behind the throne along with a very dedicated group of friends and advisors known as the "Porra"—"the political black hand."[2]

In 1913, Mexico was in the third year of a bloody revolution and civil war, which would go on for another seven years. Political unrest swept the nation from the halls of the capitol in the Federal District to the huts of campesinos in the most remote regions of the country. Eighty percent of the populace was illiterate, so Madero's lofty ideals of bestowing universal democratic rights was not conveyed to the people and proved wanting. As historian Enrique Krauze noted, he put all his "faith in the capacity of the people to govern themselves with serenity and wisdom." He surrounded himself with both family and so-called supporters, whose lofty grand presidential goals did not match his, and he alienated key business interests (both domestic and foreign investors). The federal army, political opposition, and the landed aristocracy set the stage for the inevitable counterrevolution. By mid-1913, discontent for President Madero evolved into numerous secret plans, not for recall or resignation, but for a coup d'état. Scattered armed uprising in Mexico City had been crushed, the last headed by Félix Díaz, a nephew of Don Porfirio. In the only meeting between the ousted Díaz (exiled to Cuba) and the idealistic Madero, the old president cautioned, "Señor, a man must be more than honest to govern Mexico." Yet, Madero, the "quixotic," seemed oblivious and naive to the plotting and rumors of unrest and impending dangers. He considered any reports of such treasonous action by enemies of his administration as "incredible."[3]

The William Howard Taft administration in Washington placed—with the revision of the US Arms Embargo Statute of 1898—an arms and munitions shipment prohibition (embargo) on Mexico in March 1912 and became increasingly concerned. While at first Taft was supportive of the transition of power to Madero, apprehension mounted as the Mexican president became more vocal about limiting the foreign commercial investment privileges American industry enjoyed over the past forty years. The primary protagonist in shifting official opinion in Washington was the

US ambassador to Mexico, Henry Lane Wilson.[4] His detailed cables to Washington painted a shift in attitude and questioned the viability of the Madero presidency. In Mexico since 1908, following seven years of diplomatic service in Chile, Wilson was the de facto dean of the Diplomatic Corps in Mexico City. Ambassador Wilson's primary job was to represent the United States and to promote and protect the so-called Taft policy of "dollar diplomacy" along with the growing interests of American investments in Mexico. Connected closely with American business interests and market entry, including for example, the extensive Guggenheims' American Smelting and Refining Company investment interests in Mexico, the ambassador gradually encountered a strained relationship with the Madero family members and radical cabinet members who wished to supplant US commercial concerns for personal gain where possible.

Ambassador Henry Lane Wilson, a seasoned diplomat, became a leading figure in the transition of government from President Francisco Madero and General Victoriano Huerta during the uprising of 1913. Author's collection.

The American embassy and residence of Ambassador Henry Wilson was the center of diplomatic intrigue and power. This is where the foreign diplomatic corps organized a response in the days after the violent overthrow of President Francisco Madero. Author's collection.

The Madero family business interests in mining, ranching, and smelting were a direct competitor to US companies in Mexico. Ambassador Wilson's diplomatic dispatches to Washington became increasingly alarmist as he detailed the rising discontent across the country among rival factions, ranging from inept governance and graft to the safety of US citizens increasingly in grave danger. In questioning the Mexican government's ability to enforce diplomatic protection, Wilson stocked the US embassy with arms and munitions to withstand a possible attack by radical anti-American elements. To be armed and prepared to protect the embassy staff and families was a prudent action in the war-torn country. Ambassador Wilson, on behalf of American creditors, demanded the settlement of outstanding claims against Mexico be resolved. Much of the debt and claims dated from the ousted Díaz administration. Wilson further confronted the Madero government with a growing list of Americans known killed due to lawlessness and the lack of protection. No satisfying answers were forthcoming. And the tensions soon grew to a climax.[5]

The Pacto

President Taft received a great deal of protest from border state governors and residents concerning the violence and eroding economic conditions.

The ease in crossing arms into Mexico and the ability of rebels to use Texas as a safe harbor to plan incursions into Mexico caused Texas governor Oscar B. Colquitt to assume an active role in the evolving hostile situation south of the border. Prior to entering the governorship, Colquitt, a former newspaper publisher and Texas railroad commissioner (1903–11), became increasingly involved as tensions and violence grew. All parties with business interests and family were close observers of events on the border and the reaction by the governor. Throughout 1911, Colquitt watched as attacks and threats raged in Ciudad Juárez across the Rio Grande from El Paso. In early May 1911, cross-border hostilities originating in Juárez, resulted in stray bullets that left six killed and fifteen wounded. Colquitt protested to Washington that action was needed to protect Texas citizens. The Taft administration responded by pressing Colquitt to take a stronger role in assisting the enforcement of the federal neutrality laws. The governor, with the support of Texas' US senator Joseph W. Bailey, replied he would take matters into his own hands if the federal government did not provide additional support for the expansion of the Texas Rangers. Tensions continued to escalate. In response to a threat from hostile forces on the border in Matamoros, Mexico, the governor activated Texas National Guard units to proceed to Brownsville. Once there, the troops were not needed as the threat slowly evaporated.[6]

Knowing full well that arms and munitions flowed with ease across numerous spots along the border, Colquitt met with President Taft in September 1911. The governor agreed to give increased support to the neutrality enforcement in exchange for new federal funding to put additional US Customs agents and Texas Rangers on the southern border. Colquitt further stressed that the lawlessness extended beyond the border. Texas investors in Mexico became prime targets for the roving *revolucionarias* attacking property. For example, East Texas lumber magnet John H. Kirby requested and gained the support of Colquitt to contact President Madero to address the damages to his extensive mining operations in Ojuelos, Jalisco. The governor's role in the enforcement of the neutrality law along the border soon resulted in both political and personal conflicts of interest. On the one hand, he wanted the violence to be curbed, yet on the other the governor felt the agents of the federal government and the US Army did little to forcefully assist in curbing the smuggling and unrest.[7]

Shortly after the governor's meeting with President Taft, a member of Colquitt's staff, Francisco A. Chapa, formerly a San Antonio pharmacist and Democratic Party activist, met at the governor's office in Austin with former Madero general Bernardo Reyes, who was ordered deported from Mexico. Details of the meeting are vague, but the intent was to get the governor's ear on plans to launch "rebellious" actions from Texas into Mexico. Reyes established a provisional headquarters in San Antonio, and his supporters set up operational groups in Laredo, Brownsville, Eagle Pass, and El Paso. In each of the border cities they gathered recruits, arms, and supplies. Laredo soon became a hotbed of anti-Madero activity. Under the watchful eye of Amador Sanchez, the former mayor of Laredo (1900–1911) and current Webb County sheriff, the *reyistas* coup invasion planners operated out of the county jail in downtown Laredo. Detailed plans were in process for invading Mexico along with stockpiling arms and munitions. Their activities, in clear violation of the neutrality laws, were monitored by both the US Bureau of Investigation (BOI) and Mexican government agents. As concern of Reyes's movement and intentions grew in Texas, a formal complaint from an indignant Madero to Taft resulted in sending additional US federal agents to monitor border activities. Colquitt cooperated by sending additional Texas Rangers to Laredo only as observers.

In mid-November, Bernardo Reyes, Sanchez, and Chapa, along with a number of co-conspirators, were arrested by US Marshals and indicted on federal charges for violation of US neutrality laws. General Reyes posted bond and jumped bail and immediately crossed the Rio Grande back to Mexico. Reyes attempted to launch a counterrevolution from Nuevo Leon but was captured on Christmas morning by Federal Rurales. President Madero, who by law could have him shot on treason charges, instead sent him to Santiago Tlatelolco Prison in Mexico City. What is not known of the Reyes incident is whether Governor Colquitt, most likely duped by political supporters Chapa and Sanchez, had unwittingly supported the overthrow of President Madero.[8]

Sheriff Sanchez, Chapa, and a Colquitt staff member were tried in January 1912 on multiple federal counts of the neutrality laws and were found guilty on all charges. Each paid a small fine and returned to their jobs. Although Colquitt's behind-the-scenes indirect dealings with Reyes, Chapa, and Sanchez, as well as the governor's staff's involvement in the Reyes coup, were exposed during the trial, the governor remained focused on the border hostilities and continued his outspoken concerns about the Taft administration's reactions to the festering violence on the

Francisco I. Madero assumed power as president of Mexico following the abdication of Don Porfirio Díaz. His efforts to consolidate power in the country resulted in unrest and a violent coup d'état fomented by General Huerta. Author's collection.

border. For the balance of the year, the governor become more concerned with the actions or inactions of the US Army and federal agents on the border. In response he activated units of the Texas National Guard, ordering a section of artillery to El Paso. After inspecting the border region in which most area residents were disenchanted with the response of the federal government, Texas adjutant general Henry Hutchings, reported to Colquitt, that the people are "looking to the Governor for protection." If needed, Hutchings indicated he would take any necessary action.[9]

As the border situation worsened, numerous rumors of a US military intervention swept the Mexican capital. Governor Colquitt's saber rattling in Texas and Ambassador Wilson's persistent complaining to Washington resulted in the following orders from the US State Department to the ambassador: "With the full knowledge of the President's policy and your intimate knowledge of the local situation, it is left to you to deal with the whole matter." Negotiations in Mexico City among counterrevolutionary groups never gained any footing, yet tensions rose unchecked, and on February 9 the capital city awoke to a violent civil war. General Reyes, who had avoided prosecution in Texas and the Mexican firing squad, escaped

General Victoriano Huerta and staff member Rubio Navarrete confer in February 1913 during the height of the bombardment aimed at ousting troops loyal to President Madero from their positions in the capital. Author's collection.

from prison in downtown Mexico City, along with Félix Díaz, nephew of Don Porfirio Díaz. The two rallied anti-Madero troops and rebels for an assault on the National Palace. In the frontal attack, Reyes became one of the first killed in the cuartelazo (coup), while Díaz retreated to an old military fortress, the Ciudadela. Ten days of door-to-door fighting and artillery bombardments among competing factions erupted in downtown Mexico City, then a city of some 450,000 inhabitants. The area of most action was located between Chapultepec Castle and the Zócalo facing the National Palace.[10]

Decena Trágica

The battle resulted in over eight thousand military and noncombatant casualties and was remembered as Decena Trágica. By February 18, 1913, General Victoriano Huerta outmaneuvered a number of rivals to capture the presidential palace, ordered the arrest of Madero and Vice President José María Pino Suárez and assumed the role as the supreme commander and provisional president in a secret deal brokered with Félix Díaz and Henry Lane Wilson at the US embassy. There is considerable evidence that Wilson, sublimely confident in his own unaided sagacity, knew about twenty-four hours in advance of the general details of Huerta's plans for a coup. Ambassador Wilson on February 19, accompanied by the German and Spanish ministers, met with "provisional president" Huerta to strongly request the government assurance that the life of Madero would be spared, which assurance was given. Thus, the Pacto de la Ciudadela, or better known as the Pacto de la Embajada, sealed Madero's overthrow and fate with the implied blessings of the United States ambassador.[11]

With the US interest foremost, Wilson called a meeting of the foreign diplomatic corps in the capital to urge recognition of the new government. Pressing for a speedy resolution of the hostilities, the diplomats gave carte blanche approval to Ambassador Wilson to act on their behalf. Most of them believed Washington would support Wilson and respond in kind. The plan brokered by the ambassador was for an interim federal government pending a nationwide presidential election. Huerta, as well as some seventeen members of the diplomatic corps, assumed he had de facto US recognition due to Ambassador Wilson's extensive involvement. Yet the Taft administration *never* officially recognized Huerta. Wilson's primary aim was to send a clear message to the British, German, Spanish, and French diplomatic representatives that the United States was in

The "Decena Trágica"—ten days of fighting in central Mexico City—was located at the Zócolo and Palacio National, guarded by the mounted troops loyal to General Huerta. Author's collection.

full control and expected no outside meddling in the internal affairs of Mexico. Huerta's role was to be the temporary head of state until national elections were held and foreign citizens and property were to be safe-guarded. Ambassador Wilson had struck a deal with the devil.[12]

By February 18, 1913, General Huerta formerly declared himself the supreme commander of the armed forces and president. And just before midnight, in a brief, bold, and blunt cable, Washington was informed:

> General Huerta to the President [Taft]
> /telegram/ Mexico
> February 18, 1913
>
> I have the honor to inform you that I have overthrown this Government. The forces are with me, and from now on peace and prosperity will reign.
>
> Your obedient servant,
> VICTORIANO HUERTA

An unsettled calm fell over Mexico City in the immediate days following General Huerta's coup. The general was both conciliatory and cautious with the Corps Diplomatique as his supporters moved rapidly to occupy the key offices of the national government, the central bank, railroad stations, and military garrisons. Ambassador Wilson, the dean of the diplomatic corps, in order to restore calm decided to continue with a long-planned unveiling of a large monument in white marble on February 22 of George Washington at the Glorieta Plaza de Dinamarca. Edith O'Shaughnessy noted in her memoirs, "President Huerta gave a short address and Mr. Wilson made one of his finest speeches—a happy combination of Stars and Stripes and Eagle and Cactus." Following a reception at the American embassy attended by Huerta, a number of ministers in the new cabinet were formally presented to the diplomatic corps by Foreign Minister León de la Barra. All appeared calm.[13]

Once in power, Huerta—noted by one observer as the most "sinister figure" of the Mexican Revolution—had no intention of being controlled by either Ambassador Wilson or the United States government. The grotesque treachery of the coup began with the death of Madero and his vice president, José María Pino Suárez, reportedly shot late on the night of February 22 "attempting to escape." Such acts, permitted and sanctioned under Mexican law and known as *ley de fuga*, were merely a euphemism for murder. As the martyr of the revolution, Madero attained stature in death he never enjoyed in life. While Huerta, referred to by many as *el chacal*—the jackal, was never directly connected in the murders, he was blamed for not providing adequate protection for their safety after assuring the foreign diplomatic corps that Madero and the vice president would be spared. Had they lived, he too might have survived a longer term as president.[14]

General Huerta proclaimed control of the country except the far northern states along the US border. In fact, he controlled far less of Mexico, but he did hold the capital, critical rail centers, and the most populous cities.[15] Forces loyal to the new government fanned out to eliminate any opposition. Over the protest of the Mexican Congress, Huerta seized the Hacienda (Treasury Department) and sent his representatives to take control of the Customs Office, a key source of revenue for the government. He also ordered increased armed patrols at banks and railroad stations. General Félix Díaz, who wanted to be the primary candidate for the presidency in the fall of 1913, avoided yet another firing squad and was sent (exiled) to Tokyo as the official representative of the Mexican Republic. Viewed as Huerta's personal betrayal, Díaz got no nearer to Japan than Paris, where he told friends he did not want to be too far from Mexico in case he had to return to stand for the presidency. In fact, his appointment to Japan was unceremoniously rejected by the Japanese imperial government. Huerta replaced the discredited Díaz with former provisional president and interim foreign minister Francisco León de la Barra, who arrived in Tokyo at Christmas to a grand ceremony and welcome.[16]

General Huerta's military and political domain included much of Mexico he did not or could not control. The northern frontier of Mexico comprised the states of Nuevo León, Tamaulipas, Coahuila, Chihuahua, and Sonora and the then Northern Territory, now Baja California. Their remoteness from the Federal District by some one thousand miles was only surpassed by the fierce independent nature of its people. During the balance of 1913 and through early 1914 the *norteños*—"men of the north"—would disavow the bloody Huerta dictatorship; to first independently and then

El Primero Jefe V. Carranza became the de facto leader of the opposition revolutionary groups against General Huerta. He called for the elimination of the arms embargo yet strongly protested against any form of armed intervention by the US Army or Navy. Library of Congress.

via loose agreement unite under the Constitutionalist banner—so called because the movement wanted to restore the "constitutional" order violated by Huerta—to reestablish a legitimate government for Mexico. The titular head of the anti-Huerta coalition was a fifty-five-year-old, bespectacled, white-bearded landowner—hacendado—and Madero supporter, a Coahuila state governor—Venustiano Carranza. Having no legal claim to the presidency, absent an election, he consolidated his political and military support across the north and took the title of First Chief of the Constitutionalist Army. Carranza's initial step was to outline his "Plan of Guadalupe" to restore the Mexican Constitution of 1857. He named pro-Constitutionalist governors and alcaldes, yet the power during this phase of the revolution was vested in the military leaders in each northern Mexican state. Carranza was in control of Coahuila as well as the northern border states along the Rio Grande in Nuevo León and Tamaulipas (with small garrisons of Federalist troops still partial to Huerta in Matamoros, Nuevo Laredo, Hidalgo, Ojinaga, and Piedras Negras). Roberto Pesqueira became the provisional governor of Sonora, yet the power was vested with General Álvaro Obregón. And in Chihuahua, Francisco "Pancho" Villa assumed the sole leadership of the Constitutionalists.[17]

President Taft and Secretary of State Philander C. Knox continued to receive mixed messages from Ambassador Wilson in Mexico, who badgered Washington to support the speedy recognition of Huerta and employ the possible use of US military intervention if the unrest exploded into open fighting between the many factions. Knox would not support Carranza's recognition until "assurances" from Huerta on a number of outstanding diplomatic issues on border disputes, water rights, and claims resulting in the loss of American lives and property were fully addressed. Having lost the presidential bid for reelection in late 1912, the Taft administration in the last months and weeks of its administration maintained a "hands-off" policy. The administration remained cautious on learning of rumblings from Capitol Hill that the Texas congressional delegation might force the necessity to address the growing violence and property damage in Mexico. As a precaution, the White House authorized the assembly of two thousand US Marines for transport at Guantánamo, Cuba, and ordered the US Fifth Army Brigade of five thousand troops to move to Galveston, Texas, over 150 miles from the border. Taft, Knox, and Secretary of War Henry L. Stimson were well aware of the increasing pressure from Governor Colquitt (who sent the Texas militia troops in force to Brownsville as a precaution) and border residents in Texas to take action. A request from Governor Colquitt to allow the Texas Rangers and Texas militia to cross the Rio Grande in "hot" pursuit of bandits or rebels was abruptly denied by the Knox State Department—to which Colquitt responded: "We will not hesitate to use State troops to protect Texas people."[18]

On February 21, 1913, Secretary Knox ordered, as an additional precaution, the stationing of six US warships off the coast of Mexico, writing the secretary of the navy a strong note of caution outlining the need for an "unoffensive [*sic*] display of naval power . . . *watchful to prevent any incident* which might provoke the use of this great power." Dispatches from US consular officers around Mexico to Secretary Knox reported rumors of protest following Madero's murder and Huerta's assumption of power. Ambassador Wilson was notified by the State Department on February 28, 1913, the "U.S. is in a *defacto* relation [with the government of Mexico] for the purpose of transacting all business," thus, "any such formal act of recognition is to be avoided just at the present."[19]

In a lengthy confidential dispatch on the evening of March 3, 1913 (sent at 7:00 p.m. and received at the State Department at 3:30 a.m. the following day), Ambassador Henry Lane Wilson tried one last time to have Taft extend full diplomatic recognition to General Huerta, a position, Wilson claimed, that was strongly supported by the American "colony" (American ex-pats and businessmen) in Mexico City and foreign business "concessions" (capital investments and ownership in business operations) across Mexico. Little did the Taft administration know, Great Britain had secretly extended recognition to Huerta on the same day, March 4, yet the official diplomatic correspondence did not reach Mexico until March 31. Furthermore, British ambassador James Bryce in Washington held a lengthy conversation with president-elect Woodrow Wilson in early March, during which Wilson wondered whether His Majesty's Government would entertain a joint US-European intervention to include the British, French, Japanese, and Germans. There is strong evidence that diplomatic counterparts in Mexico City and their business associates—Sir Francis Stronge of the United Kingdom, Ambassador Bernardo de Cólogan y Cólogan of Spain, and Admiral Paul von Hintze of Germany—influenced Ambassador Wilson's persistence for official recognition from Washington. And as one observer noted: "Taft quite properly delayed, leaving the entire complicated situation for [Woodrow] Wilson to deal with."[20]

Foreign capital investments and ownership in Mexico: mining, lumber, petroleum exploration, refining, steel, manufacturing, brewing, seaport development, railroads, cattle, banking.

Wilson: Mexico Sui Generis

At noon on March 4, 1913, there was a changing of the guard in Washington, DC, with the inauguration of the twenty-eighth president of the United States, Thomas Woodrow Wilson. By all reports the transition of power was smooth, with Secretary Knox and his staff briefing incoming secretary of state William J. Bryan on the four primary different yet integrated foreign policy situations immediately facing the new administration: (1) the revolution in Mexico, (2) overall relations with Latin America, (3) status of European attitude toward America over the Panama Canal toll issue, and (4) pending issues with Japan and China.[21] It was made clear in the transition that, "the Mexican Problem," as it was referred to by the administration was sui generis—an unique situation not like anything else. Foreign affairs were scarcely mentioned during the 1912 presidential campaign—and in the days prior to his inauguration President Wilson quipped, "It would be the irony of fate if my administration had to deal chiefly with foreign affairs."[22]

Wilson scholar Arthur Link concurred that the president had a great deal to learn even though he was considered at the time the most educated president to date and that there "were certain obvious deficiencies in Wilson's thought and training in foreign affairs. The most serious of these was his failure before 1913 to do any systematic thinking about the nature, complexities, and difficulties of foreign policy and his assumption that the main task of diplomacy was the simple one of "translating national ideals into a larger program of action." President Wilson's total distain of "dollar diplomacy" and anti-big-business views (he had never worked in the private sector or created any jobs) overshadowed any balanced or informed crafting of a realistic foreign policy in the face of rising competition primarily from European nation-states that were aggressively advancing the global commercial interest of their nations.[23]

While Taft toyed with the possibility of recognizing Huerta if certain assurances were provided, Wilson and Bryan at first review were against any formal recognition whatsoever. One complicating problem was that the State Department and White House received a great deal of conflicting information on the situation in Mexico. The primary source of the confused updates on the status of Mexico was determined to be those submitted by Ambassador Wilson in Mexico City. The alleged misinformation from Mexico City, according to Secretary of the Navy Josephus Daniels, was generally out of context and shaded toward his bias for Huerta. The ambassador in his diplomatic role representing the United States was determined to be complicit in the whole affair, and some feel he abused his credibility as one of the foremost US political experts on Mexico by sending slanted assessments. In one dispatch, he noted that a strong man like Don Porfirio could calm the unrest, backing up his claim by falsely informing Secretary Bryan that 90 percent of the Mexican people supported the Huerta presidency. And apparently there were others who felt the same way. Big business lobbied in Washington for a swift recognition. Taft and Knox departed without making a decision on Mexico and Huerta. Senator Henry Cabot Lodge, who viewed the new idealist President Wilson as self-righteous and a "pompous prig," wrote Sir Cecil

Spring Rice at the British Foreign Ministry in London shortly after the inauguration, "I hope they got a man now of the Porfirio Diaz type who will do sufficient throat-cutting to restore peace. That seems an unpleasant thing to say but it is apparently impossible to maintain order or any approach to decent government in Mexico upon any other terms."[24]

Distrustful and not knowing the full details of the role Ambassador Wilson played in the fall of Madero and the brokered support for Huerta, President Wilson permitted the ambassador to remain at his post. He reasoned this would buy time to determine the full magnitude of the dynamics unfolding in Mexico. Furthermore, to abruptly recall Lane Wilson and send a new ambassador could possibly have been viewed as tacit recognition of the Huerta regime. Further confusing a full and accurate picture of the events in Mexico were the newspaper media—in Texas, Mexico City, New York City, and Washington, DC. Media reports and printed events occurred faster than the diplomatic dispatches from Mexico could arrive at the US State Department. For example, William Randolph Hearst, who owned over a million acres of ranchland in northern Mexico, used his media empire to demand intervention to restore stability and protect American property, stating "the time for action has already come." And shortly after Wilson's inauguration, the *New York World* published a stinging series of articles in April 1913 attacking the ambassador for his questionable role in Huerta coming to power. Although these reports, later reprinted in *Harper's Weekly*, were considerably distorted, they influenced the president and Secretary of State Bryan.[25]

Wilson called his first White House cabinet meeting for 11:00 a.m. on March 7. The conversations of this first meeting, as well as subsequent cabinet meetings over the next few months, were dominated by the unrest in Mexico and increased reports of lawlessness along the border. Neither the president nor the cabinet had a coherent grasp of the magnitude of the revolution in Mexico, as well as discontent across Latin America in general. Other nations in Europe and Latin America waited and watched to see what would be the official position of the US administration toward Mexico. While all the cabinet members gave opinions, the primary players in the Mexico crisis were Secretary of State William J. Bryan—appointed as an olive branch for the Nebraskan's political backing and assistance at the Baltimore Democratic Convention—Secretary of War Lindsey M. Garrison, Postmaster General Albert S. Burleson, and Secretary of Agriculture David F. Houston, with the balance of the cabinet composed of

Secretary of the Treasury William G. McAdoo, Attorney General James C. McReynolds, Secretary of Commerce William C. Redfield, and Secretary of the Interior Franklin K. Lane. While there were different opinions on Huerta's recognition, President Wilson was clearly in charge, hearing out all comments before stating that in no way would that "usurper"—Huerta—get his blessing. Notwithstanding all the ramp-up for the new administration, appointments, and assignments—the first Democratic presidency in sixteen years—Wilson spent an inordinate amount of time on Mexico and Latin America issues during 1913 and 1914. He wanted to send a clear message of America's newfound progressive noninterventionist intentions in the Western Hemisphere.[26]

Collectively, Wilson and his cabinet knew very little about Latin America and even less about the political, economic, and social intricacies of the revolution in Mexico. While Wilson seemed a quick study on the issues, there were other dynamics of the cabinet and administration that shaped the debate. As early as mid-December 1912, the president-elect was briefed on the situation in Mexico by the Taft State Department, private-sector concerns with investments in Mexico, and the governor of Texas. Governor Colquitt, who did not endorse Wilson until after the Democratic Convention, assumed a belated role in the campaign as a statewide fund-raiser in Texas. From mid-September 1912 through Election Day much of the fund-raising was handled directly out of the governor's capitol office in Austin.[27] Colquitt was routinely in contact with future key players in the Wilson administration—William McAdoo, Henry Morgenthau, Walter H. Page, Texas Senator Charles A. Culberson, Colonel Edward House, and Tom Love of Dallas. After suggesting to McAdoo that Wilson address the do-nothing policies of the Taft administration on Mexico in stump speeches went ignored, in December 1912 Colquitt wrote to the president-elect directly on the failure of federal authorities to cooperate in dealing with the "perplexing and dangerous question" along the border. The governor noted that previous "Republican office holders" had not worked fully with border state officials. As an example, he noted that the US Army tended to be apprehensive and jealous of the Texas Rangers—"antagonistic federal appointees by Taft were out of harmony and out of sympathy with the state."[28] Wilson responded that he was most interested in the governor's comments on the Texas-Mexico border and would welcome any further observations in the situation. Thus, the new presidential appointees, several from Texas, placed in key positions in the new administration would be critical to the welfare of Texas citizens along the border and the crafting of a policy to deal with revolutionary Mexico.[29]

Colonel House

Other than the president-elect, the only man who knew and met with each new cabinet member was Colonel Edward Mandell House of Texas. History has consistently relegated House to the shadows of Wilson's administration—a presidential confidant who Texas historian Joe B. Franz called "a sort of benign Rasputin in Wilson's court." The shy, soft-spoken Texan, small in stature and dapper in dress, was from a wealthy merchant-banking family in Houston. Born and educated in Texas and in prep schools back East, House attended Cornell University, traveled throughout Europe, managed the family's large Texas landholdings, and by 1890, married and settled in Austin. Due to his friendship with Texas governor James S. Hogg, he was drawn into managing Hogg's 1892 winning reelection campaign for governor in a close, hotly contested three-way race. Intrigued by the political process, House slowly worked mostly behind the scenes to build a string of political contacts and allies across the state—known as "our crowd." Fascinated by the electoral process, he embedded with the Democratic Party in Texas and followed up the Hogg reelection campaign victory with additional Texas gubernatorial campaign management, resulting in victories for Charles A. Culberson (1894), Joseph D. Sayers (1898), and S. W. T. Lanham (1902). In 1898, he also secured the election of Culberson to the US Senate.[30]

By 1902, House departed from his active role in Texas politics to devote the next decade to investments in the oil and gas industry, banking, and railroads across Texas and Mexico. His financial commitments forced him to spend more and more time in the East, where he turned his interest to national politics. On November 24, 1911, House first met New Jersey governor Woodrow Wilson at the Hotel Gotham in New York City, and they quickly became fast friends. Disenchanted with the Democratic Party's preoccupation (and three defeats) with William Jennings Bryan atop the national ticket, Colonel House put all his efforts behind Wilson to be nominated as the 1912 Democratic presidential candidate.[31]

At the 1912 convention in Baltimore, House helped secure all forty votes of the Texas delegation to stand firm against a Tammany Hall–backed Champ Clark. His behind-the-scenes work obtained the endorsement of three-time Democratic presidential candidate William J. Bryan for the Wilson candidacy.[32] Wilson received the nomination on the forty-sixth convention ballot, and as T. R. Fehrenbach in *Lone Star* noted of House's behind-the-scenes work, "Wilson never forgot it." A confidant of Wilson throughout his presidency, House turned down any appointed position in the new administration—yet he confessed to one biographer in 1931, "I would have liked to be Governor of Texas." The colonel played the primary role in selecting the nine cabinet secretaries and hundreds of key administrative appointees. House submitted a tentative cabinet "slate to ponder over" to Wilson on January 9, 1913, and the president-elect concurred on the initial list of cabinet members on February 7. In addition to Bryan as secretary of state, Texans Albert S. Burleson, Thomas W. Gregory, David Houston, and Thomas B. Love were placed in key positions—as well as some 1,400 appointments of ambassadors, federal judges, postmasters, customs district posts, and agency heads. Furthermore, House and this group of Texans (the first ever in a presidential cabinet) would have substantial influence—though not necessarily well-informed influence—over the complexities of political affairs in Mexico and Latin America.[33]

As the policy toward Mexico developed in the Wilson administration, the Texas representation in the cabinet and its many ties to business interests in Mexico and Texas played heavily in the response to violence on the border, including the Vergara affair. In the meantime, Wilson and Bryan—both equally ignorant in foreign affairs—had no clear policy toward Mexico other than they did not intend to recognize Huerta. They both felt that to do so would be tantamount to a sign of approval of his past actions. During the early months of Wilson's presidency, tensions continued to grow among other Latin American nations as well as foreign investors in Mexico looking for protection of their operations. As one scholar notes: "Wilson aroused native resentment, enmeshed the United States in bewildering Mexican politics, and nearly brought the two nations to war. Wilson's idealism exposed the fallacy of applying a single American solution to vastly different problems . . . purporting to know what is best for others. The president's policy revealed his ill-concealed feelings of racial superiority and self-righteous paternalism"—captured in his classic statement: "I am going to teach the Latin American Republics to elect good men!"[34]

President Wilson, during the first year of his presidency, generally ignored the staff at the nepotistic US State Department and distrusted

From the first day of the new Wilson administration, the official policy of the president was not to recognize General Huerta. Wilson extended his dislike of radical government change to all the nations of Latin America: noting he wanted "good people elected." Source: *Literary Digest.*

reports from the American embassy in Mexico City and thus developed his own policy announcements. His reliance on his own judgment placed little confidence in such advice, and he often drafted and typed policy pronouncements on his portable typewriter in the president's residence on the second floor of the White House. Wilson's first efforts and plans were to introduce and maintain a neutral policy toward Mexico. In the first of three major policy statements during 1913 on Latin America in general and Mexico in particular, the president issued a statement typed by him and read to the cabinet for their review (Secretary Bryan, who had little or no role in formulating foreign policy nor anyone at the State Department had seen the document in advance), on March 11, 1913, and released directly to the press.[35]

Wilson declared, "one of the chief objectives" of his administration was "to cultivate friendships . . . based upon law, not upon arbitrary or irregular force" with the republics of Latin America. In an indirect blow at Huerta, who was not mentioned by name, the president noted, "We can have no sympathy with those who seek to seize power of government to advance their own personal interest and ambitions." Pulitzer Prize biographer of Woodrow Wilson, Arthur Walworth, noted that as Bryan sat quietly in the meetings, other cabinet members feared that the proposed statement by the president "seemed superfluous and amateurish" and insulted rather than consoled the nations of Latin America.[36]

By April, the weekly White House cabinet meetings were preoccupied, first, with the reports of violence toward Americans in Mexico, second, with whom to recognize as the legitimate government of Mexico, and, third, broad discussions on what actions should be taken in light of repeated queries from the British, Germans, and French on the administration's Mexico policy. From Mexico City, Ambassador Wilson wired Secretary Bryan urging the timely "moral support" of the new Mexican government to avoid unneeded chaos that could necessitate intervention. There was no change of heart from Washington. In addition to media coverage, official reports from the US-Mexico border were coming in through the State Department, the War Department, the BOI, the US Secret Service, and border state governors.

At the April 11 presidential cabinet meeting, Josephus Daniels, in detailed entries from his diary, captured the internal White House debate on Mexico, with Secretary of War Garrison reporting that there is a:

> serious question of the killing of Americans in the towns on the Mexican and Texas border. It seems that there are fifteen town[s] in which a street or the river only divides the Mexican and American people, and that when there is fighting between the Mexican troops [Federales] representing the Huerta government and those who deny that he is the actual president, the bullets fly over to American soil and injure, and in some instances kill American citizens.[37]

Secretary Garrison stressed, "something ought to be done," and strongly suggested that a "neutral zone" several miles wide be declared along the border as a no-man's-land where no fighting would be permitted. Given that different portions of the 1,900-mile-long border, portions of the Mexican side were held by Huerta's forces and the balance by a mix of rebel factions—there was concern for how this could be effectively accomplished and the possible likelihood for causing a full-scale intervention. The topic of US intervention, while not discussed publicly by the representatives of the Wilson administration, was discussed at length in the cabinet meetings. The Texans then weighed in, with Burleson noting that these "conditions" existed on the "frontier" for years, and any action at the border could further jeopardize Americans living in the interior of Mexico. He further cautioned that any provocation, such as Mexicans firing on US Army troops or harming border citizens, could escalate into a larger problem. Secretary David Houston, the former president of both A&M College of Texas (1902–5) and the University of Texas (1905–8), gave a blunt cold-hearted assessment of life on the US-Mexico border, which was an eye opener for those unfamiliar with the region: "a good many of the people in the [border] towns were Mexican anyhow and a good many of these people didn't belong to either country, who were mere bummers and that the country would suffer no loss if they were killed."[38] Such cavalier statements, even in the confidential confines of the presidential cabinet meeting, by the Texans had a strong impact on the perceptions of the other cabinet members as well as on how border incidents—particularly Clemente Vergara's murder—were handled by President Wilson. And in future decades, such racist attitudes fueled the reaction of current-day borderland scholars who properly note incidents of injustice inflicted on Mexicans and Tejanos alike.[39]

By early May 1913, the Wilson cabinet remained divided over recognition of the Huerta government. Colonel House urged the president to extend de facto recognition. All of the major European nations and most of Latin America had extended formal recognition to Huerta, in spite of pressure from the United States not to do so or to withdraw official status. Garrison and Lane were the leading proponents in the cabinet for recognition. Daniels, in his diary, notes two issues that at this stage would probably preclude any recognition: first, the northern states of Mexico were fully in rebellion under the Constitutionalists, and there was little or no chance they would agree; and second, and most importantly, "the general opinion in the Cabinet was that the chief cause of this whole situation in

Mexico was a contest between English and American oil companies to see which would control [the rich Mexican oil fields]."[40]

Daniels was correct in his assessment, and Wilson was naive. The swift recognition of the Huerta government by the British was directly linked to their broader strategic interests. Having converted the British Royal Fleet from coal to petroleum, the Admiralty was keen to source a cheap means of bunker oil "in sufficiently great quantities." The British enjoyed fabulous oil concessions under the Porfiriato, yet when Díaz fell, Madero annulled most of the concessions controlled by Weetman Pearson, who received a peerage from the British crown as "Lord Cowdray," and his oil conglomerate. When Huerta took power he immediately recognized and restored the British oil interests in Mexico, who responded in kind with diplomatic recognition. Huerta restored the British oil concession, and through them the general was able to obtain financing, arms, and an implied "official protection" of his new government.[41]

British investor Weetman D. Pearson, conveyed a peerage by the Queen as Lord Cowdray, fought to influence the Mexican government in order to control English investments in the growing petroleum sector. Source: *Literary Digest.*

In broader terms the viability of the vast array of so-called special concessions in oil and gas, mining, railroad, banking, and public works projects (that is, urban sewers as well as dams, electric generation, and harbors). Individual American investors in Mexico, as well as British, German, and French interests, took issue with the blanket use of the term "concessions," which implied they had been "given" land or special rights. In fact, except for the railroad, oil, and telegraph services, investors were required to buy and secure title to land and mining rights, then make extensive capital investments in equipment and technology. Except in limited partnerships with foreign firms or individuals, Mexican investors and citizens had very little participation prior to 1913 in investments of capital intensive industrial developments of natural resources. Instead, domestic Mexican investors concentrated on traditional agricultural endeavors, along with consumer production investments (primarily in Mexico City and Monterrey) such as steel, textiles, furniture, soap, cement, cigarettes, and beer factories.[42]

As Washington was coming to grips with its Mexico policy, the civil war in Mexico entered its bloodiest phase, spilling over into Texas as activist Texans endeavored to assist various factions in Mexico. Texas border towns for over a century were an ideal natural refuge and safe haven for *revoltosos* plotting insurgency and disorder south of the border. While the Constitutionalist forces quickly gained control of the countryside in the four Mexican border states, the twin cities along the border tended to sway toward the Federalists and Huerta. Groups of pro-Huerta activists in Texas crossed from Laredo on February 15, 1913, to capture Nuevo Laredo. Sheriff Sanchez and his eldest son assisted with the planning and allowed the group to stage its operation from the Webb County Court House in downtown Laredo, four blocks from the International Bridge. After two days of people fleeing across the border into South Texas, Governor Colquitt again demanded regular US Army assistance to protect the region. If the US Army would not respond, he threatened to order Texas National Guard units to move south at once. When Major Esteban Ramos the new Federalist commander of Matamoros garrison across the Rio Grande from Brownsville, Texas, threatened an American citizen, "Colquitt, with his unusual hyperbole, declared that the life of the Mexican commander would be forfeit if a single Texan were harmed." His words at once got Washington's attention. Fearing the governor might launch an attack into Mexico, the federal government at once dispatched troops to Brownsville.

The Texas governor was not bluffing. Harassed by the pro-Huerta council in San Antonio claiming that Texans and arms were crossing the river to fight with the rebels, Colquitt replied that the state did not have the resources or authority to enforce the neutrality laws. And unable to get any clear assurances from Mexico City or Washington, DC, on border security matters, Colquitt and Carranza in May 1913 exchanged letters to cooperate on all international matters and incidents affecting Texas and Coahuila.[43]

Thus, the first days and weeks of the Wilson administration were a confusing time for the president, inhibiting the creation of a clear foreign policy toward Mexico. An untested administration was met with a combination of nonprofessional diplomatic fores: a distrust of the holdover professional staff of the Taft Department of State, pressure from foreign capitals for the United States to clearly state its intentions with regard to the recognition of General Huerta, and a growing discontent with the violence along the Mexican border. The cabinet, largely handpicked by Colonel House, was further ignorant of the magnitude of the violent civil war in Mexico. They also did not understand the alternative motives of the British and Germans to secure strategic oil reserves, and the magnitude of the Panama Canal Toll dispute and its lasting military and political implications. This ignorance and misunderstanding resulted in the cabinet oftentimes providing misinformed personal observations and advice to the president. Postmaster General Burleson confirmed the critical role of the military and political forces in northern Mexico in the final outcome and reconfirmed that the border was still in dangerous upheaval. Additionally, Josephus Daniels noted in his diary that Burleson "told a horrible story of a young man whom he knew well, employed by an American railroad company in Mexico, who sometime last fall was surveying for a new line for the railroad and was taken by the *Insurrectos* who cut his head off and the body was shipped to Cincinnati . . . this recital of the horrible and murderous thing shocked the Cabinet."[44]

By spring 1913, Secretary David Houston captured the essence of the situation facing President Woodrow Wilson: "Mexico loomed . . . as an ugly problem."[45]

2
Seven Other Devils

The attitude of the President in Mexican affairs has been, from the origin of the difficulties there, that he understood the situation and that no one else did . . . this mental obsession he has clung in spite of an absolute collapse of his policy . . . and disastrous consequences.

—Henry Lane Wilson
US Ambassador to Mexico, 1909–13

As the situation in Mexico deteriorated, President Woodrow Wilson and his cabinet remained hesitant to determine a solution and were perplexed as to the course of action needed. Wilson distrusted the American ambassador in Mexico City and discounted the State Department's role, and furthermore the president usurped even his own secretary of state to craft foreign policy in a vacuum. Therefore, there was no clear Mexican policy. Restless foreign interests, especially those from Great Britain and Germany, were increasingly irritated and expressed concern about the lack of resolve from Washington on the protection of their investment interests and citizens in Mexico. Total multinational investments in Mexico exceeded $2.9 billion in 1913, with the United States accounting for about $1.3 billion and the British $1.1 billion, and the balance divided among Germany, Spain, France, and the Netherlands.[1] This growing foreign direct investment in Mexico, known as "concessions," had vastly expanded during the Porfirio Díaz administration, when near carte blanche was given to foreign development. The investment had indeed lifted the country's sluggish economy, but that came at the cost of abdicating much of Mexico's richest resources, railroad, seaport development, and telecommunications to foreign expropriation. Foreign investors controlled 97 percent of mining and more than 90 percent of the petroleum sector as well as the railroad and harbor facilities. In addition to billions in capital investments, the United States composed nearly 80 percent of cross border foreign trade in goods and services, leading one observer to note, "Mexico had become an economic satellite of the United States."[2]

The *Yale Review* chronicled a pointed view of foreign residents and investments in Mexico, found among the papers of Francisco Madero in the Benton Latin American Collection in Austin under the title on "La Hipocresia del Presidente Wilson":

> Over 100,000 Europeans and Americans live in Mexico and not one of them is a citizen of the republic, not one of them is there for his health. Banking, mining, plantations, water power, manufacturing, and railroads are largely in the name of this class. It's only lack is a stable government—can this be obtained except through someone like Diaz—another ruler by terror and by Force?

This vast corporate interest by US companies and individual investors in Mexico was a major stumbling block to Wilson's outspoken disgust with the "dollar diplomacy" tactics of the Taft administration—given the fact the president's stated promise during the campaign to the middle-class voters was to reel in large domestic corporate trusts. Little did Wilson know, the first major challenge to his progressive platform would be in the international realm and not in domestic issues. A number of factors concerned Wilson on how his administration should proceed. The big money corporate interests had been critical to his campaign financing and victory. Many viewed the election as skewed, given the fact that three candidates, Wilson, Roosevelt, and Taft, split the national vote and there was no winner with a clear majority in the popular vote. This assessment was based on the fact Wilson only had 42 percent of the popular vote, yet captured 435 of the 531 Electoral College votes. Notwithstanding, foreign events would, as Colonel Edward House correctly warned, shape the domestic agenda.[3]

The complicated situation Wilson faced in Mexico needs to be fully revealed to understand his policy process. Friedrich Katz, in his book *The Secret War in Mexico*, captures the underlying dynamics and lobbying that influenced Wilson's actions:

> The driving forces and motivations behind Wilson's Mexico policy remain to this day one of the most disputed questions in American

> history. In the view of many European diplomats of the time, many of his political opponents, and some historians, Wilson was an agent of the large American companies whose interests he wished to promote. In the eyes of his supporters and other historians, he appeared to be attempting to push through an idealist policy against the will of all U.S. business interest involved in Mexico.[4]

Compelling evidence exists that US corporate and foreign investment interests weighed in heavily both privately and diplomatically with the Wilson White House in hopes of settling the civil war in Mexico and protecting US influence and investments across the country. By early May, those with substantial interests in banking, oil and gas production, railroads, and mining were pivotal to the status of the Mexican government, which each day seemed to hinge on the US response for recognition. In the banking sector a great deal of anxiety revolved around the June 1913 renewal of a $10 million (at 4.5 percent interest) loan to Mexico. Those opposed to the Huerta government—primarily the United States government—argued any new or renewed loans needed to be secured by a "recognized" government. If not, a default could result in disorder and a call for prepayment by creditors. The United States wanted to avoid the need for intervention such as occurred in the early stage of the French intervention in Mexico in 1862. While not necessarily military intervention, a show of force to occupy the customhouses would allow a revenue source to cover the outstanding debt.[5]

Secretly, foreign banking representatives, with the implied knowledge and unofficial support of their respective governments in London, Paris, and Berlin, all individually negotiated with Mexico City to approve a short-term bridge loan to Mexico to support the Huerta government. It had been rumored that US ambassador Henry Lane Wilson supposedly supported this action. Unable to reach an agreement, the financial ramifications of Mexican default were further compounded when it was reported that representatives of American, British, German, and French banks met secretly in Paris and resolved that stability in the Mexican financial markets would come only from American intervention. Furthermore, a major signal of US corporate interests stepping forward to represent their investments in Mexico occurred in May 1913 when, with the assistance of Colonel House, a large group American executives and leading concessionaires in Mexico requested an audience with the White House.[6]

The meeting included some of the most powerful American industrial leaders of the era. The group was led by railroad magnate Julius Kruttschnitt of the Southern Pacific Railroad, developer of one of the principle lines across the US border states and into Mexico, Edward L. Doheny of Mexican Petroleum Company, the owner of over 620,000 acres in Mexico and vast oil and mining interests; Cleveland H. Dodge of Phelps, Dodge and Company, a classmate of Wilson at Princeton and one of the leading contributors to Wilson's 1912 campaign; and representatives of the Greene Cananea Copper Company of Sonora, Mexico. Other powerful financial interests bringing pressure on the White House included John Speyer, of Speyer and Company, a financial intermediary and large holder of Mexican bond debt; and E. N. Brown, president of the National Railways of Mexico. Wall Street contacts with both Secretary William McAdoo and Henry Morgenthau (treasurer of the Democratic National Committee) increased pressure on the administration for the need for action.[7]

In a detailed brief prepared for the president, the "big interests" presented their case for an action plan to calm the unrest in Mexico. In order to insure stability and the transition of the government, they noted that it was not necessary that Huerta be required to resign due to the fact that regardless of the White House's position—Huerta was presently the de facto president. They were clearly aware that Wilson and the Constitutionalists in northern Mexico under Carranza steadfastly refused any form of recognition. Furthermore, they argued that foreign nations were undermining the influence of the United States: "If Mexico is helped out of her troubles by the British and German influence, the American prestige will be destroyed in that country and the commerce of the United States will suffer untold loss and damage." Of further consideration was the opening of the Panama Canal. The United States had a broader interest in maintaining stability throughout Latin America. Thus, the Wilson transition plan for Mexico called for: (1) some form of temporary recognition for Huerta, (2) the US government to prevail upon Carranza to halt fighting in the north, and (3) at once to call for a presidential election in October 1913 to choose a "constitutional" president. Finally, Carranza's refusal to negotiate with Huerta would have to be overcome with two items: first, by Mexican law a president could not run for back-to-back terms, thus removing Huerta, and second, Carranza might like to be president.[8]

Close political advisors House and Dodge, who acknowledged and abhorred Huerta's grab for power, urged the president to move forward with this proposal. Again, the president, without consulting Bryan or the State Department (even though John Bassett Moore, legal counsel at State, provided a detailed and compelling background on US de facto recognition policy dating back to Thomas Jefferson), sat down at his personal typewriter and prepared a note based on the recommendations of Colonel House and industrial leaders to Ambassador Wilson to present to General Huerta. However, at the last minute he reconsidered, and the draft was voided and never sent to Mexico City. Recognition of Huerta was to President Wilson the core of the problem. Compounding his decision was the fact that he deemed Huerta "arrogant and dictatorial." Moreover, he doubted Huerta would carry out the plan in good faith, and he distrusted Ambassador Wilson. Another looming concern, if President Wilson at this late date were to recognize Huerta, was that he would only strengthen the dictator's hand and enhance the British and German investment and trade interests across the country. During the late May cabinet meetings, several members, according to Secretary David Houston, continued to oppose Wilson and Bryan in favor of recognition.[9]

Cabinet debate on recognition was fueled by a State Department memorandum on the historical practice of the United States treatment of diplomatic action regarding de facto foreign governments. The briefing, prepared by State legal counselor John Bassett Moore, bluntly noted: "The Government of the United States having originally set itself up by revolution, has always acted upon the *de facto* principle. We regard governments as existing or not existing. We do not require them to be chosen by popular vote," and that under no circumstances did the United States have the right to supervise the foreign relations of other Western Hemisphere countries. The agreement for recognition became more persuasive as seventeen nations extended recognition to Huerta, and additionally the United States had conducted de facto relations with Huerta for many months.[10] President Wilson appreciated the candor from Moore but was not swayed, remarking to Colonel House that the State Department's staff was wrapped up in legalizations and corrupted by their experience with dollar diplomacy. At the same time, the sanctimonious Secretary Bryan, who outlawed the serving of alcoholic drinks at all State functions, was to consult with the British and the French on their governments' status on loans to Mexico. He warned the European ambassadors in Washington, DC, that they, or any of their national banks, were to avoid banking with the Huerta government and if they did, the United States "could not enforce a loan guaranteed by [expecting] a pledge of [Mexican] customs duties." Furthermore, if additional pressure was warranted, Wilson ordered Bryan to be ready to extend the Monroe Doctrine to preclude "financial intervention" by Europeans in the Americas.[11]

Throughout the April–May 1913 debates at the White House, at no time were the large Wall Street business interests led by Kruttschnitt maligned or criticized for meddling. One observer notes, "Sometimes, for him [Wilson], American businessmen abroad were selfish predators; sometimes he saw them as bearers of American ideals."[12] House, Dodge, McAdoo, Houston, and Burleson assured the president the Wall Street interests were critical of a solution. To increase an already confused picture, Senator Albert B. Fall of New Mexico, a not-so-subtle spokesman for American oil companies and private investment in northern Mexico, broached the need for American armed intervention to solve all Mexico's problems. And if not intervention, Senator Fall called for an open border policy for all combatants to freely import munitions and arms. In response to his vocal stance on Mexico, the senator was accused a number of times by the Mexican government of smuggling arms and dynamite to the rebels under the ruse of mining supplies. By summer, the business coalition agreed to abstain from any mention of recognition, but strongly urged the administration's use of "its good offices" to bring about an election and urge all parties to forgo fighting. The culmination of May's activities, dominated by Mexican affairs, was about to take a new turn.[13]

"A Confidential Man"

The concerns and proposals of big business and President Wilson's ongoing mistrust of information from the State Department in general and Ambassador Lane Wilson in particular resulted in Wilson creating his own eyes and ears in Mexico to get the "right" information. Wilson, an idealist to the core, was introverted, secretive, puritanical, and not trusting of those he did not know (such as the holdover Republication appointees in the State Department). This pattern of dealing in the shadows had been well established from his days as president of Princeton and governor of New Jersey. It was his way of getting the information he wanted from those of a like mind he trusted. The practice of using special agents started long before Wilson's inauguration. Colonel House was a prime example from 1912 through his behind-the-scenes work with the post–World War I League of Nations, one Wilson biographer concluded that "the president was impatient with stereotyped reports through conventional channels and eagerly sought more comprehensive information."[14] Thus, the president, after a brief discussion with the cabinet on the need of sending "a confidential man" [men] to get "trustworthy information" to develop a policy toward Mexico, began placing a series of "special agents" in Mexico to evaluate the situation and send reports directly to the White House, bypassing all official channels. First to be dispatched was forty-four-year-old newspaperman William B. Hale, followed by Reginald Del Valle, and in late summer the former governor of Minnesota John Lind. In all, Wilson dispatched some dozen men, between mid-1913 and early 1916, to fan out across Mexico, collect data, and provide observations. While the practice of using executive or secret agents was not new to the presidency, Wilson employed such private channels far more extensively than other previous presidents.[15]

The deployment of Hale, Del Valle, and Lind was outside of State Department channels, an accommodation that suited President Wilson's management style. The agents were not on the federal payroll, but instead their expenses and salaries were paid from the president's secret White House contingent fund. This fund was managed by the president and Colonel House. It required no oversight or reporting. Furthermore, the agents held no official status and were given only "more or less uncertain credentials" of introduction for their travels. Hale and Lind, who spoke no Spanish and knew nothing of Mexican customs, were to visit under the respective covers as a newsman and a tourist. They were to remain discreet and report back. To add to the confusion, Secretary Bryan sent an old friend, W. H. Sawtelle, on the same mission; neither Sawtelle nor Del Valle gathered any results other than confusion among all the parties involved. These roving agents were not discreet and could not adequately assess the situation, and the reason for their presence in Mexico was soon known. William Hale, a former Episcopal minister and journalist for owner-editor Walter Hines Page's the *World's Work*, was the first special agent sent to Mexico. Embarrassed and diplomatically undercut by these so-called agents, a thoroughly aggravated Ambassador Wilson noted the confusion among the Mexican government as to who spoke for the United

States. He informed Secretary Bryan that "the presence here in Mexico of persons *claiming to be representatives of the president* are lowering the dignity of the embassy and detracting from the respect and deference with which the Mexican people have been taught to regard."[16]

The conflict did not miss Hale, who wrote the president that he was worried about being arrested by Huerta's authorities (for spying). Hale's reports, the first sent after only nine days of investigation, to the White House were highly critical of both Ambassador Wilson and the Huerta government. Further confusion followed in the foreign diplomatic corps in Mexico City who were in close contact with the American embassy. Thus, Ambassador Wilson, following one more attempt to get clarification on the "attitude of the administration on the question of recognition" and a formal protest to the White House on these so-called special agents on June 29 and July 1, 1913, was abruptly recalled to Washington for "consultation." Henry Lane Wilson packed in twelve hours, leaving behind most of his personal property, and traveled by railroad to board the ship at Veracruz via Havana for New York City. He never returned to Mexico.[17]

Governor John Lind, the former governor of Minnesota, was serviced as one of President Wilson's "confidential men," or agents, in Mexico. At times, he sent misleading information and constantly undercut the Huerta government. Lind was one of the first to advise President Wilson that an intervention could bring government change in Mexico. Source: *Literary Digest*.

With the removal of Ambassador Wilson, the president sent John Lind to Mexico City with a detailed plan to press the views of the administration with the Huerta government for a political settlement. Tall and slender, the loss of his left hand due to a childhood hunting accident was seldom noticed as Lind traveled from Washington to Galveston, Texas, to board the US battleship *New Hampshire* for the voyage to Veracruz. Traveling by US naval ship, Lind's passage was abruptly interpreted by the Mexican government as a threat and possible prelude to intervention—surely not intended by Wilson. Due to its large size, the warship anchored outside the Veracruz breakwater and fired a twenty-one-gun salute upon arrival—further alarming the local population. Lind, a Swedish immigrant to the United States and the former governor of Minnesota in 1898, was selected for the mission to Mexico because he "reportedly" had no interest in any concessions or investments in that country. In fact, Lind and partner Duval West of San Antonio owned extensive properties and joint ventures in Mexico, including the Mexico Land Company headquartered in Saint Paul, Minnesota! Although Lind knew little of Mexico and spoke no Spanish, Wilson and Bryan felt he was well qualified because he "was a loyal Democrat." Once again, Wilson personally typed out instructions for his new special agent.[18]

Lind was apparently unaware that William Hale had been sent to Mexico until he arrived in Veracruz and recalled that Hale was disheveled and "exceedingly nervous." Urged to work with chargé d'affaires of the US embassy Nelson O'Shaughnessy (who learned of Lind's mission to Mexico not from the US State Department or the White House but instead through an American newspaper correspondent), the two men harbored ill feelings for each other from the time they met. Lind, who carried credentials drafted and signed by the president and a proposal addressed "To Whom It May Concern" (in order not to give any recognition to General Huerta), was evasive concerning his mission and a blatant affront to the Mexican government. Given his abrupt undiplomatic attitude, Lind—who would nervously tap the stump of his left wrist to make a point—was also quickly threatened with expulsion from Mexico by General Huerta. The "American colony," a general reference to expatriate Americans living and working in Mexico, were very concerned at the less than official and amateur approach to the Huerta government. The Lind mission, given the title of "advisor to the embassy," was viewed by the Huerta government and the diplomatic corps with singular ineptness.[19]

A large American mining and property owner, Michael J. Slattery, in Mexico for over a dozen years before he was forced out by the invasion of the US military at Veracruz in April 1914, recalled the general attitude toward Wilson's "special agents":

> The President certainly picked a lot of lemons. You know John Lind's visit to Mexico City was a joke, and if it were not so serious it would be a comic opera. He came down there with his chest thrown out, that—well, he was a big fellow back in the United States, and he was coming down there to show those Mexicans how to do things, and he was the direct representative of the President, and all that sort.[20]

While writing high-minded reports that gave an air of superiority, Lind came to the conclusion the Huerta regime was the "worst pack of wolves" ever to infest any country. Much of his information was collected in casual conversations and from unsolicited petitions sent to him from various groups and individuals. Lind did confirm, however, that Lord Cowdray, managing director of "El Águila" Oil Company, and the British government were focused on maintaining a monopoly over the oil business in Mexico. Thus, within days of his arrival in Mexico, Lind concluded that intervention was the only solution—if for no other reason than to end the

After recall of Ambassador Wilson, chargé d'affaires Nelson O'Shaughnessy became the senior American diplomat in Mexico. A calm, seasoned veteran, he confers with the US consul in Veracruz, William W. Canada, on the eve of the US Marine and Navy landing on April 21, 1914. Author's collection.

strife and unrest. Lind advocated for the United States to throw its support behind the rebel Constitutionalists in the north. He further recommended that all steps that would hasten the establishment of a liberal capitalist democracy be taken. Lind's presence soon ran the course of Hale's, and though he moved from Mexico City to Veracruz to consult with US consul William W. Canada (under the watchful protection of US battleships commanded by Rear Admiral Frank F. Fletcher), Huerta kept Lind under constant surveillance by Mexican agents (as well as British and German agents). Lind too became worried that his activities may be considered clandestine and he would be arrested as a spy.[21]

"Blood-Stained Hand"

On July 3, 1913, the same day that Wilson and Bryan decided to recall Ambassador Henry Lane Wilson from Mexico City, the president's number one special White House agent, Colonel House, sat down to a private lunch of lobster and lamb cutlets with the British foreign secretary, Sir Edward Grey, in London. Concerned that the British were hampering Wilson's policy in Mexico, House was dispatched to investigate and report back. It was viewed at the White House that the British fully supported the Huerta regime and that the British ambassador in Mexico City, Sir Francis W. Stronge, was key to this relationship. The question of England's swift recognition of Huerta on the eve of his inauguration had irritated President Wilson and undercut, what they thought, any coordinated efforts that the president might have taken with the British to dethrone Huerta. In fact, the British recognition was presented to House as fully pro forma and in line with their extension of long-standing British diplomatic protocol. Furthermore, in a top secret document, Sir Edward Grey noted, "We only recognized Huerta as provisional President . . . after the . . . entire Diplomatic Body [in Mexico City] paid him a complimentary visit . . . hosted by the U.S. ambassador, this in itself constituted a certain measure of recognition and it was understood that all the foreign representatives were agreed as to the advisability of doing everything possible . . . to restore tranquility."[22]

Referring to the actions of Ambassador Henry Lane Wilson during the Decena Trágica does not change the fact that the British recognition of General Huerta, given the extensive level of British banking, mining, oil, and commercial investment, was anything but a routine affair. Restoring order would assist in the protection of British property and investments as well as allow the Mexican government to obtain loans in the international financial markets at reasonable rates. Yet as Colonel House's diary notes, the "vexatious questions at issue" were who controlled the oil interests in Mexico and the British attitude on the Panama Canal (planned for an August 1914 inaugural opening) toll exemptions. Furthermore, the British soon realized that Colonel House, "though very unobtrusive in his methods, is in fact 'the power behind the throne,' and is, perhaps, the only man who really influences the President." Thus, the luncheon in London proved timely for the establishment of complete unofficial cordiality, as Grey assured House the recognition of Huerta, viewed as "provisional," was neither "definite nor final." Furthermore, Grey said the Mexico situation (and the British access to oil), as they repeatedly reported to the print media, was not connected with the Panama tolls issue. Grey continued to be disingenuous, as these critical issues were in fact completely intertwined.[23]

In the case of Mexico oil, the real political and financial power behind Great Britain's posture in Mexico was British oilman Weetman Pearson, also known as Lord Cowdray. Strategically, Cowdray's multi-million-dollar oil holdings in northern Mexico, Mexicana de Petroleo 'El Águila' S.A. (Sociedad Anónima), were tied hand in hand with long-term contracts to supply the British naval fleet's transition from coal to bunker oil. Efforts to block British oil expansion in Mexico were led by James N. Galbraith, general manager of the Waters-Pierce Oil Company, who fronted for the Standard Oil Company and their backing of Carranza and Villa to overthrow Huerta.[24] The extraction of Mexican petroleum had dramatically increased from 3.5 million barrels in 1910 to over 25 million barrels in 1913—which accounted for some 7 percent of the world's petroleum supply. Petroleum from the Tampico and Tuxpan oil terminals was under contract by Lord Cowdray with the British Admiralty as their sole fuel supplier in the region. Wilson and Bryan assumed the British Foreign Office stood firmly behind Lord Cowdray and assisted him in influencing Huerta. They were right on both counts. Unknown to the Americans was the scope of British strategic planning and European geopolitical intrigue that far outpaced the knowledge and scope of understanding in the new Wilson administration. For England, the hint of the dark clouds of war appeared not in August 1914 but a full year earlier—"for Europe at the beginning of 1913 was a kennel of snarling dogs."[25]

The major powers of Europe became enthralled with the conclusions drawn by Alfred Thayer Mahan in his historic book *The Influence of Sea Power upon History, 1660–1783* (1890)—to date the most influential book on foreign policy ever written by an American—and prior to World War I, the critical influence on the building of a blue-water navy to support national security and commercial objectives worldwide. In reply to this situation and to anticipate the future security needs of Britain, Winston Churchill, First Lord of the Admiralty, put forth the 1913 Navy Plan for 1914–15 that called for adequate "provisions" (a veiled reference to naval "mobilization") for the future development of twelve super-dreadnought battleships, twelve cruisers, forty destroyers, and support vessels. All of these ships were to be powered by an increasingly larger amount of Mexican bunker oil. Thus the arrangement with the one major supplier was the Admiralty's contract with the Anglo-Mexican Petroleum Products Company chaired by Lord Cowdray. Furthermore, the British had fanned out in other parts of Latin America and Canada to contract additional supplies of petroleum and strategic materials—ever mindful that the new Panama Canal would forever alter global maritime operations. British strategic planning and national defense concerns eclipsed even the concern over the Panama tolls issue as secret efforts were underway to secure a secondary canal crossing site in the region. There is little question that British actions in Mexico (and throughout Latin America) to thwart the wishes of the United States were exclusively in their long-range strategic self-interest.[26]

A further concern, and a part of House's mission, was whether the strong British economic and strategic interests in Mexico challenged Wilson's policy of nonrecognition. As rumors of intervention and annexation of northern Mexico swirled in diplomatic circles, Sir Edward Grey confidentially reminded his colleagues that President Wilson was steadfast and unwilling to condone a bad example by taking "Huerta's blood-stained hand." The British had additional concerns as well, for fear that their subjects may suffer harm if the United States "took violent measure." The British ambassador in Mexico City wrote Senator Henry Cabot Lodge, bluntly stating, "the Greasers can no more distinguish between a Britisher and an American than between a crocodile and an alligator."[27] Notwithstanding the pointed remarks, the crisis in Mexico was viewed by the British as purely strategic and economic. The British wanted stability in Mexico to protect the vast investments of their citizens as well as unfettered access to mineral interests in the country and fuel oil for the fleet.[28]

By the first of August 1913, the 150th day of the Wilson administration, the British remained somewhat perplexed about the American diplomatic actions in general and Mexico in particular. The British Foreign Office of seasoned diplomats grappled with mixed messages coming from the State Department and the White House. Confusion reigned. The US ambassador in London, Walter Hines Page, was a close personal political friend of the president and Colonel House, yet with no diplomatic experience. Page often provided uninformed personal observations to British officials that were misinterpreted as administration policy. When pressed by Sir Grey on the president's position on Mexico, Page noted that President Wilson was reluctant to interfere, but "the U.S. might be compelled by disorder on their frontier [southern border] to intervene." Most perplexing to the British was the lack of experienced diplomatic professionals and the use of amateur agents. In addition to Ambassador Wilson being summoned back to Washington, the new head of the Latin American Division at the State Department, W. T. S. Doyle, was, according to Ambassador Spring-Rice, filled by "an amiable but ignorant political appointee." The one man in the State Department who knew the most about the Mexico situation, Fred M. Dearing, was sent to a new posting in Brussels. In a secret report to Sir Grey, the embassy reported, "There is only one person who knows what the policy of the United State is toward Mexico, and that one is the President . . . he takes advice from no one—least of all his Secretary of State."[29]

President Wilson, during the entire early years of his presidency, wanted and worked for regime change in Mexico and appeared to have a love-hate fascination with the fortitude of General Huerta, writing in confidence to family friend Mary A. Hulbert:

> Our friend Huerta is a diverting brute! He is always so perfectly in character: so false, so sly, so full of bravado (the bravado of ignorance, chiefly), and yet so courageous, too, and determined,—such a mixture of weak and strong, of ridiculous and respectable! One moment you long for his blood, out of mere justice for what he has done, and the next you find yourself entertaining a sneaking admiration for his nerve. He will not let go till he pulls the whole house down with him. He loves only those who advise him to do what he wants to do. He had cold lead for those who tell him the truth. He is seldom sober and always impossible, and yet what an indomitable fighter for his own land! Every day the news from Mexico City unsettles the news

> of the day before. The whole thing is quick-silver. I dare not finish my message to Congress intended for Tuesday till Tuesday's news comes, for fear the things I say in it might turn out to be untrue in fact! Any hour of the day or night I may have to revise my judgement as to what it is best to do. Do you wonder I have lost flesh a bit?[30]

The idealistic and amateur actions stretched from the top of the administration to the agents in the field. Secretary Bryan, against the advice of staff and legal counsel, ignored secret code book procedures, sending unencoded sensitive messages in the open, many times undated and improperly addressed. Once via open channels, Bryan (over the strong objections from security experts at State) asked Ambassador Lane Wilson to request the Mexican government, *which he had not and would not be recognized*, to join the United States in the recognition of the insurgent government of Yuan Shih-kai of the new Republic of China—after China's some four years of bloody civil war.[31] Little was secret, as British and German agents in Mexico City were well aware of Hale, Lind, and Del Valle, and noted they made little progress other than confuse the Mexican government. Of most concern to the British was the threat the United States' ineptness could hamper oil concessions and scuttle new loan arrangements between the major European banks and the Mexican government. Rumors constantly swirled around the intent of President Wilson's special agents. For example, Del Valle was reported to be near a deal with Huerta that implied recognition and his own appointment as US ambassador—with Sir Cecil Spring Rice noting the obvious, "such a step would imply the recognition of the Huerta regime"—which quickly proved false.[32]

British reports from Washington to the British Foreign Ministry at Whitehall, created further concern and confusion. There seemed to be a broad consensus by the US Senate, except for New Mexico senator Albert Fall and a couple of his friends who pushed for annexation of sections of northern Mexico, by the War Department, the banking sector, and industry for formal recognition of Huerta's government. The British assessment was that the American people, notwithstanding the sensational reports in the Hearst syndicated newspapers, also did not want intervention. However, one of the most telling events was an urgently requested meeting with Sir Spring Rice by Bryan, following a telegram from the secretary with the words: "Will you be here soon?" Although traveling out of the Washington area, and concerned that a hasty return trip by him might be monitored by the press, "I should not in any way give colour to any rumours that his Majesty's Government were urging drastic action" by a sudden return trip, so he dispatched his deputy, Lord Eustace Percy, to the State Department until he could arrive in good time. What followed was one of the most telling meetings and follow-up briefings to the Foreign Secretary in London.[33]

Moving discreetly, the British ambassador arrived in the capital and early on a Sunday morning called on Secretary Bryan at his private residence. Following a somewhat long recital of the details of the revolution in Mexico and the philosophy he and the president had to only "act in the interest of peace and honour"—recognition of Huerta would be breaking their solemn pledge and setting a very bad precedent for other American republics (no mention was made of China). Bryan then read "in strict confidence" the instructions given John Lind's mission in Mexico (of which the British intelligence service and government were already aware) noting now was the time for action, and the British needed to help remove Huerta and a lawful election held. Spring Rice noted in his top-secret briefing to Sir Grey in London, "I asked if they were certain that Huerta's withdrawal would not have the effect of making room for *seven other devils* worse than himself."[34] Bryan responded, "Huerta was Impossible!" And the ambassador concluded they would use their good offices to act informally and unofficially to assist special agent Lind in facilitating a peaceful settlement. Spring Rice knew full well it "might be difficult for Mr. Lind to carry his point" with the stubborn general.[35]

Watchful Waiting

The erratic nature of Wilson's approach to the Mexican crisis raised concerns at the highest levels of the British government. The president's moral and idealistic approach to the transition of power in Mexico caused them to conclude: "The President was pursuing a dangerous course in attempting to exclude from power on moral grounds the only man who seemed capable of restoring order."[36] The British determined that by avoiding the extension of recognition, they would not be drawn into taking forceful steps to restore order. The Wilson and Bryan approach left no room for negotiation or compromise, and as one scholar noted, it was near impossible for Wilson to follow even a degree of the British approach—"It was not necessary to establish formal relations with provisional governments to carry on business on a satisfactory basis."[37] Thus, no informal means to address the provisional government resulted in growing concerns of uprisings in Mexico City and some form of active response in Mexican ports. However, the major concern and flashpoint was the US-Mexico border. Arms were constantly smuggled in from the United States regardless of neutrality laws, Huerta's forces and the forces of the Constitutionalists had divided up sections of the Mexican side of the border, and allegiances on both sides of the Rio Grande were divided over the two factions. The possibility of open full-scale hostilities, if employed, would require more than just a "police force," which was commonly used by the United States to enforce customs duties collection and port protection. US and British military planners prepared reports noting that a prolonged occupation of Mexico would call for from 200,000 to 300,000 troops. The total strength of the active duty US Army in late 1913 was only 42,370 troops! The British concluded such action should be avoided and brought pressure on the president to "modify his non-possumus attitude."[38]

In an undated briefing paper to Sir Edward Grey, newly designated British ambassador to Mexico Sir Lionel Carden, a rabid pro-British business proponent, Latin America expert, and anti-American, foretold the future (that is, Tampico, April 1914) in his 1913 memo:

> The relations of the United States and Mexico have reached a phase not unlike that which immediately preceded the Spanish-American war, in which an untoward incident, even of relatively small importance, might bring about an outbreak of hostilities at a day's notice—casus belli. No one who knows Mexico can doubt that "intervention"—or, in other words, a war of invasion—by the United States would be protracted, sanguinary, and destructive beyond words.[39]

When British Ambassador Spring Rice arrived in Washington in April 1913, Sir Edward Grey charged him with two main objectives: first, deal with the Mexican crisis in the best interest of the United Kingdom, and second, keep the pressure on the new Wilson administration to honor in both the spirit and letter of the 1901 Hay-Pauncefote Treaty, which included provisions that all shippers and nations (including warships) traversing the Panama Canal would pay rates equal to shipping registered to the United States. For Grey the issue was simple. The United States in 1911 during the Taft administration decided that they, the Americans, had built the canal with "their own money and skill and enterprise," and thus they deserved a special preference toll rate lower than other merchant ships. But the treaty clearly stated there would be no preference in rates. To skirt the treaty, the US Congress decided in June 1912, "since we built it," to pass a law that lowered American shipping tolls (only from one American port to another) via the canal—and President Taft signed it. Notwithstanding the fact that the British merchant marine and Royal Navy were the largest and most competitive in the world, Wilson through Colonel House clearly signaled to the Congress and the British that he would hold the covenants of the 1901 treaty above self-interest and address the issue at the proper time. From the British, Wilson expected two items in return: first, that all talks of calling an international arbitration conference on tolls be vacated, and second, the United States' role in the Mexican crisis would be primary to all outside concerns and that clear and speedy consideration be given to the transitioning of the Huerta government. Colonel House in his diary concluded: "it was better to make concessions in regard to Panama rather than lose the support of England in our Mexican policy." This "gentlemen's" agreement would be yet another of the many brokered by House for President Wilson.[40]

By the end of August 1913, little had changed in Mexico City. Wilson's agents provided little results and much confusion. The president did, however, put a great deal of credence in John Lind's direct reports to the White House. On August 27, Wilson went before a joint session of Congress and stated that John Lind's purpose was to "offer our good offices" to obtain a settlement that includes cessation of fighting, early and free elections, and the departure of General Huerta. Lind submitted these proposals to Mexico City and they were rejected. The impatience and paternalism toward Mexico are reflected in the president's high-minded appeal:

> We shall yet prove to the Mexican people that we know how to serve them without first thinking how we shall serve ourselves. . . . War and disorder, devastation and confusion, seem to threaten to become the settled fortune of the distracted country. As friends we could wait no longer for a solution which every week seemed further away. It was our duty at least to volunteer our good offices—to offer to assist, if we might, in effecting some arrangement which could bring relief and peace and set up a universally acknowledged political authority there. . . . The steady pressure of moral force will before many days break the barriers of pride and prejudice down, and we shall triumph as Mexico's friends sooner than we could triumph as her enemies."[41]

Reviewing the situation, it was decided to "wait" for further opportunities and "vigilantly watch" the acts against Americans and their property, coining the phrase "watchful waiting"—a policy stance the president would use again in his 1913 annual message to a joint session of Congress on December 2. British diplomatic records paint a clear picture that the United States consulted extensively with Lord Grey and Ambassador Spring Rice throughout this period. Agents from both Great Britain and Germany worked actively in Mexico City and Washington to determine the plan of action of the Wilson administration. The bombshell of the August congressional presentation was that President Wilson officially "urged all Americans to leave Mexico at once." This action did not please those Americans living in Mexico, because many of those who wanted to leave had done so, and more importantly, such a proclamation from the president could result in retribution against those still in Mexico—Americans as well as British, French, and Germans citizens.[42]

On the same day that the president urged the exodus of Americans, US consuls across Mexico were cabled advising them to "convey to the

The exodus of Americans, Mexicans, and foreigners living in Mexico to Texas as the revolution intensified on the Rio Grande border communities in late 1913 and early 1914. Known only as the "Hulse family," as they crossed, they were among thousands of Americans and Mexicans who fled across the Rio Grande into Texas for safety. Library of Congress.

authorities an intimation that any maltreatment of American is likely to raise the question on intervention"—the first time the Wilson administration officially invoked the possibility of direct arms "intervention." The response to the president's proclamation from Mexico, England, and Texas was mixed. Mexico's minister of foreign relations, Federico Gamboa, responded for the government in a dispatch to John Lind, whom he repeatedly addressed officially as "Mr. Confidential Man"—noting we have no intention of taking into consultation your conditions and "if you want to do business with us send us a new ambassador without previous conditions." An action Woodrow Wilson would not allow, because a new American ambassador would be tacit recognition by the US government of the Huerta government in power.[43]

From London, official channels were very concerned with the order for Americans to depart Mexico and its impact on British citizens. Both Whitehall and the London media saw little hope in Wilson's high-minded policy working in civil-war-torn Mexico. The *Pall Mall Gazette* noted,

William Jennings Bryan served as President Woodrow Wilson's secretary of state and proved a novice in dealing with international diplomacy and incidents in Mexico during the early years of the revolution. Source: *Literary Digest.*

"we will watch the results of the steady pressure of moral force with much interest, but without much belief in its success." The *Standard* concluded that American diplomacy has been "left to a group of politicians whom in foreign affairs are the most amateurish of amateurs." And the Germans were apprehensive that a US-British coalition referred to in the media and diplomatic circles as an "anti-German alliance" would set the stage to limit German activities not only in Mexico but also across Latin America—the *Berliner Nueste-Nachrichten* dismissed the president's "imperialistic delirium" as little more than "colossal arrogance." Responses from London,

Ambassador Wilson was a growing target of the cartoon specialist during the Mexican Revolution, pointedly attacking his heavy-handed relationships with the Mexican government and his forceful request of the Wilson administration to officially recognize General Huerta in order to restore calm in Mexico. Source: *Literary Digest*.

Berlin, and Mexico City gave little comfort. The standstill in Washington now began to focus on the rising violence on the Texas border.[44]

And the harshest response came from the US-Mexico border as unrest intensified. An informative weekly, the *Literary Digest* published by Funk and Wagnall's in New York City, noted: "Texans, on Texas soil, have been killed by bullets of the combatants across the border. Texas ranchers have been raided from Mexican side, and horses and cattle commandeered for use of the Mexican fighters. It is, therefore, not surprising that Texas has shown signs of chafing under the Administration's policy of watchful waiting." Governor Colquitt's hopes that the new Wilson administration would be more responsive were dashed by the summer of 1913.[45] Speaking from the platform at the National Governors' Conference in Colorado Springs, an increasingly impatient Governor Colquitt lashed out at the Wilson policies in Mexico: "I know I am treading on dangerous ground, but the United States should not stand idly by while Americans are being murdered and outraged in the rebellious republic [of Mexico]."[46]

Unconcerned with British strategic petroleum planning, agents in Mexico City, or rumblings in Europe, the governor and Texans were focused on the unrest in South Texas on the Rio Grande border. The governor, referring to the border as "on the firing line," was intent on taking direct active action to protect citizens and property; the issue was soon to be of heightened concern in Washington.

3
On the Firing Line

> **The Northern papers seem to be afflicted with the idea I was going to have state troops invade Mexico . . . no such thought had ever entered my mind. I specifically instructed the militia on the ground not to cross the river.**
>
> **—Governor Oscar B. Colquitt**
> **March 3, 1913**

> **The majority of the population along the border were of Mexican extraction, they inevitably became caught up in the factional struggle, as, for that matter, did many Anglos, either out of sympathy or because the Revolution became a lucrative business.**
>
> **—Charles H. Harris and Louis R. Sadler**
> **1982**

As the White House worked through the late summer of 1913 to determine a policy toward General Huerta's government and console American and European financial and business interests, the US-Mexico border was in a state of open hostilities. By August, most of the American public had only limited general knowledge of the internal situation in Mexico or the scope of problems the administration was dealing with in Mexico. Between January and August 1913, scores of Americans, in addition to hundreds of Mexican casualities, were reported killed/murdered in the border region alone. The killings of foreigners were classified variously as killed by bandits or by stray bullets, and one victim hung by rebels was charged with being a Madero spy—bringing the total Americans killed since the start of the revolution in November 1910 to 116 known deaths.[1] The growing unrest along the border was almost exclusively limited to the border states, and many of the rumors and most of the news were misleading. Ambassador Henry Lane Wilson's recall and dismissal as well as media articles began to appear on the rise regarding the Huerta government and the questionable death of President Madero. While returning Ambassador Wilson was reported to have "rather shocked the press and the public by his undiplomatic discussions of Mexican matters," scant attention was given to the turmoil on the border. Unless you worked or lived on the US-Mexico border or in a community around a Mexican seaport, you did not know of the incidents of border violence, the redeployment and concentration of US Army troops into Texas, or the ongoing rotation of over a dozen US battle cruisers along both coasts of Mexico. Henry Bamford Parkes, in his classic *History of Mexico* (1950), captured the attitude of the day: "across the border, the United States was watching this spectacle of a nation in chaos with self-righteous amazement."[2]

The turmoil and magnitude of the Mexican situation were formally presented to the American public in an address by President Wilson to Congress on August 27, 1913. The bluntness of the president's presentation was bolstered by the increased pressure from the European financial community, which held millions in loans and bonds with Mexico, backed by the assets and projected revenue of the National Railways of Mexico, which daily was losing value as it was routinely under attack and thus the loss of revenue. Also, special agent John Lind's mission to present a plan for Huerta to vacate the presidency, hold national elections, and then gain official recognition was abruptly rejected. With Lind's failed attempt in question, Major William A. Burnside, military attaché at the US embassy in Mexico City, reported to the army chief of staff at the War Department, "Huerta would take a chance in precipitating a foreign war rather than compromise." Similarly, Manuel Calero, former Mexican secretary of foreign relations and ambassador to Washington, DC, concluded that Wilson's blatant efforts and demands to undercut Huerta actually strengthened Huerta in the short term with both Mexicans and foreign observers.[3]

In reporting Governor Lind's unsuccessful mission to Congress, Wilson announced his plans to alter all arms shipments to Mexico. He followed with a dramatic pronouncement ordering all Americans to leave Mexico and stay out until further notice, clearly all of which received the attention of the American public. Figures for the number of Americans living and working in Mexico ranged from 38,000 to 50,000, with 7,000 to 10,000 residing in Mexico City. The exodus of Americans triggered a corresponding response from thousands of British, Spaniards, Chinese, Italians, French, Japanese, and even a stranded group of Syrians who flooded the US-Mexico border, crossing into the United States at El Paso, Eagle Pass, and Laredo.[4] Railroad, mining, cattle ranches, port facilities, and petroleum operations across northern Mexico as well as merchants and bankers in the urban areas were mostly affected. Neither President Wilson nor the State Department nor anyone in the administration had any authoritative knowledge of the magnitude of American investment and business ownership in Mexico. One scholar estimates that some 15,000 Americans owned 130 million acres, equaling almost 27 percent of Mexico's land. In addition to control of key areas on the coastlines, borders, and vast railroad rights-of-way, some 160 American individuals and companies owned landed estates each of 100,000 acres or more of prime agricultural, timber, and pasturelands. Property ownership and investment included all the major financial houses in New York, California, and Texas, railroads, numerous US senators and congressmen, members of the Wilson cabinet, and Colonel House and his family. For example, newspaper publisher William Randolph Hearst, his family, and business partners purchased over 7 million acres of land in northern Mexico beginning in the 1890s on the speculative assumption the United States would eventually annex northern Mexico. The concern about filibustering efforts to somehow separate northern Mexico and then apply for and/or be annexed to the United States was raised by Ambassador Wilson in mid-May 1913.[5]

Americans across Mexico, many of whom had lived south of the border for decades, responded with bitterness to Wilson's hollow pronouncement that placed all expatriates, their families, and their business investments in harm's way. A circular telegram and instructions from the US State Department were sent to some twenty US consuls across Mexico and read to American groups. One American businessman with accumulated investments over $7 million in Colima and Jalisco, for over a decade, noted, "the one thing that seemed to stick in the craw of everyone was [the implied comment] 'your remaining there [Mexico]—mind you—will get your government into trouble!' How could we possibly get our Government in trouble? . . . Any trouble we had in Mexico was given to us by the United States Government, by their meddling in the affairs of the Mexican Republic." Unlike the lukewarm response to similar warnings during the Taft administration, many Americans packed up and abandoned their homes and businesses. Two overlooked American groups in Mexico since the 1860s were the hundreds of missionaries who established protestant churches, hospitals, and schools. The Protestants were followed by the first Mormon settlements in Chihuahua in 1885.[6] Their abrupt exodus was recalled by preacher David Hardeman LeSueur and his family in Torreón, "we packed provisions enough to last 48 hours, the time required to reach Laredo . . . bread, eggs, sardines, and malted milk." However, the two-day trip took nearly three weeks as rebels stopped and robbed the train numerous times and damaged tracks, diverting the train to Tampico where the LeSueur family boarded a Norwegian cattle boat bound for Galveston. And at the Rio Grande thousands of expatriates and Mexicans began to flood into cities on the US side of the border. US Customs and Immigration personnel were overwhelmed, with most of the refugees entering the United States unchecked and undocumented.[7]

Few better understood the impact of Wilson's statements to Congress on the border region than Texas governor Oscar Colquitt. Fully frustrated with the inaction of the Wilson administration to work with Texas border officials to stem violence, Colquitt ordered state officers to stop "cooperating" with any active enforcement of the federal neutrality laws. Furthermore, in spite of efforts by local law enforcement, arms and munitions flowed across the border. For example, the arms and munitions were smuggled to rebels in boxes labeled as pharmaceutical supplies, hidden in watermelons and bales of hay, or packed in bodiless coffins. US Customs officers and the Texas Rangers as well as local law enforcement officials were understaffed and hence unable to deal with the problem. The US Army wanted no part in enforcing a law that might create an incident or bring them in direct confrontation with Mexican federal forces or the rebels. The governor had hoped the new Wilson administration, since they were both of the same political party, would be more perceptive and cooperative to limit federal-state friction. However, the August speech only reinforced that Wilson's idealism and evangelical nature were out of touch with the rough-and-tumble politics and spreading violence across revolutionary northern Mexico. The vast region and the southwest section of the United States were sparsely populated and poorly policed.[8] Both the Mexican consul in San Antonio, Texas, J. A. Fernández, and federal officials in

Washington protested the Texas governor's stance on neutrality. Colquitt responded, saying he would use whatever force was at his command to protect the citizens of the state of Texas. Calls for action from the governor and landowners along the border increased. Washington needed to invoke an ultimatum to Mexico to restore border order or intervene with force to settle the violence. Thus, Wilson's policy of "watchful waiting" was filled with hollow promises and seen in Texas as "too little, too late."[9]

An example of border friction was the constant efforts to enforce and/or exercise jurisdiction, and, when needed, extradition proceedings. On the US side of the border there are four adjacent states: Texas, New Mexico, Arizona, and California, and along the 1,900-mile boundary there are six northern Mexican states—Tamaulipas, Nuevo León, Coahuila, Chihuahua, the Baja territory, and Sonora. In the case of Texas, Colquitt's dealing with the governing authority in Mexico—or identifying who was in control given that various parts of the border were alternately governed by Huerta's Federalist or regional Constitutionalist forces, made extradition nearly impossible. Without formal recognition by Washington, the problems of governance were compounded as towns changed hands. The US consuls along the border were equally handicapped, able only to deal with the rebel faction in control on any particular day. Small-scale raids spread on both sides of the border as well as arms and munitions smuggling and cattle rustling; these were compounded by the absence of legal rights or the rule of law on either side to follow bandits in "hot pursuit" across the Rio Grande—known in Mexico as the Río Bravo.[10]

The failure of the Wilson administration to recognize a de facto government in Mexico City, while at the same time negotiating through back channels with the Carranza forces in northern Mexico—to include lax enforcement of cross-border arms movements—confused and complicated any clear policy of how to address border depredations. Since the Constitutionalists were landlocked in northern Mexico, the arms embargo favored Huerta (who received a steady clandestine supply of arms and munitions via seaports from Germany, Japan, and Britain). Notwithstanding Washington's inability to remove Huerta by threats, the United States shifted its policy to combat Huerta by covertly strengthening Carranza and the Constitutionalist rebels. Wilson's rush to explore a solution with the Constitutionalists, after months of being ignored, was at first rebuffed by First Chief Carranza. Arthur S. Link observed, "Wilson and Bryan proceeded throughout the summer and early autumn of 1913 very much as if the Constitutionalists did not exist."[11] Carranza was insulted and viewed the White House approach as further proof of American attempts at interventionism. Thus, to establish better communication, Wilson and Bryan shifted the efforts of special agents Del Valle and Hale to northern Mexico after consultations with both agents in Washington, with mixed results. While Del Valle made some inroads with Carranza agents in the Tucson, Arizona, area, his less than discreet actions with the press soon retired him home to California. Hale, in contrast, was able to establish contact with the Constitutionalists through their agent, Manuel Pérez Romero. Efforts at mediation were stalled as the "men of the north" won more battles in the field and demanded no mediation with Huerta or any of his representatives—"on the ground that it is incompatible with the national dignity."[12]

In August–September 1913, there was a concerted notion in Washington that "military" intervention was not advisable or even feasible on a large scale. There continued an implied "political" intervention by Wilson via his many "agents" to control the internal affairs of Mexico. This argument is fully supported by Berta Ulloa, who concluded the Mexican Revolution was an "intervened-in revolution." At every decisive moment—due in large part to geographic proximity, the American business interest, and risk to citizens—of the complex Mexican struggle, the US exerted influence and oversight.[13] In the case of the Taft administration, the concern of the United States from 1909 to 1912 was deemed to be fully justified, as Taft noted in a letter to his wife, "the simple fact is this country has an investment of 'a billion dollars' in Mexico, which meant the U.S. had a vested interest to be involved!" The British Ministry of Foreign Relations concurred: "as a neighbor of Mexico they [US] are affected by considerations that did not arise in the case of European Powers . . . the U.S. might be compelled by disorder on their frontier to intervene." And for Wilson, who abhorred and campaigned against the notion of "dollar diplomacy," and demanded the removal of the usurper Huerta, the approach was much more complicated and would soon involve serious detailed planning for a military option.[14]

Spies among Us

A mention, at this point, must be made of the amount and scope of spying and intrigue, collectively labeled today as counterintelligence, that transpired in Mexico and in the United States during the early years surrounding the revolution. This wide range of espionage activity was first attributed to the rising violence in Mexico that might itself cause peril for both American and foreign investments, which in fact morphed into a group of foreign powers' efforts to exploit the instability not just in Mexico but also in other fragile areas of Latin America. Their objective and goal was to advance their own national interests, source raw materials and new markets, and foster global ambitions. Following the increased unstable atmosphere around the extensive foreign investments in Mexico there were additional international concerns about how the United States would manage (and possibly limit) access to the Panama Canal scheduled to open in August 1914. As President Taft bragged, "we built it so we will determine who uses it and at what cost!" The British were at odds with the United States over Taft's special exclusion clause to allow American shippers reduced transisthmian canal tolls. And other rising global maritime nations' interests followed the lead of the British Admiralty in their protest.[15]

During the last years of the Porfirio Díaz administration and extending into the Madero presidency, both the Germans and Japanese had "military" advisors in Mexico, either covertly or in official acknowledged status. The Germans were active with line and staff units of the Mexican Federal Army and provided instruction and military books and manuals for use in the Mexican Military Academy for future officers. Additionally, the German embassy under the direction of Admiral Paul von Hintze, assisted arms merchants such as Krupp with extensively lobbying for the adoption of German arms and munitions. German strategists envisioned a trained, well-led, and armed Mexican army that "could" prove a vital counterweight on the US-Mexico border if war broke out in Europe, and "certain" powers wanted to limit or delay the involvement and military assistance from the United States. American policy and war plans, first and foremost, called for the defense of the homeland, that is, any possible invasion from Mexico, before any commitments to Europe.[16]

The level of Japanese intrigue in Mexico, beyond efforts to sell mostly small arms to Mexico or efforts to monitor the Panama Canal, took a new level of concern with the California state legislature passage of the Alien Land Exclusion Act. As it is bluntly titled and indicates, the act forbade Japanese nationals from owning or leasing property in the state. Expressing shock at the state's action (notwithstanding the fact that there was a century's old imperial edict that no American or foreigner could own land in Japan!), the Japanese imperial government protested and could not believe diplomatic clarification from the US State Department that it could not under federal law, amend, void, or overturn the state law. Incensed at the blatant xenophobic policy, Japan dispatched additional intelligence agents to Mexico and the Rio Grande border as well as ordering the cruiser *Izumo* on a "port-call" to Manzanillo and doubling arms shipments to the Mexico army. Additionally, a new Japanese ambassador, Mineichirō Adachi, was authorized to offer a foreign aid package that included a contract with Mitsui Company to design and construct five coastal defense ships for Mexico as well as provide a loan to pay for the ships. Soon after Ambassador León de la Barra arrived in Tokyo, arms shipments increased to Huerta's army—shipped by the Japanese hidden in loads of coal. And rumors surfaced, while erroneous, that Japan intended to establish a naval base on the Baja peninsula, possibly at Magdalena Bay. The United States strongly protested both the increased arms shipments and the Japanese naval activity in the Gulf of California.[17]

Meanwhile, agents of both the British Secret Intelligence and German Intelligence Agency (both agencies were a great deal more discreet), spies employed first by Madero and then Huerta, and rebel agents and arms buyers on the US-Mexico border daily played a cat-and-mouse game with the US Bureau of Investigation (renamed the FBI in 1935), US Customs agents, the US Army, the Texas Rangers, and a varied cross section of local civic and rural law enforcement officers on both sides of the Rio Grande. Over time, there were some seven US government agencies daily involved in detective and espionage activities in cooperation with Mexican authorities. Smuggling and the trade in cross-border contraband, including arms and munitions, started decades before and thrived annually long in advance of the start of the 1910 Revolution. The arms embargo imposed by Taft in March 1912 (and modified to allow shipments to the Madero regime) was little more than a nuisance to seasoned border gunrunners, filibusters, rebels, and exiles—often one in the same—as they took advantage of sanctuary in the United States. Concerned with security along the border, *huertista* representatives corresponded with Governor Colquitt, strongly requesting he do something about smuggling along the border. The governor responded that the issue of illegal arms and supplies was entirely in the hands of US federal officials.[18]

The arms business, a very lucrative enterprise, was fueled by border merchants who avoided prosecution on neutrality violations as long as they sold the arms locally and had no business with outbound shipments to Mexico or dealings with the end user. While US federal authorities attempted to prosecute a number of border merchants and arms dealers, their case proved ineffective, since according to international law, the only punishment for "smuggling" was the seizure of the so-called contraband in question. Notwithstanding, high-profile arms and neutrality cases were taken to the grand jury in November and December 1913 against Phelps Dodge Mercantile Company (owned by Cleve Dodge, Wilson's college classmate and the largest contributor to his 1912 presidential campaign) and arms merchants Isadore Ilitsky, W. C. Shwamm, and N. M Trickey in Arizona as well as noted Laredo merchant Joseph Netzer, yet all were dismissed for lack of evidence. This resulted in a near de facto sanctioning of cross-border shipments. As the smugglers operated on a brisk cash-and-carry basis, the US federal government's (with less than enthusiastic support from local law enforcement) ability to enforce the neutrality laws was tenuous, as foreign agents had conflicting priorities and intermingled daily with the smugglers who operated on both sides of the border.[19]

The Mexican Secret Service had an active cadre of spies and informers, in addition to operations from San Diego to Brownsville, that extended into Texas as far as Houston, San Antonio, and Austin as well as agents in Phoenix, Tucson, New Orleans, and Washington, DC. President Madero, with his personal approval, deployed "confidential agents" to the United States long before Woodrow Wilson was even inaugurated as president and prior to his death had established a very effective agent network in the border communities. Due to his previous control of the Mexican Federal Army, General Huerta in February 1913 inherited much of the spy apparatus established by Madero. And the scores of double agents were as replete as informers.[20]

Foregone Conclusion

As tension built on the southern border, Governor Colquitt became increasingly vocal. Unknown to the general public and him was the growing concern at the War Department that the US Army and US Navy did not have the manpower, training, or equipment to invade and occupy Mexico while simultaneously protecting the 1,900-mile US-Mexico border.[21] This was further confirmed by British intelligence who had completed an assessment following their lingering experiences in Egypt. Lord Grey knew full well the United States, without a massive joint force with European assistance (even then a challenge to mass the needed troop strength) could not fully prevail.[22] Avoiding "mission creep" was something the British gained insightful experience in, as well as untapped wisdom, long before the US experiences in Mexico, Vietnam, or Iraq-Afghanistan. Newly appointed British ambassador to Mexico City, Lord Lionel Carden, had over two decades of diplomatic service in Latin America, much of it in Mexico, and he was no friend of American businesses "actuated by feelings of hostility to the United States" he felt bullied the region. In a confidential memorandum to Lord Grey, the new ambassador captured the essence of the magnitude of the Mexico situation:

> No one who knows Mexico can doubt that "intervention"—or, in other words, a war of invasion—by the United States would be protracted, sanguinary, and destructive beyond words. The climax has been reached in Mexico, where the ineptitude and bad faith of the United States Government must be held largely responsible for the very great losses already suffered by British investors since the commencement of the Madero insurrection, and for the present imminent danger that these losses may culminate in the complete destruction of British interest of immense magnitude, as would undoubtedly be the case were an American force to cross the border.[23]

US armed forces' estimates, in the fall of 1913, appeared in unofficial print media calling for a full-scale invasion of Mexico ranging from 300,000 to 500,000 troops. Throughout the late summer and fall the US Army had no response to such reports, in spite of the fact that increasingly more troops were being deployed to Texas. There were many concerns over any action involving Mexico: first, it could lead to a protracted occupation that would be unsustainable; second, there was a question of how to deal with the possible deployment of European troops on Mexican soil given the Monroe Doctrine; and third, and more telling on the deep interworking's of the leading European powers, was the more immediate concern with continental affairs—addressing Churchill's "kennel of snarling dogs."[24]

In spite of recommendations from the War Department to move with caution, Wilson turned from an ongoing informal diplomatic handling of Huerta's overthrow to authorizing American war planning against Mexico.[25] The US Army War College at Carlisle Barracks, Pennsylvania, was tasked with the prime responsibility for both the army and navy operations to draft and review detailed plans for a coordinated land and sea invasion. General William Crozier, chief of planning at the Army War College, assumed that the purpose of intervention was to restore the "constitutional government." He believed to do so would require a total occupation of the Mexican territory. There were no plans for any "limited invasion" or "police action" such as in Cuba (1898–1902) or the Philippines (1902–4), nor would it be a low-key customs collection "protectorate" similar to the use of a US Marine Corps constabulary as in Nicaragua (1907 and 1911), Honduras (1911), or Panama (1913–early 1914). In preparation for an armed invasion and capture of Mexico City, US Navy and Marine officers (undercover in civilian dress as railroad employees) were sent into Mexico to photograph bridges, railways, troops' locations, and defenses around the Presidential Palace. The War College estimates for a prolonged war were for deployment of 265,000 troops—with one major caution, that if not executed swiftly, the conflict would pass from traditional warfare into a protracted occupation and/or guerrilla war. Finally, in spite of repeated reports and speculation from both the British and the Germans that the US plan was to not only occupy Mexico but also take over Central America and "carry the flag to the Panama Canal." Other than print media speculation, there were no known official US political or military plans to annex any part of Mexico, either as territory or as a protectorate.[26]

Supply ships were provisioned and rerouted to the Gulf of Mexico, additional army units transferred to the border (along with one of the first airplane units in the army), and US Marine units were consolidated in Cuba for possible redeployment. Several intriguing options were explored to limit the need of armed intervention—primarily directed at an accommodation with Carranza. The first top secret efforts involved Major General Leonard Wood's back-channel contact with Carranza in October to determine if the First Chief had an interest in declaring independence for the northern section of Mexico between the Rio Grande and the 26th parallel north. The second plan involved Colonel House working behind the scenes with special agent Hale to urge the president to impose a naval blockade. A blockade could be potentially problematic because such an action could be roundly recognized as an "act of war." And occupying the Mexican ports with American troops to control inbound arms shipments and to prevent possible European interference, thus allowing the Constitutionalists to concentrate on defeating Huerta, faced a number of diplomatic hurdles. Carranza opposed both the Wood and the House plans and broke off all negotiations with Wilson's "agents." One explanation for rejecting the long-sought recognition is provided by historian Friedrich Katz: "Carranza saw the secession [and recognition] of the northern provinces merely as a prelude to their annexation by the northern neighbor."[27]

Wilson complained to Colonel House that the European powers and Japan had "perpetuated" Huerta in power by recognizing him when he seized the presidency. Now Carranza, after months of talks, rejected the opportunity to accept formal recognition. Beginning in late 1913, some fifteen US warships patrolled both the east and west coast of Mexico. Additionally, the waters off the coast of Mexico became increasingly crowded by more than a dozen warships from the British, Germans, French, and Japanese, and thus prone to an inadvertent incident that could spark a larger conflict. The major European powers were advised, in the president's October foreign policy address at the Southern Commercial Congress at Mobile, Alabama, to avoid any action that may cause concern in Mexico, to include strong pressure not to recognize or aid the Huerta government. Furthermore, repudiating economic imperialism in Latin America, the president—to calm and assure the European nations of America's intentions—boldly announced the "United States will never again seek one additional foot of territory by conquest."[28]

As the pressure mounted in Mexico City, Huerta in October—in what he felt was a necessary move to preserve his power—dissolved the Mexican Congress and arrested eighty-four elected members opting for an arbitrarily convened Congress of handpicked *huertistas*. US chargé d'affaires in Mexico City O'Shaughnessy wired Washington on October 11: "Huerta has his back to the wall and may now be considered an absolute military dictator."[29] And in Edith O'Shaughnessy's diary, later released as *A Diplomat's Wife in Mexico* (1916), she bluntly concluded in what can only be interpreted as a pro-Huerta stance: "Only by the hand of iron can this passionate, tenacious, mysterious, gifted, undisciplined race, composed of countless unlike elements, be kept in order. In the States . . . this isn't quite understood." Admiral Hintze from the legation in Mexico City concurred, sending a cable to Berlin: "Huerta is a man of many means and, at times, flabbergasting disconcertedness as far as the constitution and the law are concerned."[30]

These actions were followed by a sham national election on October 26, which was nullified due to very low voter turnout and reset by Huerta's handpicked Congress for July 1914. To shore up his hold on the country, he authorized the army to be increased to 150,000. To raise funding for the army, Huerta received "forced loans" from the large Mexican landowners and industrialists. When customhouse receipts fell considerably, he increased import duties 50 percent and called on each state government to pay additional taxes to support the national government. The military buildup was the result of Huerta's agents in the north warning of expanded rebel military operations. In northern Mexico, the Constitutionalists were in fact preparing for their boldest action to date—to capture major urban areas, disrupt rail and communication service, and to limit the effectiveness of federal forces across the northern border states.[31]

Dollarless Diplomacy

A group closely watching the actions of the White House and the US Army's movements was a broad cross section of US and foreign investors and financial institutes. Huerta's special agents in Europe maintained an active search for government financing to shore up the depleted government treasury. Both France and Germany kept their options open, providing short-term funding, along with Japan, in hopes they could arrange a loan amounting to twenty million pesos by December. While most of the government loans had historically been secured by customs receipts, Huerta considered issuing new oil concessions to the British and railway lines to a Belgian financial syndicate to raise revenue.[32] Wilson and Bryan held extensive meetings at the White House with Senator Augustus Octavius Bacon of Georgia, chairman of the Foreign Relations Committee, and Republican Senators William Borah and Porter J. McCumber of North Dakota to insure backing to craft a plan of "inflexible determination" to block any efforts by Huerta to secure foreign loans or aid.[33]

Able to daily track the attitude and planning of Washington, DC, often called "*Watch*ington" in the Mexico City newspapers, via coverage by the *New York Times*, *The Economist* of London, and the *Mexican Herald*, Huerta was quick to react. In addition to requesting more state revenue, the embattled general demanded the government in Mexico City handle all gold and silver purchases and pricing, and if needed, devalue the peso further by printing more currency. All bills issued by the various individual Mexican state banks would be discounted by 10 percent. In early November, there was a small currency run on the banks in Mexico City, as specie in circulation began to dry up due to hoardings of coinage and small bills. This resulted in a new government law ending the convertibility of paper money into gold and silver coinage.[34] Between February 1913 and August 1914 the purchasing power of the Mexican peso in terms of the US dollar fell 74.6 percent. These actions sent financial markets in London, Paris, Berlin, and New York into a tailspin as oil prices, bond values, and stocks rapidly varied in price. The London *Daily Mail* noted the concern of the financial markets:

> Paper currency [in Mexico], not being immediately convertible into coin, would inevitably depreciate in value and drive gold and silver money out of circulation; for nobody would pay his debts in good gold and silver with a world-wide value when he could legally satisfy them in [devaluated] paper.
>
> This would disorganize foreign trade and send commodities up to famine prices, the depreciated currency possessing so much less purchasing power. Moreover, it would seriously affect British and other railway companies operating in Mexico, which would be forced to

By late 1913, there were a dozen different Mexican currencies in circulation, all rapidly devalued, which was a prime cause for capital flight and loss of investors. Notes were printed by Mexican state banks in competition with the federal government in Mexico City: (*Top*) $20 peso note, of rebel Gobiero Constitucionalista de Mexico, May 1913; (*Center*) $5 peso note, El Banco del Estado de Chihuahua, December 1913; (*Bottom*) $1 peso note, El Estado de Sonora, August 1913. Author's collection.

> receive payments in depreciated currency, while interest and dividends due to bondholders and stockholders would have to be met in gold.[35]

In spite of repeated failed demands by Wilson for Huerta to resign, John Lind was ordered to meet with the Russian, Norwegian, French, and German ministers in Veracruz to insure support from each country to counter any efforts to gain loans or aid. Notwithstanding the pledge from London by Prime Minister Herbert Asquith to cooperate with the Wilson administration on the situation in Mexico, there is little doubt that the British and Germans, in spite of the fact that they had recognized "that the U.S. has a special interest in Mexico," continued both the float of short-term financing and arms via the Lord Cowdray's petroleum interest donations to the government and British imperialist and outspoken anti-American Ambassador Lionel Carden (who was recalled to London in January 1914).[36] Not just thc British had special interests, but the French financial institutions, while expressing an interest in cooperating, stood ready to provide Huerta loans at favorable rates and collateral. The Germans maintained a steady flow of arms and munitions via procurement agents in Pittsburgh, Pennsylvania, routed through neutral ports such as Hamburg and reshipped and landed at Veracruz throughout the summer and fall of 1913. And partly in response to the controversy over the California Alien Exclusion Act, the Japanese landed additional amounts of weapons in Mexico in support of Huerta—noting such arms shipments were "merely a matter of business and [were] not indicative of any unfriendliness to the United States."[37]

Colonel House warned President Wilson of European interest in not only Mexico but all of South America; he worked with the British Foreign Office to smooth over ill feelings—with the promise that the United States would protect all foreign citizens and property investments in Mexico. Among all the European powers, the Germans seemed most prone to challenge the letter and spirit of the Monroe Doctrine. As one commentary noted, "Laughing in her sleeve at the Monroe Doctrine as an antiquated policy . . . Germany is engaged in the peaceful conquest of Spanish America."[38] Notwithstanding the buildup of US naval forces in the Gulf of Mexico, a dozen American battleships and some 6,000 men were anchored off Veracruz; this did not deter the British and the Germans from dispatching additional naval forces to the Western Hemisphere to protect their interests.[39]

The Wilson cabinet held extensive meetings in early November 1913. Still split over the need for a unified action, the pressure increased anew as reports of Americans killed in Mexico were further fueled by an increase in Federalist-rebel military action across the north.[40] Bryan wired the American diplomatic corps the strongest telegram to date: "If General Huerta does not retire by force of circumstances it will be the duty of the United Sates to use less peaceful means to put him out"—leading the *London News* to conclude, "Intervention will ultimately be inevitable." In dealing with Carranza and his agents, it became apparent that with numerous military victories in the north, the Constitutionalists were becoming bolder in their demands on the White House. Carranza, a former Coahuila state governor, was known by a number of the Texas cabinet members, as well as bankers in Texas, as a politician and no firebrand. Although carrying a quasi-military title as First Chief, his stated goal was to protect the integrity of Mexico professed by Madero and to oust Huerta. In this regard, he demonstrated the same degree of high-minded idealist objectives as President Wilson. Thus, while at first irate about the lack of attention from Washington toward the acceptance of the loftier goals of the Constitutionalist movement, Carranza became more adept at public relations and the use of his own "agents" to shape the message of the Constitutionalists in Washington.[41]

President Wilson dispatched special agent William Hale to work with Manuel Pérez Romero to gain access to Carranza. Hale's first meeting with Carranza in mid-November in Nogales at the Sonora-Arizona border crossing was cold and confrontational. The First Chief, far more nationalistic and antiforeign than Huerta, was very vocal, with three main concerns: first, armed intervention or blockade by the United States for whatever reason would be a grave mistake; second, lift the arms embargo at once and let Mexico settle its own struggle for constitutional liberty; and third, the Constitutionalists would not negotiate with Huerta or any of his representatives. Little room was allowed for compromise. The Constitutionalist distrusted Wilson and feared the president was stalling for time and playing them off against Huerta. They had no positive sign that the United States would lift the arms embargo. Greatly annoyed at the Constitutionalist's tough stance, Wilson's hope to work directly with Carranza was derailed, placing the administration at odds with both Huerta and Carranza. The British in their secret assessment captured the situation in a briefing to the prime minister: "Thus the policy which

General Pancho Villa at Ojinaga in January 1914. This picture was taken as a Hollywood film crew filmed the general and his army in action attacking a federal stronghold. Once believed he could bring calm to the revolution, his popularity was soon overshadowed by rivals within Mexico. Library of Congress.

began in the maxim that 'we will never condone iniquity because it is convenient to do so' had led him [Wilson], within nine months, into an intimate alliance with the most notorious bandit in Mexico"—Pancho Villa.[42]

Pretended Governments

The failures of the Wilson policy toward Mexico soon broadened the preoccupation and considerations of new options to remove Huerta from office. In late November, US ambassador to London Walter Page received the following (most likely to be passed on to Lord Grey) from Secretary Bryan:

> The President feels it is his duty to force Huerta's retirement, peaceably if possible but forcibly if necessary. The steps which he has in mind are (A) withdrawing of diplomatic representatives (B) raising

> of embargo on arms shipped to Constitutionalist (C) blockading of ports (D) use of army. This is the order contemplated but subject to change to meet new conditions. He still hopes Huerta can be induced to retire or, if not, that Constitutionalist can compel his retirement without necessity for employment of force by us.[43]

In a detailed memo to the president, Ambassador Page in London explored the options of a joint European-American intervention force to include the British, French, and Germans (along the line of the joint force used against the Boxer Rebellion in China). During late December 1913 and January 1914, the German Foreign Office reviewed and rejected the proposals crafted by the British and French of a joint landing on the grounds that Germany wanted to avoid any conflict with the United States over Mexico. Rising tensions on the continent among the European powers took primary position over American hegemony in Mexico.[44] As the year closed, the resolution of the situation in Mexico was no closer and the Wilson administration had made little forward progress other than demanding that the European nations, which each interpreted the demands in his own way, allow only the United States to be involved with Mexico and that in so doing their foreign investments and citizens would be under US protection. The Wilson policy to oust Huerta and restore a constitutional government of his liking had fallen flat. And the president's first annual message to Congress on December 2, 1913, offered little encouragement, only a backhanded assessment of not just Mexico (denying any intention of intervention) but of all Latin America—"that such pretended governments will not be countenanced and will be dealt with."[45] The *New York World* in late December, a very pro-Wilson newspaper, wondered if the president was touting a "new American or Wilson Doctrine":

> Exactly ninety years to a day after James Monroe in a message to Congress defined the Monroe Doctrine, Woodrow Wilson in an address to Congress defined the Wilson Doctrine. The former was designed to protect the Latin America republics from European colonization. The later to save these republics from recurrent anarchy. . . .

As the Monroe Doctrine was aimed at the Holy Alliance, so the Wilson Doctrine was aimed at the professional revolutionist, the corrupting concessionaires, and the corrupt dictators of all Latin America. If language

The international bridges across the Rio Grande were critical to the flow of supplies to Mexico and a constant target of rebel forces; pictured here is the strategic rail bridge between Laredo and Nuevo Laredo. Author's collection.

means anything, it means that so far as this Administration is concerned the United States will not recognize the constitutional authority of Latin American governments established by usurpation without the free consent of the unintimidated inhabitants thereof.[46]

In spite of Wilson's lofty idealistic statements, the revolution in Mexico continued unabated. While the resourceful General Huerta was unable to secure loans from European sources, he manipulated his own banks, allowing them to print daily more worthless regional currency, and he continued to control the silver and gold exchange price. In late December, General Huerta declared the first of four decrees on the moratorium to pay interest on the national debt. The suspended payments of interest, while vastly unpopular with European creditors, would earn interest at the same coupon rate as the bonds to which they were assigned. The abrupt suspension of payment of interest, surely no surprise to the bondholders, was met with strong diplomatic protest to the Huerta government along with threats of seizure of Mexican customhouses—to include raising duties on petroleum and cotton exports as well as increasing the tax on alcohol and tobacco. Such "forced collection" threats were without the force of international law given the terms of the 1907 Hague Convention, signed by thirty-four nations, which allowed collection only by means of arbitration on behalf of the bondholders. As the Mexican financial crisis deteriorated, the pressure on the central government in Mexico City intensified. Thus, by late December 1913, the attention was once again on the border.[47]

The flamboyant General Villa proved an able commander and did in fact turn the tide in the field against the federals with sweeping victories in Torreón, Chihuahua, Culiacán, Ciudad Victoria, and Ciudad Juárez. The increased military action across northern Mexico in late 1913 drove more refugees to the US-Mexico border, destabilized the federal garrisons, interrupted supply lines and customs collection, and resulted in increased random border violence against Mexicans, Americans, and foreigners. And the angst on the Texas border grew as weekly US troop strength intensified and war supplies were stockpiled at Texas City near Galveston. There continued an increase in the numbers of American citizens being killed. Thus, the heightened sense of insecurity and belligerence along the Mexican border led Texans of all persuasions to call on Washington for intervention. And an exacerbated and irritated observer, Governor Colquitt—stated bluntly the United States should intervene immediately to restore order—a front page *Washington Post* story again put the Wilson administration on notice that "we will protect our citizens and not wait for Washington to act!" Both Colquitt and Wilson knew it was only a matter of time before an incident would tip the uneasy, hostile state of affairs along the border.[48]

4
A Thorn in My Side

The thorn in my side is of course Mexico. I have a sneaking admiration for at least the indomitable, dogged determination of Huerta. It makes the task of smoking him out so much the more interesting. . . . I am now paying the price of having told other people what they ought to do when I never had the slightest idea that I should ever be thrust into their place.

—Woodrow Wilson
February 3, 1914

War erupted on the Texas-Mexico border on New Year's Eve 1913/14. Simultaneously, the Constitutionalist rebels launched frontal attacks against the federal garrisons at Nuevo Laredo across from Laredo, Texas, and at Ojinaga across from Presidio, Texas. Although there had been fighting for over two years around Ciudad Juárez, with little direct impact on El Paso, this time the revolution threatened to spill over into Texas. Border towns on the Rio Grande—connected by a cross-river bridge—are unique because of the close daily interaction by private citizens, who often had generations of strong familial ties with members living of each side, and commercial interests in trans-border trade. Thus, any disruption on either side of the border impacted their daily lives. As the battles raged in these border cities, considered Huerta strongholds, crowds of onlookers in Laredo, El Paso, and Presidio watched from across the Rio Grande as bullets flashed overhead and the fighting engulfed each Mexican town. These attacks were all a part of a grand strategy by the rebels to cut off the four primary railroad US-Mexico border crossings (and if possible burn

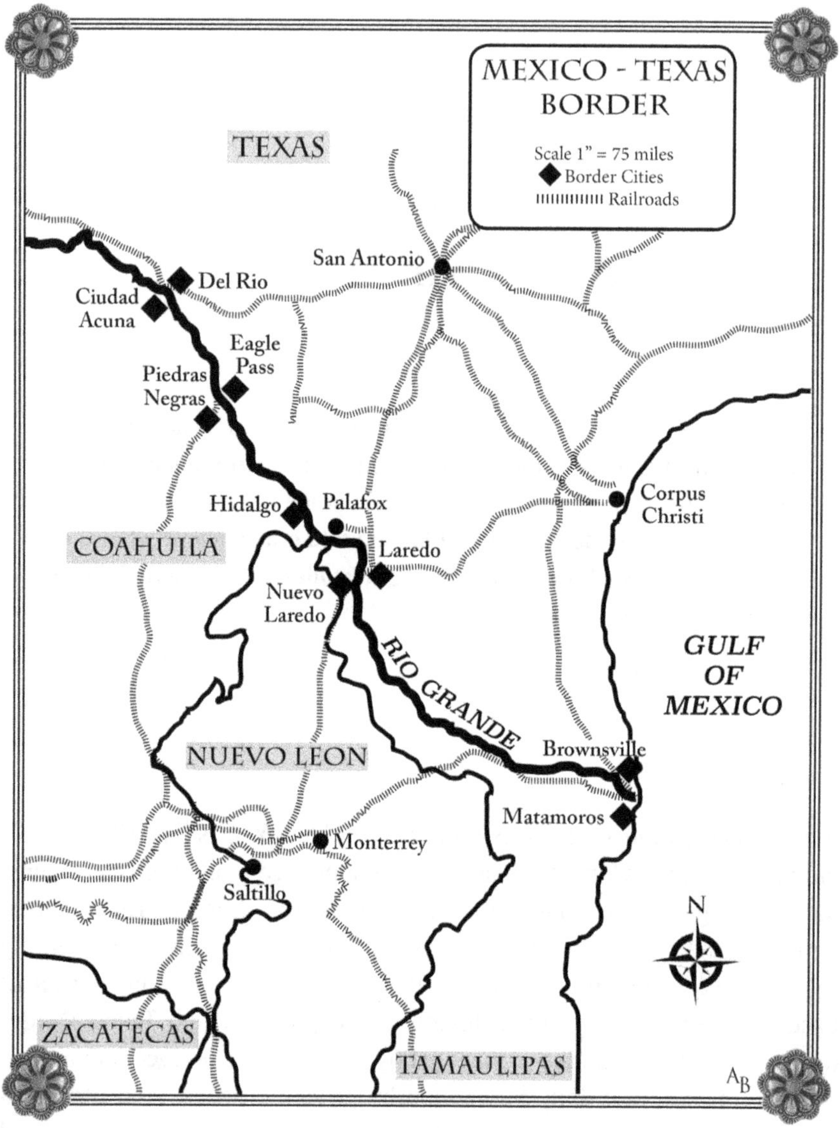

the bridges), controlled throughout 1913 by General Huerta. The crossings were at Nuevo Laredo, Piedras Negras, Ciudad Juárez, and Ojinaga. Of these key northern transportation and supply lines, Nuevo Laredo–Laredo was the principal strategic Texas-Mexico border location connecting the cross-border bridge of the Mexican National Railroad—842 miles from Laredo to Mexico City—with three railroads in Texas.[1]

The Constitutionalist attack on Nuevo Laredo, a city of about 13,000 in late 1913, was led by General Pablo González. González first planned for a night assault on New Year's Eve in hopes of catching the federal garrison of 1,800 troops asleep. This plan failed due to ill-equipped organization and poor execution. Instead, the general opted for a frontal attack at daybreak on January 1. Fully alerted to the rebel's intentions, the federals prepared rudimentary fortifications and positioned artillery. The primary targets of the attack were the railroad facilities and the regional federal customhouse. The result was a total disaster for González and the rebels, numbering about 1,500 casualties. While the rebels never reached their targets, they continued the battle for two days without entering the city. While Nuevo Laredo was defended, federal forces in Ojinaga also repulsed the initial attack, resulting in a victory for Huerta's troops. The victory was short-lived as an irritated Pancho Villa took personal charge of a massive counterattack and captured the border crossing into Presidio on January 10. Angered at the delay, Villa ordered the seriously wounded shot and all Federalist prisoners disposed by firing squad. With the victory at Ojinaga, Villa had sole control of the state of Chihuahua. The revolution was now at the right bank of the Rio Grande, as graphic reports filled the

The Nuevo Laredo Custom House was a considerable source of revenue to the Mexican government, at one time handling as much as eighty percent of the imports within its district. Author's collection.

print media nationwide, which shocked Americans with the news of the savage fighting and "barbarism" on both sides.[2]

US Army surgeon Captain Hiram Philips, from nearby Fort McIntosh, west of downtown Laredo, witnessed both sides of the battle in Nuevo Laredo and wrote a firsthand report on the combatant wounds suffered. He was amazed at the valor and drive of the ordinary raw soldier: "The Mexican soldier is fearless and has no regard for his life. Mexicans would expose themselves to fire merely to shout, 'Viva Carranza!' and when wounded considered it a matter of course. They were stoical and seemed not to suffer at all from shock and demonstrated remarkable vitality."[3] One possible reason for their fearlessness was the knowledge that there was no quarter—victory or death. Captured combatants from both sides were either shot or hung without delay or trial. Reports of torture were routine; for example, "a wounded Constitutionalist, his arms tied behind him, his knees tied to his body was spitted on a pole and paraded in front of the Federal lines from the shoulders of Federals like water carriers of Southern Mexico carry their wares through the street."[4] Exact numbers of casualties in Nuevo Laredo are hard to determine but some estimated the federals suffered three hundred killed and the rebels over five hundred. In the fields around Nuevo Laredo and Ojinaga, the dead were piled in layers with cord wood, saturated in kerosene, and burned. Over 150 of the seriously wounded in Nuevo Laredo were brought across the International Bridge to Laredo and housed in a temporary emergency hospital set up in an old school building near the Rio Grande. And at both Laredo and Presidio, thousands of Mexicans and foreigners of numerous nationalities took the opportunity, due to the turmoil and fighting, to flee to Texas, many never to return to Mexico again. The *Austin American* banner headlines read: "Stampede from Ojinaga: Two Thousand Mexicans Cross Border into Texas."[5] As one observer noted:

> Never in border history had there been a scene equal to that of Federal wounded and deserters who scrambled to reach the United States, while upon their rear there still poured a parting shower of shells and bullets. The river's edge was a ragged fringe of smoke-begrimed, maimed and half-naked soldiers, some of them rushing pell-mell into the river, some crying from pain of their wounds, others crawling, because of shattered limbs, over the rocks and cacti, some greedily stopping to drink the muddy water, and all begging the Americans on the opposite side for shelter from the horrible turmoil from which they had fled.[6]

As war raged in northern Mexico, Wilson spent the 1914 New Year's Eve as part of a three-week vacation resting in Pass Christian, Mississippi, recovering from a bout with influenza. Eager to obtain a firsthand report on the situation in Mexico, the president recalled agent John Lind from Veracruz for consultations. Lind failed to be discreet and much to the irritation of both Wilson and Bryan the pending conference became front-page news nationwide.[7] The president opted, following the breach of security, to meet on the scout cruiser USS *Chester* off the coast of Gulfport to avoid the media. Special agent Lind's candid assessments and pro-Carranza stance helped shape the next phase of the confrontation with Huerta. Lind's primary advise to the president was to land US troops in Mexico to oust Huerta—a recommendation he had first encouraged since October 1913 in dispatches to Secretary Bryan. The administration's plans were detailed by Secretary Bryan in a lengthy cable to Ambassador Page in London (to which there was no objection from the British). The cable outlined the progression of the administration's response from diplomatic recall, open border for arms shipments, and blockade. If needed, the use of the army and navy was again fully endorsed by the president. The military intervention to facilitate government change and restoration of peace suddenly became high on the list of options. The timing and level of armed force to be deployed had not been determined. Wilson pressed the army chief of staff for options short of all-out war. The military professed to foster no other course than full-on armed invasion, even though they only had engaged in a limited number of warfare actions in Cuba, the Philippines, and in so-called constable duty across Central America over the past decade.[8]

One ongoing aspect of the discussions in Washington, and with Carranza's agents in the field, questioned when and to what extent the US would support the Constitutionalists. Carranza's agent in Washington, Luis Cabrera Lobato, along with detailed conversations with the State Department and agents Lind and Hale in Mexico, continually argued there was no substitution for the immediate lifting of the arms embargo. Wilson, seeking a resolution to the unrest, signaled his gradual change of outward support to the Constitutionalists by way of agent Lind during a mid-January 1914 dispute with the German ambassador in Mexico City. Admiral von Hintze represented German businessmen concerning payments on outstanding obligations from the Huerta government due German banks. The message from Washington to Lind to deliver to the ambassador on the losses to German financiers was clear and to the point.

The president reconfirmed that the payment situation (to include the possible loss of money) was "inevitable" and regrettable. However, the "suspension of payments was a step toward Huerta's full elimination" and "the men of the north have our sympathy and will know our active support if necessary."[9] Yet still Wilson continued to reject a full open border policy. He was daily aware, from US intelligence reports provided by the US Army, US customs agents, and the Federal Bureau, that large amounts of munitions "slip through" getting to the Constitutionalists. Special agent Hale, for example, reported directly to Wilson that there were, "carloads of ammunition through Douglas, Arizona [for the rebels] with a little indulgence."[10]

The Wilson administration from the time of its inauguration in March 1913 through January 1914 walked a thin line in its interpretation of both the arms embargo passed by a Joint Resolution of Congress in March 1912 and the overall enforcement of the neutrality laws. Arms flowed freely to both Huerta and the Constitutionalists, in spite of the fact the rebels wanted carte blanche approval to import arms. One complicating factor is that the mining, railroad, and ranching sectors needed access to explosives, the same items used by the combatants on both sides. These so-called commercial/industrial shipments were highly prone to being diverted away from their intended purpose. In contrast to small "carloads" of weapons and munitions spirited across the border, these commercial orders were significantly larger and more dangerous. Each required a preapproval by the signature of President Wilson under the following proviso:

> Satisfactory proof has been submitted that it is probable that the shipment enumerated below will reach their respective destination in safety, and that they are not to be used in promoting conditions of domestic violence which I have found to exist in Mexico, exceptions are hereby made to the prohibition against export created by the joint resolution of Congress, approved March 14, 1912, and the President's proclamation of that date; and you will please instruct the collector of the port and other officers of the Treasury Department to permit to be exported through the United States custom house specified the following munitions of war for industrial purposes:[11]

A sample of such "commercial" munitions of war shipments to Mexico on December 15 and 19, 1913, include:[12]

Table 1.

Item*	from	ship via	consignee
dynamite: 262,500 lbs.	Hercules Powder	Manzanillo	Compañía Mocional
caps: 100,000 ea.	Hercules Powder	Naco	Cananea Copper Co.
dynamite: 100,000 lbs.	L. Gray Agent	Pachuca	Cía de Real del Monte
dynamite: 30,000 lbs.	E. I du Pont Nemours	Oaxaca	Adrian Spitalier

* Note: to transport these four orders would require 6–7 large railroad cars

As the rebels and federals battled and traded occupied territory these war munitions continued to be in high demand and subject to confiscation for military purposes. Thus, the mining operations and railroads were prime targets by the combatants on both sides of the revolution, and these supplies fueled a great deal of the violence and destruction, as commercial interests continued to import supplies to remain in business.

Sword of the Revolution

While Huerta grew continuously more isolated in Mexico City, pressure mounted in the *carrancista* ranks over the direction and leadership of the revolution. Having control of the state of Chihuahua, General Pancho Villa outlawed the use of federal bank currency, seized property of the *huertistas* and Spaniards, and expanded the size of his army. Many in the diplomatic corps and media, reacting from secondhand information and dramatic newspaper accounts, were drawn to the magnetism of General Villa. Little of the rebel's bloody battles, destruction, hangings, and firing squads was reported. Those impressed by Villa, with the strongest military force among the rebel generals, included the British ambassador in Washington, who reported back to Whitehall, "among the so-called Constitutionalist . . . Carranza is a mere respectable figure, and the real man is Villa . . . a sort of Robin Hood. . . . Villa is the sword of the revolution." Many in early 1914 wanted to lift Villa to the status of presidential material. The *New York Times* headline noted, "Villa, Bandit, and Brute, May Be Mexican President"—a prospect that even the old bandit himself said he would never accept. General Pancho Villa's allegiance was repeated many times, that "*mi Jefe*," as he always referred to First Chief Venustiano Carranza, was the lone supreme commander of the Constitutionalists—and the heir apparent to be president of Mexico.[13] Bragging to Governor William C.

General Huerta increasingly appealed to European banks and investors for assistance, hoping to weaken the American influence in Washington, DC. Author's collection.

McDonald of New Mexico during a meeting in Juárez, Villa boasted: "I never will be President of Mexico. I never went to school a day of my life, and I am not educated enough for the post. My alphabet has been the sight and trigger of a rifle; my books have been the movements of the enemy."[14]

Villa's dash and command in a string of military victories across the north created immediate worldwide notice. With success and media attention, open confrontation and tension were always present between the headstrong rebel leaders. Villa was beloved by his men and feared by the Federalists. A Hollywood movie company, the Mutual Film Corporation, began documenting the daring and actions of the Men of the North—signing an exclusive $25,000 film production contract with Villa on January 3, 1914—all done in time to capture on film General Villa riding a "spirited horse" into battle during the final assault on Ojinaga.[15]

Special agent Lind advised the president that while Villa had his faults, he could be a promising leader—if the administration could "restrain his violent tendencies." Lind's recommendation proved very interesting, given the fact that rebel depredations under Villa's command continued unchecked, and in particular there was a blanket threat against most foreigners, with a special order against all Spaniards. Viewed as active supporters of the *huertistas*, the property of Spaniards was to be expropriated, and all not loyal to the revolution were to be expelled within ten days "under penalty of death."[16]

The Mexican Revolution, by mid-January 1914, was at a critical crossroads. The civil war in Mexico between Huerta and the Constitutionalists was at a stalemate. The Federalists were in a constant search for funding to ease the financial shortfall, yet in spite of more pressure from Washington to cut all contacts in Europe, Huerta continued to survive. And although the División del Norte had an impressive series of victories, there was little organization or effort to move south to engage the major body of Federalists and capture Mexico City. Thus, the mounting circumstances and the repeated urgings of Lind, highlighted by his detailed New Year's conversation on the USS *Chester*, were gaining the president's attention. Lind's primary argument to the president was to swiftly end the civil war to prevent a full military intervention. Lind's recommended steps for the New Year were the culmination of months of no defined policy that factored in all the previous options discussed, including: publicly endorse and support the Constitutionalists; lift the arms embargo; take Huerta out of power; and, if required, invade and capture Mexico City. While William R. Hearst and a small group of filibusters demanded swift action by the Wilson administration, there was no serious discussion of the secession or annexation of the northern Mexican provinces.[17]

If the rebels were to succeed within their own civil war and revolution there would be no need for full-scale intervention by the United States. And while the rebels were receiving copious amounts of arms and funding, they wanted and needed the arms embargo to be lifted. Incidents of cross-border arms-for-cattle-and-horses, while quite profitable, grew more violent daily as ranches were plundered for cattle along the border. Concerned with the response from the American public as well as the European nations, Wilson and Bryan, while they stated to the press there was no change in policy toward Mexico, strategized that the lifting of the embargo would be presented as an act of "neutrality." It was, in fact, "an act that was decidedly unneutral [*sic*] and meant to do so."[18] Lind strongly argued that the action would have a positive psychological impact on the Constitutionalist movement and serve as a tacit endorsement of the Constitutionalists and First Chief Carranza. The secondary effect would be to demoralize Huerta and the Federalists. Lind was convinced his plan was the best course of action.[19]

Rebel leader Enfemio Zapata worked closely with his famed brother Emiliano to rally opposition to Huerta in southern Mexico. Author's collection.

Still Wilson wavered. Quite possibly, the president's hesitation was the result of a major source of advice coming from the Texans in his cabinet and administration. Edward House, David Houston, Charles Culberson, Albert Burleson, Thomas W. Gregory, and Sidney Mezes all held extensive capital investments in Mexico and along the border. The scope of this investment and the involvement of these Texans and their business partners has seldom been mentioned by previous researchers. Relationships and business dealings in Texas among those actively invested in Mexico dated to the 1870s and posed an extensive conflict of interest. Included in this group of investors were Secretary of State Bryan, who was a large landowner in the Rio Grande Valley of Texas, numerous New York and Texas banks, and a dozen American oil and gas companies. One of the most vocally and politically active was represented in Mexico City by legal counsel William F. Buckley Sr., also a Texan, who demanded intervention to protect massive oil interests in Tampico of the Texas Company. Major stockholders of the Texas Company (the forerunner of Texaco) included Joseph Cullinan, Will Hogg, Frost Brothers Bank of San Antonio, and members of the Edward House family. The House family along with Jesse Jones formed the Houston Bank and Trust in 1905. The Texas business and political elite who had close contact with both the Colonel House machine and Wall Street power brokers included Walter B. Sharp of Hughes Tool Company, lumber magnates William Marsh Rice and John Henry Kirby, and San Antonio cattle baron and US consul at Parral during the revolution, John Blocker. For many of these investors, intervention in Mexico seemed the best course of action to protect their property and investments.[20]

Some have portrayed Colonel House as disinterested in Mexico based on his diary entry of May 14, 1913: "I not only have not a dollar invested there, but never had further than a few hundred dollars of worthless silver mining stock." The diary notation, clearly not the full truth, was likely in response to rumors circulated by William R. Hearst about the House family investments and partnerships in banking, land, oil, and mining in Mexico—which were extensive. House and his family maintained contacts and investments dating from the early 1890s with investor groups dealing in Mexico ranging from political, banking, mining, and business contacts in Houston, Austin, and New York City. Thus, Colonel House, the chief advisor to President Wilson, carefully shrouded his family investments in Mexico as he helped craft US policy.[21]

Colonel House inherited large landholdings in South Texas and along the border from his father, Thomas W. House, an English immigrant and founder of the House Cotton Exchange in Houston. Family investments in northern Mexico included silver mines in Guanajuato, cotton mills, and real-estate interests. A common tie of the House family to the US and Mexican investors was the Stillman family of the Lower Rio Grande Valley. Charles "Don Carlos" Stillman built a dynasty in real estate and banking; he partnered after the Civil War with the Richard King and Mifflin Kenedy families of South Texas and the Patricio Milmo and Pablo Martínez del Río financial and business partnerships in Monterrey,

Mexico. After the illness and incapacitation of Charles Stillman in 1872, son James, age twenty-two, extended his father's empire into railroads, mining, land development, ranching, and interstate banking. Close association with Porfirio Díaz's rise to power helped advance Stillman's developments on both sides of the border. James Stillman took control of the City National Bank in New York City as chairman in 1892, which assisted the various projects of the railroad consortium composed of Collis Huntington, Jay Gould, William Rockefeller, E. H. Harriman, and former US president U. S. Grant. The group opened new railroad lines across the Southwest United States and into Mexico—to include one of the most profitable lines over the past century, the Tex-Mex Railroad narrow-gauge line from Laredo to Corpus Christi. Powerful board members of the City National Bank included Cleveland Dodge, claimed by some to be—next to Colonel House—the closest friend of President Wilson, along with Cyrus McCormick of International Harvester, and Joseph P. Grace of W. R. Grace and Company. All of these men held large investments in Mexico. In addition to railroad expansion, a bonanza followed in the mining production of silver, copper, iron, and lead in Mexico from 1890 to 1907. A financial depression in 1907–8, known as the Panic of '07, briefly slowed the economy and investments as well as crashing the Wall Street and London stock exchanges, while the long-range foreign investment interest in Mexico cooled. There is some evidence that indicated the Panic of '07 had a cascading impact on slowing the Mexican economy and ultimately resulting in some Mexican banks and foreign financiers losing confidence in the role and power of President Porfirio Díaz.[22]

What followed was the rise of the petroleum industry on the eve of the Mexican Revolution. The first major well was drilled near Tampico in 1901, but extensive investment did not begin until 1910. By 1913, American investment in Mexican petroleum exceeded British investment. Soon the Mexican Oil Company, Doheny's Mexican Petroleum Company, Standard Oil, Pearson's Mexican Eagle Company, Houston-based Texas Oil Company, and Gulf Oil acquired vast acreage and drilling rights. A new generation of financiers and promoters ushered in still-closer ties with Mexico, operating in association with the Colonel House political machine, which linked the Texas oil and gas and political elites. The colonel's brothers, John House and T. W. House Jr., along with their cousin Henry C. House, built a network of investment interests, banking, and political influence via the Texas Company and dominated the Texas Democratic

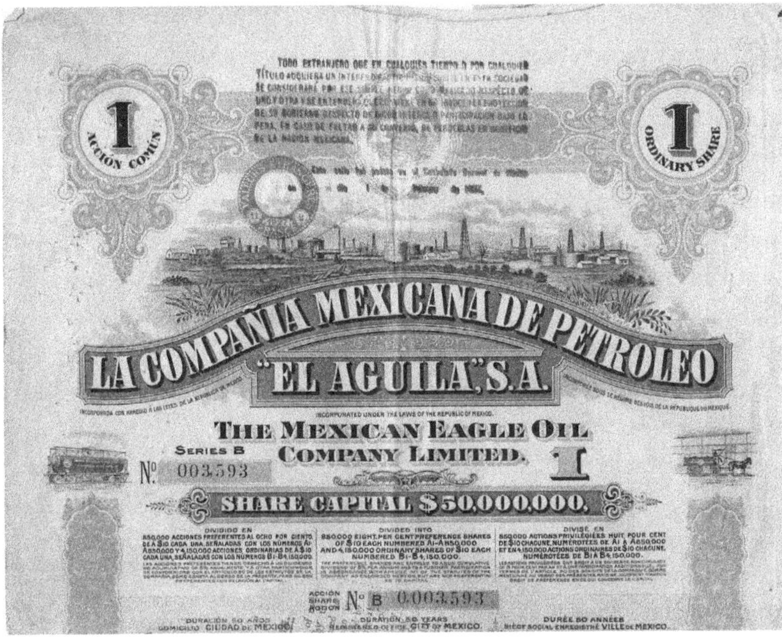

Capitalization of the Mexican petroleum industry was supported by stock sold in both the United States and Europe. This is one ordinary share of the Mexican Eagle Oil Company Limited. Author's collection.

Party from 1890 to the eve of the election of Woodrow Wilson. By 1912, friendships and business relations, developed over two decades, included leading politicians, financial institutions, and industrialists—including the colonel's Austin neighbor and legal counsel William F. Buckley Sr. In addition to assisting the brokering of the Wilson presidential nomination, House arranged for campaign donations from the leading investors and businessmen in Texas and on Wall Street—many, if not most, held investments and partnerships in Mexico[23] (see appendix D).

Following nearly four decades of close dealings and a protected environment for foreign investments with the Díaz administration, American and British business operations and investors in Mexico were quick to back whomever could bring stability to the national government and protect their assets. Huerta was a strong hand in the mold of Díaz, yet he failed to gain the support of Wilson and Bryan. Investors, especially from Texas, soon turned to Carranza. European interests remained perplexed by the actions of the White House and, in spite, of Wilson's demands and badgering, tilted toward supporting Huerta. Notwithstanding, the *villistas* had threatened oil production facilities in the Tampico region, causing the suspension of production for ninety days. However, most in the Wilson administration were favorable to Carranza after the Constitutionalists, for publicity purposes, returned some two million acres of the Sautema oil field tract in Tamaulipas back to the control of the Texas Company.[24]

A vivid snapshot of the impact and disruption of the revolution on business in Mexico is evident in the 1913 annual report of the American Smelting and Refining Company (ASARCO) headed by David Guggenheim. Daniel and Isaac Guggenheim of New York City first obtained mining concessions from President Díaz in 1890. They slowly expanded their operations whereby in 1907 the company held a monopoly in northern Mexico via their holding company, Guggemex, with over 600,000 acres in mineral interests and smelters in Monterrey, Aguascalientes, Chihuahua, Durango, and El Paso.[25] Earnings for 1913 declined to over $3.5 million compared to 1912, on gross income of $12.1 million from a combination of smelting operations and mining. The company reported retained earnings of $18.5 million and the value of total assets of $190 million. In spite of the fall in income, due to "a large part of the company's property is at present unproductive," the company paid $8 million in dividends to shareholders for fiscal year 1913, or 7.5 percent per common share. While very profitable in spite of its inability to operate at maximum capacity due to lack of fuel and ore, the company was ahead of its time in having a fully funded workers' pension plan, which in January 1914 carried forty employees "on the pension rolls whose days of usefulness have passed." This reflects only one of a score of American conglomerates with extensive investments in Mexico. Clearly these companies were eager for a settlement of the revolution, a stable national government, and a return to orderly business operations.[26]

Economic Reforms

The publicity agents for the Constitutionalists were led by Luis Cabrera Lobato, who operated as the Confidential Agency of the Constitutionalist Government of Mexico with agents and operatives in Washington, DC, Mexico City, Veracruz, and with agents in European capitals (Juan Sánchez Azcona).[27] The expressed objective of the publicity agency was to block all of Huerta's efforts for diplomatic recognition and financial support while gaining the endorsement of the Wilson administration for the Constitutionalist cause. Luis Cabrera, well known to the elites in both

Mexico and Washington, penned a detailed pamphlet released in early January 1914 and widely distributed: "The Mexican Situation from a Mexican Point of View." This became the cornerstone of the Constitutionalist argument to be the rightful group to lead Mexico out of chaos. Cabrera's well-crafted argument that the revolution and civil war, fully the making of the Mexicans, was not just a political fight but a major transition in the Mexican socioeconomic fabric as well as the agricultural structure and the system of rural landownership. Thus, a broad "constitutional" approach was the best course to establish a true democratic government in Mexico. Cabrera's arguments for a constitutional democracy soon gained the attention of Wilson and Bryan. The rise of democratic government determined by the people and with no US intervention, unless absolutely necessary, meshed neatly with the idealism espoused by President Wilson for Mexico and Latin America. After a detailed review of the situation leading up to the revolution, Cabrera's candor and detailed review of events in *The Mexican Situation* was critical in gaining the support of the Wilson administration:

> The truth is that the Mexican disturbances constitute a real revolution, of apparently political aspect, but at the very bottom are of the economic and social character. The present revolution is only the culmination of the revolution begun in 1910 . . . the Constitutionalist mean to begin immediately such economic reforms, and especially such agrarian reforms as are necessary . . . to impress the public mind with the idea that the present revolution in Mexico is really a social, political and economic revolution, and as such, requires for its accomplishment a certain lapse of time and further sacrifice.[28]

Confirmation of the role and success of Cabrera's message in Washington to influence support for the Constitutionalist views can be found in an early February dispatch to London from British Ambassador Spring Rice. Following a conversation with the president at the White House "on the Mexico question," Wilson paraphrases Cabrera's key points of *The Mexican Situation*:

> [In] the rather frank expressions of opinion he [President] was good enough to give me . . . he said that, after long and serious considerations of the whole subject and after consulting all sorts and conditions of men who had experience of the country, he had come to the

> conclusion that the real cause of troubles in Mexico was not political but economic. The real cause, in fact, was the land question.[29]

John Mason Hart, in *Revolutionary Mexico* (1987), captures the economic and political dynamics and crosscurrents of the revolution that made it difficult for the White House to understand the magnitude of centuries-old pent-up frustrations and inequities. Thus, it could be argued that Wilson's "idealism," criticized by so many, did in fact allow him over time to grasp the appeals of Cabrera and Carranza: "The violence that swept Mexico stemmed from central issues rather than diffuse minutia . . . the Mexican state had attempted to undergo a socioeconomic transformation in collusion with foreign capital without broad domestic participation. Its economic program placed the provincial elites in open competition with much stronger foreign capital."[30]

As Cabrera lobbied for a free hand to allow the Constitutionalists to control the economic and social reform in Mexico, change was underway in the United States. Across the country, those who had direct interest in Mexico were watching the Wilson administration closely. The majority of the American business and banking interests focused on absorption of the sweeping year-end congressional legislation in the Underwood Tariff Act, which lowered import tariffs for the first time since the Civil War. This legislation was followed by the passage of the landmark bill to enact the Federal Reserve Act in December 1913. This act overhauled the currency system nationwide in order to eliminate recurring bank panics such as that of 1907–8. South Texas representative John Nance Garner (whose district bordered the Rio Grande), was a close personal friend of Colonel House and was very instrumental in steering the controversial banking bill through Congress. In the months that followed, Garner, while vocal about strengthening the US military presence on the border, would become a trusted ally in the president's efforts to enhance the administration's plans for military preparedness.[31]

Attention soon turned to the selection of the locations of some dozen nationwide venues for the new Federal Reserve banks. The Texas connections in the cabinet were once again a major voice. During January, a twenty-city nationwide series of hearings was held by Reserve Bank Organization Committee, made up of Secretary of the Treasury McAdoo, Secretary of Agriculture Houston, and the Comptroller of the Currency John Skelton Williams. These individuals worked to determine the number and composition of between eight and twelve new Federal Reserve districts. Secretary Houston noted, "It soon appeared that city, state, and sectional pride was involved; and that we were in for a great deal of roasting no matter what we decided." Thus, there was a tremendous amount of jockeying and lobbying to be named one of the prime Federal Reserve district locations. Much like the determination of congressional districts to draw lines, over a dozen different nationwide maps were drawn taking into account regional bank deposits, population, and industrial base, with the final decision naming twelve districts. There was little doubt that after Texas and the Edward House Democrats helped carry the election for President Wilson, the state could select where it wanted a Federal Reserve district bank. While Colonel House, John Kirby, and Congressman Garner favored Houston, in the end Dallas—favored by Secretary Burleson, Secretary Houston, Senator Culberson, and Ben Love—was designated the site of the Eleventh District Federal Reserve Bank.[32]

Unqualified Disgust

As the nation was learning more about the new tariff and the Federal Reserve System, at the White House secret meetings were underway to prepare the armed forces for an invasion of Mexico. Secretary of War Lindley Garrison and Secretary of the Navy Josephus Daniels were charged with making arrangements and deployment. Since "intervention had already been agreed upon . . . [it was] only a question of an opportune time and sufficient arrangement."[33] Publicly, both Wilson and Bryan repeatedly said they were opposed to intervention. And the general sentiment was the American public did not want intervention. To muster broad public backing Garrison and Daniels would have to prove what the British termed a "popular necessity." However, the weakening and gradual isolation of the Huerta government was hampered by the inability of the Wilson administration to grasp the full nature of the Mexican civil war and whom among the Constitutionalist leaders to back. Carranza was clearly the titular head of the rebels, yet popular support during January swung to Villa. A general assessment concluded, "No one of the Constitutionalists was strong enough or respectable enough to deserve recognition."[34] In spite of Agent Lane's impatience and reports to Wilson, there remained a great deal of indecision in the White House. Also very frustrated were the US Army General Staff and the commanders along the border.[35]

The US Army did not have the manpower called for in the War College mobilization planning to both invade and occupy Mexico as well as protect the 1,900-mile-long border—much less of more concern, the possibility of large-scale cross-border invasion by Mexican forces. While a reserve force waited in Texas City, the total strength of the US Army on the border from Texas to California was no more than 4,000 troops. In comparison, there were over 5,000 Mexican troops in Ciudad Juárez alone.[36] The most concerned was US Army chief of staff General Leonard Wood. The general, a Harvard-trained surgeon, was no amateur; he had transferred to the infantry after winning the Congressional Medal of Honor fighting Geronimo in the late 1880s, and by 1900 commanded forces in Cuba. Yet, during January 1914, neither Wood nor the chief of naval operations had access to the president, and it was "difficult to ascertain what was the White House policy." The president requested no new funding to prepare the army after Wood had submitted a confidential assessment, including "a long and detailed memorandum explaining the deficiencies of the military," to the House Armed Services committee. The assessment was released to the media, "who promptly published it." This was much to the annoyance of the General Staff. The leaked document resulted in German and Japanese operatives reporting the unpreparedness of US Army for large-scale operations in Mexico. Edith O'Shaughnessy, in her 1914 diary, noted that the German envoy in Mexico City chided her that the United States was not prepared for war: "you can't make soldiers overnight."[37]

In a secret report from Ambassador Spring Rice to Sir Edward Grey in London, Spring Rice noted, "He [Wood] described the attitude of the American army and people to the whole question as one of unqualified disgust, like that of a sick man to an organ-grinder . . . at the present moment, however, the organ-grinder had removed himself from the immediate neighborhood. Wood did not believe for a moment that, 'the administration now, or ever had, a deliberate plan in Mexico.'" General Wood's frustration was further heightened by the fact that Secretary of Navy Daniels, responding in part to the naval arms race between Germany and Great Britain, had just concluded a congressional recommendation and request for $19 million to complete and arm warships in the final construction process and an additional $19.3 million for two new dreadnoughts, eight torpedo destroyers, and three submarines and no new funding for the army. Notwithstanding rumors on the readiness of the US Army, the general advised the British ambassador that an expeditionary force was indeed in place to take Mexico City. The force would protect both Americans and foreigners in the "case of dangerous disturbances," which were not defined, yet, "the necessary—the absolutely necessary—result was some form of intervention."[38]

The Fatal Days

On January 26, Wilson hosted a meeting of the Senate Foreign Relations Committee at the White House to review the Mexican situation. It was time for new action, and the president outlined his intent to extend open support to the Constitutionalists. Baker noted in the *Wilson Papers*, "America was growing weary of the constant irritation and wanted something done: Europe was cynical."[39] Rumors of the possible lifting of the embargo became public and were printed in the *New York Times* on the twenty-eighth. Alarmists in Congress and the media reported that this action would create mass anarchy across Mexico and the expulsion of American embassy personnel, both of which soon proved false. Thus, on February 3, Wilson formerly lifted the arms embargo imposed by President Taft on March 12, 1912, and advised foreign governments this action amounted to the recognition of the Constitutionalists. Secretary Bryan opposed lifting the arms embargo on the grounds that providing weapons in already-volatile circumstances was a risky step. Luis Cabrera and Lind assured President Wilson that the Constitutionalists offered assurances that foreign-owned properties would be respected. Reluctantly, Bryan followed the president's decision, commenting to British Ambassador Spring Rice, "the Constitutionalist party seemed at the present moment to offer the best hopes for an ultimate settlement."[40]

The lifting of the arms embargo to Mexico was greeted with mixed reactions by the foreign diplomatic corps in Mexico City. While the termination of the embargo was an important milestone for Wilson's Mexican policy, many thought the president's attitude toward the turmoil was grossly irresponsible since it stripped away the last illusion of safety and left foreigners exposed to all sorts of atrocities. There was a great deal of unspoken reproach. The Spanish ambassador felt helpless in protecting his citizens or determining who had killed Spaniards. The French secretary was impassive, reflecting on the status of loans. The always suspicious German minister, Admiral von Hintze "quietly and very coldly," remarked, the change in US policy was nothing more than "another step to [America occupying] Panama."[41] Edith O'Shaughnessy, wife of the US chargé d'affaires, reflected in her 1920 memoir:

> When therefore on the 3rd of February the Embargo was raised, the Mexicans were committed to a fratricidal war that still, after seven years, is in full vigor; for only from the blood of brothers could the etiolated being of the Carranza faction gain size and strength to fight the strong central power. The possibility of this hideous nourishment was supplied from abroad. The war that we brought about leading to the triumph of Carranza over the established governments of his country is as sanguinary, as anti-social, as destructive of the rights of men and of property. Such was the fatal day in early February 1914.[42]

Public opinion in the United States remained mixed—while Carranza and the rebels obtained an immediate advantage. Wilson's agents in Mexico, Lind and Hale, were pleased but wanted more action to back the rebels. Agent Lind expressed impatience that he was "very angry because the Carrancistas had not made more rapid progress since the embargo on arms was lifted," and "that the friendship of O'Shaughnessy for Huerta had prevented the administration from carrying out plans for Huerta's undoing." The pressure on Huerta continued, yet without a rebel offensive southward against the federals the old general would hang on. Shortly after the lifting of the embargo, both Mexican officials and the media harshly attacked President Wilson for lacking honor and diplomatic protocol in extending recognition to the new Peruvian government that took control after a bloody revolution lasting only four days: "this was done in the face of the declaration from the White House in March 1913, that the purpose of the United States is to deny sympathy to all [new] revolutionary governments."[43] *El Imparcial*, the pro-Huerta Mexico City newspaper, was quick to vilify the president in a detailed front-page attack, "The Word of Wilson Lacks Honor," noting that the United States' unconditional recognition of Peru "was done in the face of the declaration from the White House in March that the purpose of the United States is to deny to all revolutionary Governments. Yankee processes work only along the line of evil passions." And as one observer concluded in early 1914, the "'watchful waiting' murmurs of discontent were quickly heard. The watchdog had barked, but it showed no indication of biting."[44]

Deadly Drifting

February 1914 was a pivotal month for the Wilson administration and their handling of the Mexico crisis. Critical funding to Huerta from Europe had been all but halted. The lone remaining support were arms shipments from Japan and brokered deals by German agents, whose official position from Berlin was "the United States is making a mistake in refusing to recognize Huerta." The US State Department notified foreign governments in a strongly worded cable that payment to arms agents would be regarded as "an unfriendly act." Even so, this occurred because the full financial boycott envisioned by President Wilson was not enforceable on banks in Mexico controlled by foreign capitals. These institutions still desired to do business with Huerta. This led Samuel F. Bemis to conclude, "he [Huerta] knew the European powers were not really opposed to him." And to shore up domestic finances, General Huerta, in a state of crisis, printed worthless inflationary pesos, raised taxes, forced citizens to join the army, and daily

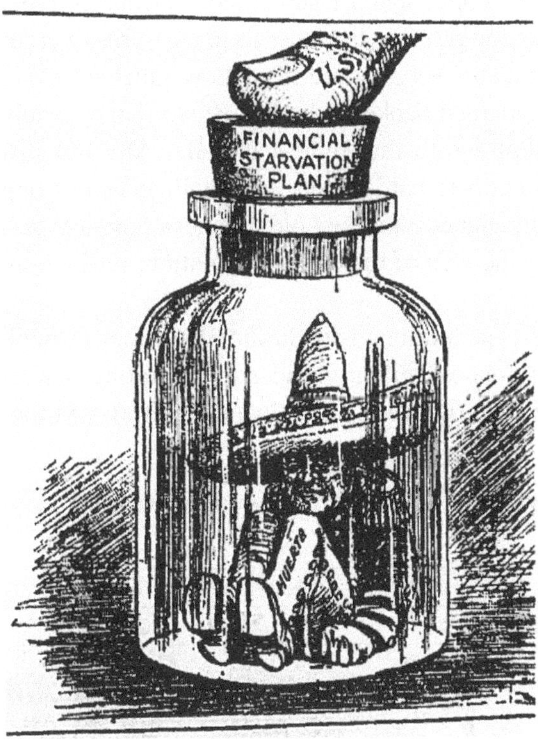

Financial Starvation Plan: One prime objective of the Wilson administration in ousting General Huerta was to prevent any new foreign loans to Mexico. Cartoons were a widely used means of conveying ideas in newspapers across Mexico and the United States. Source: *Literary Digest*.

eroded the backing of his most loyal supporters. Huerta's true passion, to gain full recognition, was dashed. Reports surfaced that the general was more erratic in dealing with his ministers; he moved from one tavern in the capital to another to avoid assassination and drank heavily—yet an ever-clever politician, he was still in power.[45]

Border Contraband

The lifting of the arms embargo in early February 1914 emboldened the actions of the *huertistas*; they quickly reached out and destroyed any perceived threats from the seemingly energized rebels in northern Mexico. Legal shipments were often commingled with illegal contraband crossings. For example, legal exports of livestock through the Port of Laredo, consisting of the consular district for documented crossings at Nuevo Laredo, Palafox, and San Ignacio, totaled $2.6 million for the period from February to December 1913 (see table 2). One indication of the harsher reaction was that the Rio Grande garrisons were given or assumed on their own a more aggressive stance against smugglers—primarily rebel arms. Among those who were targeted by the federals to curb cross-border activity were men like Clemente Vergara and his fellow ranchers along the uncharted and sparsely guarded banks of the Río Bravo that routinely smuggled and brokered supplies to the highest bidders. And not just arms and munitions but also horses, cattle, food, and intelligence of troop movements. Such mixed allegiances and age-old business practices unwittingly lured Vergara into the web of the border revolution, retribution, and violence.[46]

In northern Mexico, the Constitutionalists, during December through late January, had made the greatest military strides in disrupting federal supply trains and gradually capturing key cities. Given the efforts of Lind,

Table 2. Exportation of Livestock through the Port of Laredo February to March 1913

	Laredo	Palafox	San Ignacio	Total
Cattle	$1,032,875	574,467	683,234	2,290,573
Horses & mules	31,410	27,784	45,098	104,492
Sheep & goats	42,882	164,331	27,273	234,486
Grand total:				$2,629,551

Source: Laredo Daily Times, March 3, 1913.

Cabrera, and others to promote the Constitutionalists as the one true body to determine the future of Mexico, Carranza was gradually receiving more backing from the White House and US investors, and property owners in Mexico realized Huerta's days in Mexico City may be numbered. Shortly after the lifting of the arms embargo by Wilson, rumors, although while premature, spread that a coup d'état was imminent and Huerta was soon leaving Mexico. Further concern arose as anti-America threats appeared in Mexico City newspapers amid predictions of a mass unrest if the United States used force in Mexico.[47] Much of the first half of February seemed an uneasy stalemate, as neither the Federalists nor rebels made any moves. The White House received more complaints from Capitol Hill on the course of events in Mexico and the protection of Americans along the border. Congress wanted to know if the US Army was prepared to launch a large offensive into Mexico. Furthermore, what would be the response to an "incident" against the United States or one of its citizens that would precipitate an appropriate action? Random murders continued during late 1913 and into early 1914, yet they now rose to the level of armed response, except for the continued vocal irritation of Governor Colquitt concerning raids along the Texas border and the lack of federal

Governor Oscar Colquitt constantly demanded more protection from the US Army on the Texas border. While troop strength in Texas did increase, army commanders were advised to avoid all contact with the revolutionaries across the border, "unless fired upon first." The army began to deploy some of its first "armored" vehicles, mostly a novelty and of little use in stemming the cross-border violence. Author's collection.

response. Juárez–El Paso was in a state of armed standoff; Laredoans had been killed by stray bullets during the 1914 New Year's Day Battle of Nuevo Laredo; and the US Army came perilously close to blows against both the armed federals and Constitutionalist troops fleeing across the Rio Grande at Presidio following ten days of bloody fighting at Ojinaga—yet still the "dog did not bite."[48]

In Washington and in the national media, awareness was raised about the increased number of Americans murdered in Mexico. Declaring the Wilson policy of "watchful waiting" a failure, Congressmen Julius Kahn (R) of California and William Ainey (R) of Pennsylvania, during the floor debate on the Army Appropriations Bill, labeled the president's actions as "deadly drifting." The total unofficial number killed was 120 Americans through January 1914, causing Kahn to suggest a commission of Argentina, Brazil, and Chile (ABC) be held to end the chaos in Mexico. The ABC group was endorsed as a face-saving means by President Wilson in late April 1914 to extricate the US Marines and Navy blue coats from Veracruz. The list of American dead did not include the hundreds of murdered foreign nationals—Chinese, Spanish, Japanese, and French—that went uncounted. However, none of these senseless killings of Americans and Mexicans gained any notoriety or action by Washington. The Wilson administration preferred not to let a single incident grow into a full-blown dispute with Mexico. Protests were leveled by the State Department in Washington and by each of the foreign governments on the death of their citizens, but to no avail. Washington feared an incident at the border could spill over and escalate to intervention. Thus, while US troops were routinely fired at, Washington ordered the army to take care not to engage or pursue either the *huertistas* or any of the rebel factions—in hot pursuit, notwithstanding the increased cross-border raids to steal cattle and arms. As time passed, this became increasingly more difficult, as was confirmed in the 1914 New Year's pitched close-quarter battles at Nuevo Laredo–Laredo and Ojinaga-Presidio and in the flow of refugees and combatants across the Rio Grande. This pattern of murder along the border soon included an increased number of Americans being killed on US territory. Such depredations dated from the earliest days of the revolution and intensified through early 1914.[49]

The border region is where there was the greatest likelihood that an incident could escalate, but to date none had. A rebel attack at Agua Prieta in April 1911 resulted in two deaths and eleven wounded Americans in the cross-border town of Douglas, Arizona. This was followed days later by rebel attacks in Ciudad Juárez, with six killed and fifteen wounded Americans in the cross-border town of El Paso. Ciudad Juárez changed hands seven times during a decade of fighting. In March 1913, fighting in Nogales, Sonora, spilled into the streets of adjacent Nogales, Arizona, and citizen onlookers were wounded in both Laredo and Presidio on January 1 and 2, 1914. Given the increased rebel attacks in northern Mexico beginning in late 1913, more noncombatants were in harm's way. Three incidents, for example, focused increased attention on the US-Mexico border, and a fourth—the Vergara incident—would gain international notoriety and response. In late January, there was a shift in those committing the killings from "bandits, rebels, and *villistas*" to the active incidents involving Huerta's federal officers and soldiers. During the last three days of January 1914, an incident involved three Americans: Frank Smith, Robert W. Hardwood, and Mortimer Miller (along with the murder of Harry Compton on February 15) were killed by *huertista* troops. And there was little or no mention of their fate in the media or an investigation by the US government.[50]

Freelance writer John Reed, sent to cover the revolution for the New York *Metropolitan* magazine, witnessed firsthand the confusion and mixed loyalties in northern Mexico that placed many foreigners in danger. The distrust of Americans was demonstrated one late evening when Reed approached a group of drunken Mexican officers in a hotel lobby bar; upon seeing the American, one officer began "to sing a pleasant little song":

Yo tengo una pistol	I have pistol
Con mango de marfil	With an ivory handle
Para matar todos los gringos	With which to kill all the Americans
Que vienen por ferrocarril!	Who come by the railroad![51]

The second tragedy was the mass murder by bandits on February 4, hours after the lifting of the arms embargo, in the Cumbre Train Tunnel in Chihuahua. Renegade bandits, under the leadership of notorious bandit Máximo Castillo, sent a blazing freight train into the shaft, setting the timbers in the tunnel on fire and wrecking the train. Unaware of the wreck, a passenger train carrying over two dozen Americans, including Mrs. Lee Carruth and her five children, entered the tunnel; all passengers were trapped and killed. Castillo's picture was posted in papers nationwide, and

General Villa ordered his capture and immediate execution. Yet, after he was captured, he soon escaped to the United States.[52]

The third incident that gained wide notoriety was the cold-blooded killing by Pancho Villa and his men of British rancher William S. Benton. Protesting the theft of his cattle by the rebel soldiers, Benton went to Villa headquarters and demanded payment. A heated discussion followed, which, in some accounts, report the rancher pulled a pistol on Villa, but was prevented to fire by his guards. Next there were claims Benton was jailed, tried, and shot for attacking Villa (not true), yet in fact he was loaded on a train, shipped into the desert, made to dig his own shallow grave, clubbed repeatedly, and left for dead. Accounts of Benton's killing were soon flashed to London and Washington, both of which demanded a full reporting. The incident received the attention of the prime minister and Parliament and the wrath of the British media, which demanded immediate justice. Wilson and Bryan were in a difficult position; they had pledged to the British they would handle all affairs of state and violence in Mexico, and they expected no outside intervention. General Villa made more conflicting statements about Benton's disappearance; he was ordered by Carranza to abstain from further action, and the First Chief would be the sole contact point between the British and Americans. Some in Washington suggested a US Army Cavalry escort be sent across the Rio Grande into Juárez to recover Benton's body, and advise Mexico in advance this would not be an act of war, but humanitarian in nature. Such cross-border intervention did not occur. Since the revolution, the Benton case—possibly because he was British and murdered by Pancho Villa—has been one of the few cases cited by scholars, with little or no mention of the scores of other killings.[53]

On Friday, February 13 (ten days after Wilson revoked the arms embargo), a week prior to Benton's confrontation with General Villa, Palafox rancher Clemente Vergara became the primary American noncombatant diplomatic case handled by the White House and the US government during the Mexican Revolution. Unlike scores of foreign deaths in Mexico that went largely unnoticed during the revolution, the Vergara affair quickly escalated into an international incident with worldwide media coverage. The killing of Vergara, out of nearly five hundred Americans murdered during the revolution, would take the United States and Texas to the brink of hostile actions with Mexico. It was the first US case to receive immediate attention from the highest levels in Washington, and in many regards set the tone and backdrop for the fall of Huerta and actions of US intervention that would follow in late April 1914 at Veracruz. The alarm and reaction from both official Washington and London to these murders, over all other incidents against foreigners during the revolution, caused the American chargé d'affaires' wife to record: "there is intense indignation on the [murders on the] frontier. The fat is, at last, in the fire."[54]

5
Vergara Affair

Colquitt must be, I am afraid, a "handful" to Washington.

—Sir Christopher F. Cradock
Rear Admiral to Admiralty in London

Give me 100 Texas Rangers and I can do more toward keeping law and order in Texas than 10,000 United States troops.

—Oscar Branch Colquitt,
Governor of Texas (1911–15)

It is uncertain when official word of the death of Webb County Texas rancher Clemente Vergara reached President Woodrow Wilson at the White House. The president was routinely briefed on incidents perpetrated against Americans on the border and in Mexico. Most were senseless murders of unknown citizens meaning no harm, only caught in the violence of the revolution—as Walter Prescott Webb noted, "one must not forget the psychology of fear and racial antagonism that made the Rio Grande a battle-line and the border a battle-field." Unlike those who were killed prior to him, the Vergara kidnapping and murder was no accident or routine affair. Within days events near Laredo on the Rio Grande would be worldwide news and become a complicated affair bringing the United States and Mexico to the brink of war long before the March 1914 Tampico incident and the April 21, 1914, Veracruz landing.[1]

February–March 1914 would, in hindsight, be a pivotal period for US-Mexico relations. These two months set the stage for the eventual American intervention and forced abdication of General Huerta. Tensions in Mexico City mixed with high-profile murders on the border fueled speculation on the ultimate course of Huerta's fate and the degree to which the United States interjected itself in the revolution. Lifting the arms embargo on February 3 was viewed by most as a tremendous moral boost to the rebel cause. It placed Wilson clearly in support of the insurgents. A London *Daily Chronicle* editorial noted, "the importation of arms into Mexico will immediately strengthen the rebels against Huerta, but will also contingently strengthen Mexico against any American invasion." In a secret briefing of Sir Edward Grey at Whitehall, the British Foreign Ministry was advised that Washington sentiment had turned fully to the rebels: "the Constitutionalist party seems at the present moment to offer the best hopes for an ultimate settlement." And the White House continued to apply economic pressure on Huerta by lobbying to prevent outside financial support or loans. Mexican ports, primarily Tampico's oil terminals and Veracruz's import/export operations, were under a virtual blockade and under close watch by the US Navy, ostensibly to evacuate Americans and foreigners if necessary. The economic stability of the country deteriorated as the peso was daily devalued, there was little or no hard currency in circulation. Most financiers and bankers in the United States and Europe gave up hope for Huerta's ability to survive much longer.[2]

Rumors of a coup d'état or abdication of General Huerta were rampant in the capital, many blaming the problems of the country on the United States. Helping to fuel tension in the capital was British envoy Lord Carden, who, against direct orders from London to not interfere with American intentions, strongly lobbied the French and German legations to back General Huerta. The German government continued its support of Huerta, if for no other reason than to attempt to upset the balance of power between the Americans and British. The semiofficial *Cologne Gazette* paid a glowing tribute to the general: "Huerta is, all in all, the man whom Mexico needs and must have if she is not to be swallowed up by the United States."[3] The role and safety of British subjects in Mexico was also dubious. Oilman Weetman Pearson, Lord Cowdray, the de facto representative of British business interests in Mexico, added support and "operating" funding to Carden's efforts. Carden worked repeatedly to win over the British Foreign Office, who viewed the revolution as an American problem as a result of Washington's pledge to protect British citizens and property. Carden argued, based on the power struggle and revolution in Mexico, that Britain needed to reassess its long-term interest in Latin

America in general and the Panama Canal in particular. He worked to persuade the French and Germans, as well as the British Foreign Office, that a great deal was at stake beyond Mexico and the Panama Canal, "the real goal of American policy is to not stop at Panama, but take the entire South American Continent."[4]

Carden's lobbying, along with backing from the British business sector, gave Huerta a ray of hope, allowing him to hold out until July 1914. In the meantime, the rising tensions were met in the progovernment Mexico City press. *El Imparcial* used salvos of "libelous and scurrilous" editorial attacks on President Wilson and his heavy-handed policies. American chargé d'affaires O'Shaughnessy, whose life had been threatened by the editor of *El Imparcial*, Salvador Díaz Mirón (and who resorted to carrying a gun), protested to Huerta and Foreign Affairs Minister Querido Moheno y Tabares that such attacks on the president enflamed anti-American sentiments against expatriates living and working in Mexico.[5] Additionally, the rebels expressed antiforeign views. They spread the message that "foreign interest and prominent families resident here cannot expect mercy

Clemente Vergara. Source: Briscoe American History Library.

at the hands of the Constitutionalist if they in any way assisted President Huerta." The main target of the rebel decree was landed Spanish gentry.[6] And the problems spilled over with increased violence on the border near Laredo.

As the war of words and intrigue continued in Mexico City and Washington, DC, Clemente Vergara became the center of official attention in both capitals. The US consul in Nuevo Laredo, Alonzo Beaver Garrett, immediately notified Washington on the evening of February 13, 1914, apparently in his initial notice bypassing protocol and the US embassy in Mexico City, of the reported "kidnapping" of an American rancher near Palafox, Texas (originally San José de Palafox). By early February 14, the US State Department at once demanded that US citizen Clemente Vergara be released and a full accounting given of the circumstances for his detention. Swift action was paramount in such cases, as six months earlier Federalist troops arrested US citizen Porfirio Laurel, also of Laredo and Webb County, and charged him with aiding the rebels. Laurel was transferred to the Federalist garrison in Nuevo Laredo, interrogated, and reported released to return to Laredo. However, he was never seen again.[7] The first public notice of Vergara's "alleged" kidnapping was reported on Saturday in the *Laredo Daily Times*, and on Sunday February 15, in both the *Austin Statesmen* and the *New York Times*.[8]

A "Slight" Cold

President Wilson, after nearly a year of micromanaging the Mexico crisis policy and strategy, and absent an informed and active role by Secretary of State William J. Bryan and the State Department on how to handle General Huerta and the rebel faction led by Venustiano Carranza, may have read the small article on the Vergara incident in the Sunday *New York Times*. The president did not receive official notice until Tuesday, February 17, after spending nearly five days bedridden with, what his personal physician reported was, a "slight" cold. The president's very poor health during his first year in office was generally not noticed and, when it was, erroneously attributed to overwork. As most remember, his failing health during the post–World War I struggle over the League of Nations, was, however, a factor long before the first day in the presidency. His continued poor medical history was not reported during the 1912 presidential campaign, nor does it seem there were any questions asked. However, within a month of his inauguration, Wilson, in the White House, sustained a "probable stroke," causing paralysis to his left upper extremity.[9]

Wilson's weak immune system, poor stress tolerance, and history of hypertension-caused strokes dating back to 1896 resulted in numbness in his right hand and fingers as well as pain in his right arm. He was unable to write with his right hand for nearly a year, opting to type most of his correspondence left handed. Wilson, clearly aware of his deteriorating medical condition, referred to the numbness and pain only to family and close friends as a neurological disorder or "neuritis." One sympathetic biographer attributed the condition in Wilson's right hand as nothing but "writer's cramp!" The perpetuation and the obfuscation of the true seriousness of the president's medical condition continued undetected. While minimized, once in the White House the president's illness became a much-guarded secret, kept by his personal physician, Dr. Carl T. Grayson—along with the president's wife and confidant Colonel House. Wilson's health problems, coupled with bouts of depression, diminishing sight, and severe indigestion oftentimes found him irritable and curt with those around him. Following the April 1913 White House stroke, he complained to Colonel House, "That some members of the cabinet bothered him by taking up his time threshing out matters with him instead of presenting them in condensed fashion."[10]

During the two-month period from early December 1913 until mid-February 1914, the president was constantly ill and was bedridden three separate extended times. While his illness was reported as only a "cold," in fact there were complications of hypertension and respiratory problems caused by influenza. The period of illness included hemiplegia (paralysis of the side of the body) and attacks of blindness. This ten weeks of illness began the night after he gave his State of the Union report (during which he denied any intention to intervene in Mexico) on December 2. This illness was caused by, according to the White House, the transition from "the heated chamber of the House of Representatives to the cloudy weather outside." Dr. Grayson, who was thoroughly devoted to the president, was astute in playing down this string of illnesses; he gave an optimistic forecast, as only preventative measures were needed to keep the President Wilson from "catching a cold." The problems were more than a mere cold—as the president denied any incapacity whatsoever. However, due to his physical weakness and lingering illnesses, cabinet meetings were moved to the second-floor family study. By late December, his health moderately improved. Thus, to escape the damp cold of Washington, Wilson, with his family; Dr. Grayson; his personal stenographer, Charles M. Swen; and four Secret Service agents, boarded a special presidential car of the Southern Railway on December 23 (the day after he signed into law the Federal Reserve Act) and headed for a three-week visit to warmer climes to fully recover from what Dr. Grayson told reporters was an "attack of grippe." It was during this trip to Pass Christian on the Gulf Coast that the president met with Special Agent Lind to review the situation in Mexico. In the meantime, along the border, both the rebels and the Federalists increased attacks, refugees and deserters from the fighting flowed northward across the Rio Grande into Texas, and land and cities in northern Mexico changed hands to the extent it was difficult to determine who was in control. The lifting of the arms embargo on February 3 only intensified the struggle on both sides.[11]

Returning to Washington from the warm southern Gulf Coast vacation in mid-January, just ahead of the opening of the congressional session, Wilson's health was fair. Colds plagued the president throughout January 1914, and he was once again confined to bed on February 10, forcing him to cancel a number of highly visible events, including a presentation to a delegation of old friends and officials from New Jersey, visiting Capitol Hill for "Jersey Day," as well as a private dinner for key congressional members given for the president by Postmaster General Burleson. Bold front-page headlines in the *Austin Statesman* noted: "President Ill: Engagements Are Canceled," only days after returning from his "southern vacation." Once again Dr. Grayson managed the White House news media, cheerfully noting, "President Wilson is somewhat hoarse, and would be at his desk in the executive offices tomorrow"—Tuesday the seventeenth—the day he "officially" learned of the Vergara incident. Thus, the affairs of state were at a virtual standstill for over two months from early December 1913 to mid-February 1914, casting doubt on Wilson's interest in and capacity to focus on the problems in Mexico and on the border. President Wilson's lingering poor health surely affected his ability to address the mounting tensions with Mexico, such as the heightened pressure in February with the Vergara affair, immediate British concerns to address the Benton murder, the business sectors' demands to protect their investments, hostile protest from border governors, and calls from Congress to address the deteriorating situation. This was long in advance of the US invasion at Veracruz.[12]

Border Bitterness

The increased Constitutionalist attacks across northern Mexico had the border in chaos. Federal garrisons fought to contain and push back the rebel's attacks—with each faction concentrating forces at points where the railroad crosses the border. As the lines of communication were cut along the border to Huerta's Federalist garrisons—who had been ordered to take great care to avoid provocation with the Americans—panic, suspicion of spies in the ranks, and unrest spread. General Huerta ordered his troops to be on the offensive, dispatching the garrison of over 1,000 troops at Nuevo Laredo to curb the rebel buildup and cut their supply lines. With open borders, battle lines and loyalties of the locals were blurred. Communities and families were divided in their support of the different political factions. Loyalties to different groups of *revoltosos* running guns, munitions, horses, and supplies across the river further complicated the situation. Laredo and the surrounding area along the river was no exception as different groups in South Texas, Mexicans and Texans, harbored support and connections, as well as grudges, with their opposition in Mexico.[13]

Webb County Sheriff Amador Sánchez was an active political leader in Laredo. He was also heavily involved in the revolution in northern Mexico. Source: Laredo Public Library.

For decades Laredo served as the natural north–south crossing for cattle drives and commerce between Mexico and Texas. So located, it served as an ample launching site for rebel groups going south and as a safe harbor from Federalists or rebels seeking safety in the United States. In Laredo, arms and money could be laundered to support nefarious plotting. Nuevo Laredo changed hands three times, and with the bloody battles of early January 1914, Nuevo Laredo remained, for a time, in Huerta control. Laredoans, many with family members divided on both sides of the Rio Grande, were caught in the day-to-day activities of all the factions as they avoided both local and US federal agents attempting to enforce the neutrality law and limit stock raids along the border. Weapons, ammunitions, and good horses were in high demand by all sides.[14]

Leading the South Texas efforts to assist the Federalists in northern Mexico was Laredo sheriff Amador Sánchez; having beaten the indictment during the Reyes–Neutrality Law conspiracy in 1911, he had a firm hand on all of Webb County. A distant relative of the founding pioneer of Laredo in 1755, Don Tomás Sánchez, the sheriff, Amador Sánchez, had maintained large landholdings and cattle ranches in both Texas and across the river in the state of Tamaulipas south of Nuevo Laredo (where he owned a 100,000-acre cattle ranch). Since his pardon by President Taft for the Reyes case in early 1913, Sánchez maintained total political power in the Webb County. In addition to sheriff, he served as president of the Laredo School Board and controlled the Webb County tax office, which was located across the hall from his first-floor office in the Webb County Courthouse. A chief leader of machine politics in Texas, the sheriff's Democratic Party ties were solid with his boastful credentials of having lined up the 1912 vote across South Texas to elect both President Wilson and Governor Colquitt. A staunch facilitator of the Federalists in northern Mexico, little took place in either Webb Country or across the river with his counterparts in Nuevo Laredo and northern Mexico without his knowledge or approval—to including financing, monitoring, and facilitating smuggling operations across the Rio Grande. Furthermore, Sánchez's close political ties to the Texas governor would soon cloud the handling of the Vergara case.[15]

As the rebels intensified their attacks along the border, relationships among ranchers, merchants, and government agents grew strained due to the competing factions and demands for arms, supplies, and horses. Refugees from Mexico crowded the Texas border towns, bringing with them mixed loyalties. Cattle were important and would be rustled to be sold by the head to raise money for supplies, but the greatest demand as the revolution widened, following arms and munitions, was solid broken horses. The chaotic border conditions made it ripe for unexpected incidents and violence—and in the name of the "revolution" proved convenient cover for random killings. Reports of violence and trespassing were well known in the Palafox region of the Rio Grande. Ranchers Otto R. Winter and Jeff R. Randolph wrote Texas Adjutant General Henry Hutchings a typical letter from that period, which was forwarded by Governor Colquitt to the US Secretary of War: "refugees from Mexico cut fences as fast at night as we can repair them in daytime, and that these refugees erect willow houses on his land and subsist on his crops . . . there are at least 50 carbines in the hands of the Mexicans." They also noted that the US Army patrols, border customs and immigration agents, and county officials failed to "afford any relief by positive action."[16] The US Army found itself attempting to deliver a complicated mission affected by the sheer size of the border, the shortage of troops and supplies, and ongoing racial hatred among certain groups of Anglos and Mexicans. As one scholar noted:

> The responsibility of keeping the revolution south of the Rio Grande belonged in part to the U.S. Army. American troops were ordered not to cross the border and not to fire across the border unless the Mexicans intentionally shot into American onlookers and their property—the mission was frustrating. The traditional Anglo-Mexican hostility among border citizens was stimulated by the revolution and complicated by the fact that some Anglo and Mexican groups wanted either to provoke a military intervention or to aid one or the other of the revolutionary factions. *Ordinary crimes masqueraded as revolutionary activity.* Civilian law enforcement was confused and often ineffective, since Anglo peace officers became increasingly trigger-happy, vigilantism flourished, and Mexican-American constables and judges were paralyzed by the fear of persecuting their *companeros*.[17]

A member of one of the earliest families to locate in South Texas, Clemente Vergara, forty-five, was an active rancher and trader of saddle horses at his ranch at Palafox, 30 miles upriver from Laredo. He lived in a two-room limestone block house with his wife, Antonia, and their two children on a high bluff overlooking the Rio Grande.[18] Clemente, on the morning of Friday, February 13, was called by Federalist soldiers to come across the river and discuss payment for his "missing" horses. Rumors later circulated that he was trading horses in Mexico with both the rebels and the Federalists, not unlike numerous other Texas and Mexican ranchers and smugglers, and that somehow this was the root of his problem. In a page one story in Mexico City, *El Imparcial* labeled Vergara "*un peligroso filibustero*." For over a decade he grazed his horses on a long, narrow 113-acre island-sandbar running down the middle of the Rio Grande below the town of Palafox, to take advantage of the lush vegetation. He rotated his horses from his Palafox ranch, using some for the ranch's operation and selling others in both Mexico and Texas. His livestock carried a distinctive brand of the "V" with the half-moon across the top on the hind quarter, "V̂," and a single smaller "v̂" on the cheek of each horse. All of the horses grazing on the river island on the twelfth and thirteenth were branded with his markings, except one mare.[19]

The request from the Federalist officer, Captain Apolonio Rodríguez, for Vergara to come over, was the result of an advance meeting arranged by Sheriff Sánchez and the Hidalgo, Mexico, garrison commander, Major

One of the lesser-known key individuals during the early years of the Mexican Revolution, was the US consul in Nuevo Laredo, A. B. Garret, pictured here with his wife at the consulate. Garrett's investigation and reports on the Vergara incident proved to be the most detailed assessment of the events. Author's collection.

Juan [Andrés] Garza Galán. Sánchez and Galán were reported to have given Vergara, who probably was very suspicious about the actual intent of the Federalist, a handwritten note for safe passage across the river. However, a Texas Ranger, stationed near Palafox, Private Henry Felps, warned the rancher early on the thirteenth not to cross due to the mounting border unrest and bandits. Ignoring the advice, Vergara crossed at noon, and the Ranger did not see him. Once across the river, accompanied by his nephew Marcelo Villarreal, Vergara was captured by the Federals, pistol-whipped, taken captive, and marched a short distance to the Hidalgo army barracks stockade. The nephew avoided capture by diving into the river and hiding in the tall grass along the banks, then he swam back across to Palafox.[20]

Conspiracy

Word of Clemente Vergara's capture spread fast to both Laredo and Nuevo Laredo. For the next four weeks, there would be claims and counterclaims as well as rumors and reaction in Washington, Mexico City, London, and Austin, trying to resolve the incident. This was not another random event—according to Harris and Sadler, "The evidence indicates that Sanchez set Vergara up." However, the initial local rumors (as well as newspapers in Mexico City) did much to vilify Vergara as a supporter of the rebels, some claiming he, as a part of an extensive smuggling ring, had crossed to join the Constitutionalist fight. It is doubtful he would leave his wife and children and vast ranch to actively join the rebels. In addition to being a well-known rancher in Webb County, he was an active member of the fraternal order of the Woodsman of the World and was engaged in local county politics. Federalist officials in Nuevo Laredo, Piedras Negras, and Hidalgo all responded with a different and confused report of the events surrounding the kidnapping. On the day after his abrupt abduction, his wife, Antonia, and niece, Dolores, crossed the Rio Grande on Saturday and found Clemente alive, tied to a chair in a small holding room at the Federalist barracks. His face was badly cut and bruised and his hair matted in blood—yet he was alive. He had no medical care or food. His wife comforted him with a meal and a blanket to keep the evening chill at bay. Staying until late into the night, the women departed to spend the remainder of the night with friends in Hidalgo. Antonia was summoned before sunrise by a soldier knocking at the door and giving her a package with the bedding and informing the family that her husband had been taken upriver to the military garrison at Piedras Negras.[21]

Unable to find a Captain Apolonio Rodríguez or any other authority, Señora Vergara returned to the ranch at Palafox. Nuevo Laredo US Consul Garrett's quick action resulted in demands to Mexico to account for Vergara and to release him at once. The Federalist garrison in Nuevo Laredo, under the command of General Guardiola, was in the process of launching a campaign downriver and stated they had no information. Major Garza Galán, the commander at Hidalgo, had claimed to be in Nuevo Laredo during February 12 and 13 and had no information. Finally, the garrison at Piedras Negras commanded by *huertista* General Alberto Guajardo had no record or report of Vergara being transferred to them. Still there was some hope he was alive. The US State Department, even before Governor Colquitt or the Texas Rangers were involved in the incident, ordered Garrett to conduct a full investigation. The first, of some five inquiries that would eventually be opened by different agencies, into Vergara's disappearance. By Monday, the sixteenth, Garrett visited both Hidalgo and Palafox to piece together the incident from unnamed eyewitnesses and report to the State Department that Vergara had indeed been kidnapped and was summarily executed, his body buried in an undisclosed location. Garrett, an experienced hand on the border, soon realized the incident was part of a broader conspiracy.[22]

Dr. Alonzo Beaver Garrett had been American consul in Nuevo Laredo since 1901. A medical doctor by training, the sixty-six-year-old Lavalette, West Virginia, native practiced medicine for some thirty years in his home state and in southern Ohio. At age fourteen he enlisted in the Union Army as a drummer boy in the 14th Kentucky Infantry, only to be ordered home by his parents, due to his young age. Later he returned as a corporal in a line infantry unit, Company B, 45th Kentucky, for the balance of the war. He served a brief term in the West Virginia Senate before being appointed as US consul in Nuevo Laredo in 1901. Prior to the start of the revolution, his job was rather routine, dealing with routine visas, the US customs inspector, and trade issues. However, two years prior to the Vergara murder he was involved with a Nuevo Laredo bank robbery, when revolutionaries captured an American-owned bank in 1912. To free the bank president, Garrett made a deal with the bandits that he would open the safe (knowing there were no sizable valuables) if they would release their hostage and forgo dynamiting the safe and the building. They agreed and no one was hurt. Staff at the State Department referred to Garrett as the “fighting consul,” which soon became applicable. In another incident, when, with the help of the US Army commander of nearby Fort McIntosh west of Laredo, he threatened a Constitutionalist commander, Major Múzquiz (nephew of Venustiano Carranza) in Nuevo León that if he would not release rancher Robert Hazelrigg and a dozen American hostages, he would make Mexico “too hot for him” by use of the full force of the United States Army. The reluctant major agreed and all were safe. The Vergara case would prove an equal challenge.[23]

During the first week, the Vergara murder was primarily a diplomatic issue with Washington and Mexico City seeking to obtain a full account and to bring those guilty to trial. A week after Vergara’s abduction, the news was released that a British citizen and landed hacendado, William S. Benton, a rancher in Chihuahua, had a heated confrontation with Pancho Villa at his headquarters in northern Mexico over the theft of cattle from his multi-million-dollar ranch, Los Remedios. Insults were exchanged and Benton was accused of trying to shoot General Villa, who in turn had him executed after a “quick trial” by either Villa or his loyal right-hand man Rodolfo Fierro. This incident occurred only days after the Vergara murder.[24] The Benton cold-blooded killing soon added increased pressure on the Wilson White House to address the violence in northern Mexico. Having pledged to protect all foreigners in Mexico, and especially the British, Washington was suddenly under mounting pressure from London to account for the Benton incident. Of the over 1,000 foreigners killed or murdered in Mexico during the revolution, the Vergara and Benton cases would make worldwide news and bring all parties to near-open cross-border hostilities.[25]

Sir Edward Grey, in London, indicated he would send British consular representatives to assist the investigation into the Benton case and agreed to allow the American “good offices” to take the investigative lead in the Benton incident. In Washington, the spreading crisis on the border raised questions in Congress about an armed American intervention. And to further complicate the diplomatic discourse, the British, who had quickly recognized the Huerta government in February 1913, stated publicly, “England Will Never Recognize Carranza”—the very candidate for the next Mexican president that Wilson, Bryan, and Lind supported! The Wilson administration—firmly against intervention, denied any claims that the Vergara, Benton, and scores of additional incidents warranted any favorable action or confrontation. A suggestion, fueled by the Hearst newspapers (who used the Benton incident as valuable propaganda material against the rebel Constitutionalist), that the northern rebel factions clamored to declare a "separate new republic" in order to join the United States yet proved little more than a rumor.[26]

The mounting news from the border soon involved Governor Oscar B. Colquitt, who requested a detailed report from the Texas Ranger captain of Company B in the Laredo sector, Captain John Jesse Sanders. The fifty-eight-year-old Sanders from Lockhart, Texas, had been in law enforcement and ranching much of his career and served as one of only three Ranger captains in 1914. Sanders had a six-foot, two-inch frame with a slight pot belly, and with his pearl-handled Colt 45 was an imposing

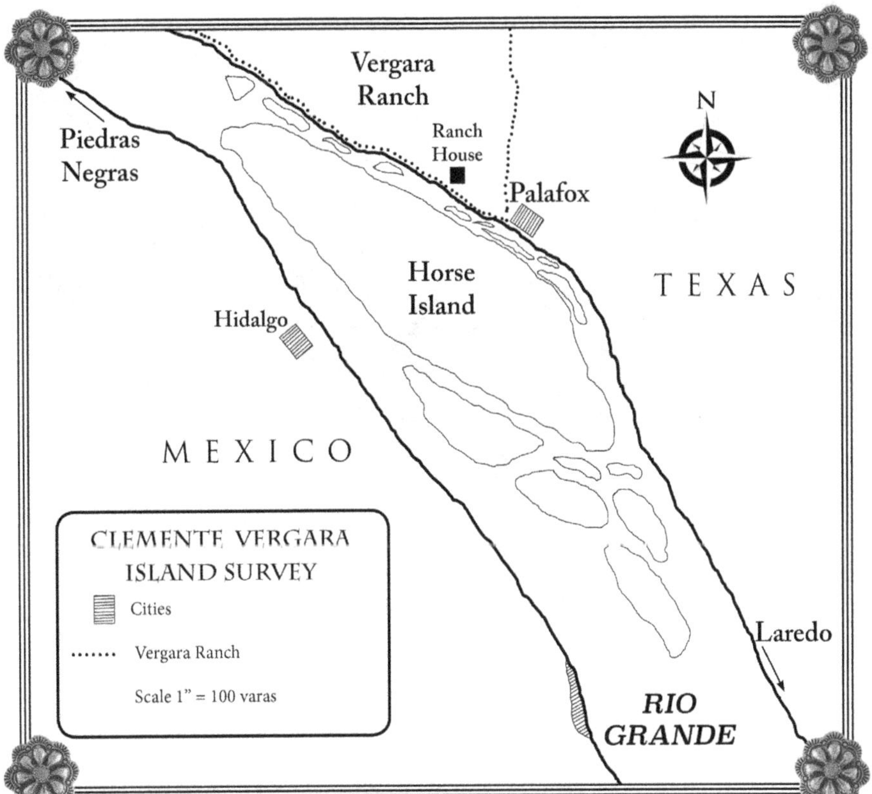

Survey of the 113-acre island claimed by Clemente Vergara in the Rio Grande in 1912 approximately 40 miles north of Laredo, Texas, by E. J. Foster, Deputy County Surveyor.

Texas Ranger John Jesse Sanders became the focus of the investigation into returning Clement Vergara from Mexico after the rancher was killed. Sanders's famed telegram of the recovery of the Vergara body was the source of a major diplomatic incident in both Washington, DC, and Mexico City. Author's collection.

figure when mounted. The investigation would not be left to the Rangers alone. Texas Adjutant General Henry Hutchings wired the Texas National Guard commander in Laredo, Captain Edward M. Matson, to make a map of the island in question, gather information, and to work with Consul Garrett. Hutchings' staff, in a rush to investigate and respond to the governor and provide a detailed report, initially failed to contact the Texas General Land Office in Austin, which housed the maps and surveys of the border region.[27]

The intent of the detailed map request was to prove the Rio Grande island was indeed Texas territory—when in fact it was "no-man's land." However, the governor quickly rushed to the conclusion, even as facts were being determined, that Vergara—an American citizen—had been abducted from Texas soil and the Federalist troops had crossed into Texas, which constituted an "invasion." Therefore, the legal status of the island in the Rio Grande, Isla Grande, opposite the mouth of San Pedro Creek, would possibly prove to be a critical factor in determining if in fact US (and Texas) sovereignty had been violated. The Texas land commissioner J. T. Robison, issued a statement that the state had never owned or leased the island due to its questionable legal status. Furthermore, records in Austin clearly indicated that in August 1910, Clemente Vergara filed a formal application with the county surveyor in Webb County to purchase and obtain title to the 113-acre island, deemed by the state as unoccupied "scrap land." The application was sent to Commissioner Robison in Austin; he refused to grant a clear title on May 20, 1912, due to doubt whether it was on the Texas or Mexican side of the river.[28]

After reviewing Ranger Sanders's first report from Laredo, Colquitt telegraphed the White House to determine who had jurisdiction in the Vergara case:[29]

> President, White House 26 February 1914
> Washington, D.C.
>
> Clemente Vergara, a citizen of Texas, who complained that his property had been unlawfully taken by Mexican troops, appealed to State authorities for protection and Texas Rangers were sent to give him protection asked for. On the theory that Mexicans wanted to confer with a view of settling for the stolen property, Vergara was induced to meet them on a small island in the Rio Grande in Webb County, Texas, where he was assaulted, abducted and carried into

> Mexico and hung, it is alleged by soldiers of the Mexican army. Under treaty between the United States and Mexico, the Governor of Texas has the right to apply to the governor of the border states for surrender of the men committing this crime to Texas authorities. I am not advised whom the United States Government now recognizes as the constitutional authority in Mexican states bordering on the Rio Grande, these border state are in a state of revolution and anarchy. To whom shall we present demand for surrender of abductors, and murderers of Vergara? Shall we appeal to Huerta or the Carranza government? In view of the condition of anarchy, can the State of Texas obtain consent of the United States Government to send Rangers across the Rio Grande to pursuit of the lawless faction when they cross into Texas and commit crimes? I insist, Mr. President, that Texas as a sovereign State is entitled to the protection of Texas citizens on the border from an unbearable condition like that which now exists.
>
> O. B. Colquitt[30]
> Governor of Texas

The governor's telegram was not well received at the White House. The request to send the Texas Rangers across the Rio Grande to arrest those responsible in Vergara's death received a rapid reply from Secretary Bryan that "any armed men into Mexico" would be the sole responsibility of the federal government. In order to "smother" the sensational suggestion from Austin, Bryan immediately released Colquitt's telegram and the White House's answer to the print media. Following a lengthy White House cabinet meeting, focused entirely on the crisis in Mexico, the secretary briefed the media that the Texas governor's actions were "a grandstand play." Bryan recalled that Colquitt had told the Taft administration that if he had the authority for Rangers to cross the border the Mexican "disorders would be ended in ten minutes." President Wilson was not happy and followed up with a statement "that any movement of American troops [to include the Texas Rangers] across the international border, even with the object of merely protecting the lives and property of American foreign nationals, would be an act of war." To further avert any possible confusion of American intent or troop movements, Wilson ordered Admiral Fletcher, stationed off Veracruz, not to send any US Marines to protect the US Embassy in Mexico City, and Nelson O'Shaughnessy, the ranking diplomat after the departure of Ambassador Wilson, reluctantly concurred.[31]

The Wilson administration seemed to be more concerned with the William S. Benton murder and the relationship with the British than with the Vergara murder near Laredo. Wilson wrote to Colonel House, "The Benton case in Mexico gives a great deal of uneasiness." And Ambassador Page in London telegrammed the president, "strong feelings here that the policy of 'watching and waiting' in Mexico has gone on long enough . . . excitement about Benton is general and intense."[32] Washington and London were in the process of coming to an agreement on the Panama toll confrontation and Wilson's struggle to repeal the Panama Canal Toll Act. There also existed the looming threat that Great Britain may construct a rival canal by way of Lake Nicaragua and the Río San Juan through Nicaragua. To curb British intentions, the State Department was already in secret negotiations with President José Santos Zelaya López in Nicaragua to block British claims in the region and secured "a lease" for a US controlled alternate "inter-oceanic canal site"—which resulted in the Bryan-Chamorro Treaty in August 1914.[33]

However, the immediate concern was the crisis with the Texas governor and Vergara. In response, Secretary Bryan complained to the media that Governor Colquitt's actions and saber rattling were having an impact on "other cases" of missing and/or killed foreigners. At the end of February 1914, neither of the bodies of Benton or Vergara had been located, nor any action taken against those accused of the crimes. Mexican officials once again made an official announcement that Vergara had been released and recently seen in northern Mexico. In the case of Benton, Pancho Villa submitted a phony transcript of the court-martial—that never took place—to the US consul in Torreón. With the insistence of rebel Chief Carranza, a five-person commission, two Americans, two British, and a doctor, were allowed to travel to Chihuahua to investigate the fate of Benton.[34]

In what apparently was a coincidence, and in no way intended to be a show of force, the HMS *Essex*, commanded by Rear Admiral Sir Cecil Cradock, docked in Galveston, Texas, on February 28. It was the first British man-of-war visit to Texas in thirty years. The Texas governor's office hosted British officers and crew, not the US Navy or the US War Department. Following visits to Houston and San Antonio, the admiral arrived in Austin. After a tour of the capitol, which included a special viewing of England's treaty with the Republic of Texas, signed by Queen Victoria and Lord Palmerston, Cradock had a private dinner with the governor. He expressed his thanks for the grand Texas hospitality and noted Great Britain's "disinterestedness in the matter of intervention" in Mexico.[35]

Admiral Cradock conveyed Colquitt's outspoken and headstrong actions and comments to London's Admiralty and Foreign Office. He felt some actions could bring war, and his impression Colquitt was of a "man intensely patriotic regarding the State of Texas"; the admiral concluded:

> He said he had a country [Texas] to administer bigger than Germany; that Washington did not understand the situation; that he did not care who was in power—Huerta or Carranza (he, like all others, detests Villa)—but that Governors of United States frontier States, by treaty, had powers to deal direct with the frontier States of Mexico without reference to Washington. Texans were being daily murdered and the Central Government had got matters into such a mess that neither he nor they could tell who to deal with in Mexico to obtain redress and protection of Texans. He said his plan would be to occupy all Mexican frontier towns on the Mexican side of the Rio Grande—whether they were in possession of the Federals or Rebels—blockade Mexican ports and then call on Mexican in general to settle their differences.[36]

While the British port of call may have been a goodwill gesture, Cradock's intelligence staff was able to compile and relay a vivid picture of the US Army strength and positions in Texas. He reported that General Bliss was "much perturbed by the smallness of the American Army." He also reported on the status of fordable crossings across the Rio Grande, the increase in shipments of arms and munitions across the border, and concern that many felt the Japanese may come to the aid of Huerta, "should they become engaged and tied by Mexican complications." In the conclusion of his report to the British Admiralty and Lord Grey on the temperament of Governor Colquitt, he noted, "He must be, I am afraid, a 'handful' to Washington."[37]

An Unmitigated Lie

The Vergara and Benton murders were front-page news for weeks in scores of newspapers across America, Latin America, and Europe and attracted extensive media coverage that no victims of the revolution received. The two cases caused many to question the Wilson policy in

Mexico. The *Austin Statesman*, the state's leading paper in 1914, noted, "a widespread howl has gone up that something must be done in Mexico." In Mexico City, General Huerta condemned the rebel execution of Benton and in a letter to Governor Colquitt pledged his support to obtain the facts and "avenge" the Vergara murder. The general sent a memorandum to the foreign diplomatic corps in Mexico City declaring that the recent "outrage on foreigners" was all because of the raising of the arms embargo; he urged Washington to reconsider its actions. On sending the Texas Rangers across the border, *El Imparcial* in Mexico City labeled Governor Colquitt "El Mexicanofobo," and a Huerta representative at the Foreign Relations Ministry remarked, "That is the species of hysteria not uncommon in the State of Texas."[38]

As the war of words intensified between the governor and the White House and State Department, Colquitt requested an opinion from the Texas attorney general:

> February 26, 1914 Hon. B. F. Looney
> Attorney General
> Austin, Texas
>
> Dear Sir:—
>
> I am advised that Clemente Vergara, a citizen of the State of Texas, was enveigled [*sic*] to a small island in the Rio Grande River, in Webb County, by soldiers attached to the Mexican Army; was there assaulted, kidnapped, and carried into Mexico, and hung.
>
> Prior to this occurrence, Vergara had complained that Mexican soldiers had stolen his horses, and had appealed to the State of Texas to protect his property. We had sent Rangers to do so.
>
> I am writing you to ask a thorough investigation, and your advice as to what is the best course for the Governor of this State to take to protect the lives and property of our people on the border.
>
> The Constitution on this State gives the Governor authority to repel invasion, and to raise and use troops for the protection of the border. Please advise me what the rights of an American citizen in Texas are, and what is the duty of the Governor of this State, and how far he can go in protecting those rights. A careful investigation of the question, and your advice in full, at the earliest moment possible, will be appreciated.
>
> The situation is acute, and I consider the honor and integrity of this State involved. I invite your attention to the treaty between the

United States and Mexico, which authorizes the Governor of a border state to surrender fugitives for justice.

Please advise me if we have the right, under the facts in the Vergara case to demand the surrender of the soldiers guilty of the abduction and murder of Vergara, assuming that the island in the Rio Grande either belongs to Texas, or is neutral.

Yours Truly
O. B. Colquitt[39]

As tension increased on the border and in Washington, Austin, London, and Mexico City, two unrelated reports soon enflamed the Vergara incident. On February 27, 1914, Texas attorney general B. F. Looney (AG), at the request of Governor Colquitt, prepared an opinion on the state's reaction and claims to action in the Vergara case. In a detailed letter, the AG reviewed the "United States of America and United Mexican States Treaty of February 22, 1899," stating that a person of either nation charged with crimes, to include "theft of horses," given the terms of the convention allowed for extradition. Thus, the AG argued the case of Texas regarding Vergara not on the charge of kidnapping or murder, but instead invoked an age-old clause on horse theft. In addition to the earlier response from Secretary Bryan to the letter saying that Washington would not assist in and would conveniently ignore any identification of the "chief civil or judicial" authority in northern Mexico, was the fact there were two governors in Nuevo León, one Federalist and one Constitutionalist. The Texas AG advised the governor "that under the conditions existing in Mexico, all civil authority is probably suspended due to the war, and that the chief executive authority is the military chieftain. Hence the requisition should be made to such military officer . . . thus, there is no doubt about the right of the State to have Rodriguez [and his men] extradited" for the theft of Vergara's horses. Once in Texas, he would be tried for the Vergara murder. Invoking the "military option" of the 1899 treaty, not just the State Department was now engaged, but also the US Secretary of War and regular army commanders on the border.[40]

Alarm over Colquitt's demands soon spread to the US Army commander at El Paso, General Hugh Scott, at Fort Bliss. The army had developed highly secret plans as early as 1904, and refined by the Army War College in 1913, to both defend an attack from Mexico and a plan to invade Mexico if needed "postulated on the event of a revolution in

Mexico." Known by army planners as "War Plan Green," there was no political or military consensus by the Wilson administration to engage in an intervention or major military action with Mexico.[41] While nonintervention was the official position of the White House, additional regular army troops were weekly mustered and dispatched by pro-interventionist Secretary of War Garrison to Texas with additional US Marine detachments assigned to the Naval Fleet off Veracruz. However, the threat in South Texas was that possible cross-border actions by the Texas Rangers or Texas National Guard, of which General Scott had no direct control, could further escalate the tense situation. The Rangers, although authorized for a strength of four companies totaling eighty-eight Rangers, in March 1914 had only sixteen active Rangers on the muster roll (three captains and thirteen privates), to cover the Texas border. The Laredo sector, which was primarily Webb County, had five active Texas Rangers, including Captain Sanders—not a very large invasion force to match Colquitt's tough talk![42]

By the end of February, Consul Garrett submitted his report to the secretary of state. His posting of over a decade on the Rio Grande border provided a tremendous window into the political, commercial, and social dynamics of the region. His investigation, while not public at the time, provided an entirely new light on the local feud turned international

Texas Rangers' patrols attempted to address the violence on the Rio Grande during the revolution, but due to the size of the border and the small number of Rangers there was little chance they could protect and prevent the growing number of hostile incidents. Author's collection.

incident. Violence, political rivalries, feuds, and gunplay dated from the settlement of the region, albeit with growth and new investment spurred on by a rivalry of the two groups. The more aristocratic citizens and merchants were known as the *botas* [boots] party, and the opposing faction as the *Huaraches*—so-called for the sandals, footwear, worn by the lower classes in Mexico. The coming of the Mexican Revolution only antagonized land disputes, smuggling, loyalties, and political rivalries.[43]

The consul personally interviewed all involved. His first step was to go to Hidalgo where he confronted Captain Rodríguez, demanded an explanation and Vergara's body so it could be properly interred. The captain denied any knowledge of the events and execution and only indicated Vergara had been sent to Piedras Negras for questioning. Garrett asked for the immediate return of the eleven horses, and he again denied any knowledge of their whereabouts, in spite of the fact that three of Rodríguez's mounted bodyguards were riding horses branded with the half-moon "V̂" of the Vergara Ranch. No charges or extradition documents had been filed against the captain and his men, leaving the consul with no recourse but to leave.[44]

On the Texas side of the river, Consul Garrett was able to locate a number of eyewitnesses to the theft of the horses and ranch hands who witnessed the capture of the rancher. Señora Vergara and her niece did cross and visit in the jail, the last time he was seen alive. Both provided detailed depositions to the Texas attorney general. Witnesses recalled hearing the volley of shots fired between two and three o'clock Sunday morning February 15. This occurred when he was executed, ostensibly on his transfer to Piedras Negras. There were no known claims by the Federalist in Hidalgo of the famous *ley de fuga*, or known attempts by Vergara to escape. Confirmed reports detailed that at first light on Sunday many in Hidalgo saw the body "hung on a tree."[45]

Over the past century there has been a great deal of speculation on the events surrounding the death of Vergara. Dr. Garrett's official report to Washington is the key to opening new light on the events. Rodríguez and his men were merely the triggermen. Garrett concluded, Clemente Vergara's death was "planned and sanctioned" by Webb County Sheriff Sanchez and Hidalgo commander Garza Galván. The two men had met the day before the capture and arranged for a handwritten safe passage note for Vergara "to inspire confidence in him so that he would cross the river." Shortly after Garrett had contacted the State Department on

Vergara's kidnapping and before he was executed, Galván, knowing the incident had been reported to Washington, boasted, "To Hell with Consul Garrett. We will show him that we are running things in Mexico."[46]

It was a well-known fact that Sánchez and his sons, Amador Jr. and Juan, were actively connected with the Huerta government and closely tied with the Federalist commanders in Nuevo Laredo, Hidalgo, and Piedras Negras. Friends of the sheriff wrote the governor that Sánchez was the "victim of a well-organized conspiracy headed by local *carrancista* leaders." Was rancher Vergara a party to the attacks on the sheriff? Furthermore, there was a long-standing grudge between Sánchez and Vergara that manifested itself into numerous efforts by the sheriff and his friends to have Vergara indicted by the Webb County grand jury and court on bogus charges. In addition to Sánchez and Galván meeting before the kidnapping, Garrett reported the two met again on Sunday morning after the rancher was executed. This pattern was a part of ongoing crimes and reprisals during the revolution in the border region. As part of this ongoing conspiracy against their Laredo enemies, they were involved with the execution of Laredoan Porfirio Laurel, when the sheriff claimed he *was not* an American citizen (which he was) "and many claim that it was at his instigation that General Guardiola [in Nuevo Laredo] ordered Laurel shot."[47] The web of intrigue, reprisals, and murder on the border was masked by the violence and bloody civil war raging across northern Mexico.

There is strong evidence supported by the news media that Vergara, Laurel, Otto Winter, George Sneckner, and Dario Sánchez were smuggling and served as potential spies for the *carrancistas* and possibly were double agents. They were not just arms and munitions runners, cattle brokers, and traders of saddle horses. The crossing at Palafox, near Vergara's home and ranch, had been a remote strategic staging area and had been linked to contraband smuggling across the border for decades. As the Federalist forces came under intensified attacks on the border following the lifting of the arms embargo in early February, the *huertista* spies worked to counter and eliminate those attempting to assist the rebels. As Friedrich Schuler notes, Huerta did his upmost to hang on to power, even if it meant inciting with racial clashes along the US-Mexico border. He spent 300,000 pesos to pay bandits inside Texas "to attack U.S. citizens and properties," with one aim, "to cause an overreaction by the U.S. Army."[48] Consul Garrett informed the State Department on numerous occasions of these clandestine activities. In his confidential report to the secretary of state, Consul Garrett strongly concluded:

> The Huerta forces have keep paid spies constantly in Laredo, Texas, and the principal points along the border, and the Sheriff of Webb County, Texas, is the man who dominates this force of spies in Webb County, and as I have before told the department all of the outrages against American citizens along the border are directly traced to either this force of spies, or the force on the Constitutionalists side [Mexico], all of whom are personally known to me.[49]

Thus, the killing of Clemente Vergara was not a random kidnapping and murder aggravated by a horse trade or unrest on the border, but instead a preplanned sanctioned execution to eliminate his influence and support of the rebel Constitutionalists.

Consul Garrett's letter to the State Department helps to explain the immediate coolness Bryan and Wilson expressed toward the Vergara incident, as well as the claims made by the Texas AG regarding extradition. News media reports across the country made headlines out of the fact that Vergara had been "given a note" (confirmed by Garrett) for safe passage to cross the Rio Grande to recover his stolen horses. The status of the ownership of the island in the Rio Grande did not resurface and had little or no bearing on the tragic event. And Sheriff Sánchez, concerned with being directly implicated in the death of Vergara, issued a vocal denial of any role in the events in a heated telegram to Governor Colquitt, which was passed to the media for publication:

> February 28, 1914
> Gov. O. B. Colquitt, Austin;
>
> I see by today's [San Antonio] *Express* that Capt. Sanders of the Texas Rangers telegraphed to you that had been informed that Clemente Vergara whom it is alleged was captured by soldiers in Hidalgo had a pass from me and one Garza Galvan to cross to Mexico what object this information man have said know but it is an *unmitigated lie* and I thus declare.
>
> Amador Sánchez[50]

By mid-March 1914, some six investigations had been made into the kidnapping and murder of Clemente Vergara, in addition to three state of Texas investigations by Ranger Sanders, Ranger Hughes, and the adjutant general, Henry Hutchings—all on the request of the governor's office. These investigations were followed by the review of the case by Dr. Garrett at the Nuevo Laredo consulate and representatives from the US Army in San Antonio. This occurred with assistance from numerous federal agencies, which included US Customs agents and the (Federal) Bureau of Investigation. This was most likely the most extensively investigated murder incident of a foreign national during the decade-long Mexican Revolution. There were a number of site visits to Hidalgo and Palafox, where the crime occurred, and over twenty witnesses were interviewed and provided written affidavits. Governor Colquitt was in constant contact with both the White House and Secretary of State Bryan. He also fielded communication and demands for resolution from President Huerta and Mexican border commanders who were charged with the investigation in Mexico. Reports by Ranger Hughes and Consul Garret implicated a spy ring in Laredo led by Sheriff Sánchez and his network of contraband agents, who had either a major role and/or knowledge of the events. It was speculated that the Vergara murder was connected with a disruption of a lucrative smuggling operation across the border and Palafox and the small adjacent village of Minerva near the terminus of the Rio Grande and Eagle Pass Railroad. In a lengthy report to Secretary Bryan, Colquitt abandoned his old political friend Sánchez to offer the secretary that chance to consider charges against the sheriff (formerly convicted in federal court of the violation of the US Neutrality Laws)—noting, "Mr. Sánchez has been connected with the Huerta Government in an official capacity since its inception [of the revolution]."[51]

The editorial board of the *Laredo Daily Times* thus provided the most telling analysis of the "Vergara Case," pointing fingers at the ongoing confusion and true intentions of the federal government:

> Much dissatisfaction is expressed here as to the outcome of the case of the killing of Clemente Vergara, Secretary Bryan having apparently dropped the matter entirely, leaving to Gov. Colquitt to demand the extradition of the slayers of the American citizen. The Huerta government has failed to clear up the mystery surrounding

> the alleged kidnapping and killing of Vergara. So far it has not been put up [to] the Huerta government to clear the mystery. But Washington authorities have not made the demands on the Huerta government in the case of Vergara, an American citizen, that they hastened to make in the case of William Benton[,] an English subject.
>
> The only crime for which Gov. Colquitt can demand the extradition of the Mexican—the only crime, this is committed on Texas soil—is the stealing of eleven of Vergara's horses. The bandits cannot be tried in Texas for murder committed on Mexican soil.
>
> There seem to be in Washington circles at present a desire to defer to England in everything, rather than to insist upon our rights. As soon as the murder of Benton was announce[d] [one week after Vergara's death], there was a great activity on the part of our state department for the Benton case than there had been over the entire lot of more than a hundred killings of American citizens during the past year in Mexico.[52]

News of the investigation as well as the Colquitt and Garret reports to Washington soon became nationwide news, causing an angered Sheriff Sánchez to write a second telegram to the Texas Governor:

> Laredo April 1st 1914
> His Excellency O. B. Colquitt
> Austin, Texas
>
> Upon my arrival last night I read in last Sundays [San Antonio] Express that Consul Garrett in his report to Mr. Bryan in reference to the Vergara case says that certain Texas peace officer has been connected with the Huerta government in an official capacity and that the officer participated in alleged kidnapping or Vergara certain libelous sheet edited in Spanish by irresponsible and unprincipled Mexican refuges and influenced by personal and political enemies of mine charge me with being that officer. I wish to state to you that regardless of who the parties may be whether Consul Garrett or anybody else it is a malicious lie and intrigue and I dare all the lying cowards to file the proper charges against me even though they may have to resort to the unprincipled elements to their partisan.
>
> Amador Sánchez[53]

Colquitt, who toyed with the idea of running for the US Senate, began to receive criticism from state newspapers and his Texas political rival, US Senator Morris Sheppard, responding to the governor's overreaction to the border incidents and claims that he was prepared to order an invasion of Mexico. Sheppard had been elected in 1913 to serve the unexpired term of Senator Joseph Bailey, a close friend of Colquitt. Notwithstanding the pressure from Washington, the governor remained on the defensive and defiant. The official Mexican version was that Vergara was a bandit aiding the revolution; he had been captured, detained, and escaped. More attention was given to the recovery of the stolen horses than to the circumstances of Vergara's capture and death—and the efforts to bring the killers to justice. At the White House and State Department, there was hope that the Vergara incident would die down so they could give their full attention to the Benton case and salvage the relationship with the British.[54]

One last item needed to be settled: the return of Vergara body. Clemente's son, Jesús, and brother-in-law, S. J. Hill, began their own visits to Hidalgo to locate the body. Captain Rodríguez and his men fled Hidalgo, leaving behind a small force. Local friends secretly directed ranch hands to the shal-

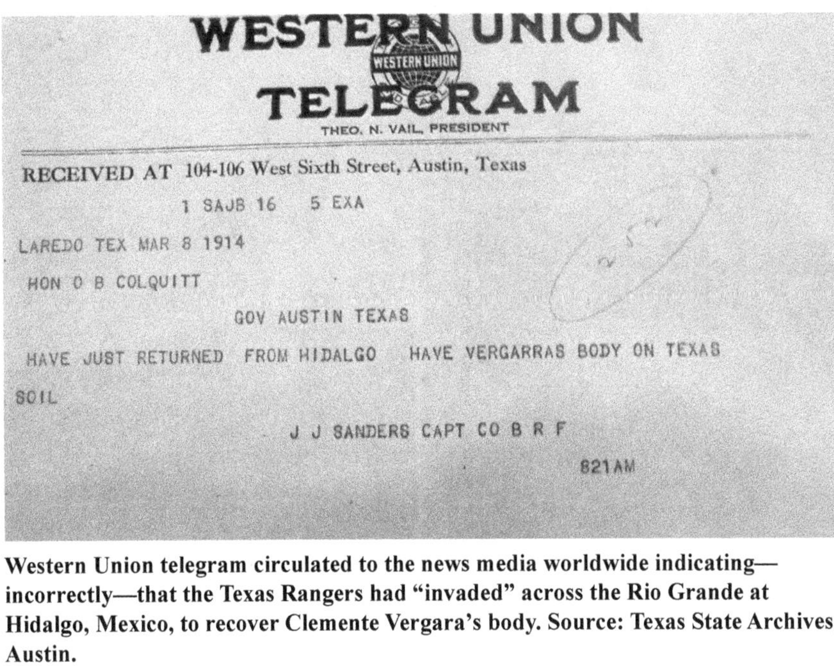

WESTERN UNION TELEGRAM

THEO. N. VAIL, PRESIDENT

RECEIVED AT 104-106 West Sixth Street, Austin, Texas

1 SAJB 16 5 EXA

LAREDO TEX MAR 8 1914

HON O B COLQUITT

GOV AUSTIN TEXAS

HAVE JUST RETURNED FROM HIDALGO HAVE VERGARRAS BODY ON TEXAS SOIL

J J SANDERS CAPT CO B R F

821AM

Western Union telegram circulated to the news media worldwide indicating—incorrectly—that the Texas Rangers had "invaded" across the Rio Grande at Hidalgo, Mexico, to recover Clemente Vergara's body. Source: Texas State Archives, Austin.

low grave on the outskirts of town. Only family, the Texas Rangers, and Garrett were shown the body's location. Aware that an armed confrontation was possible, Garrett and the Texas Rangers, Sanders, Felps, and Hines built a bonfire a mile upriver along the banks to divert any remaining Federalist patrols at Hidalgo to be mustered on the rumor that a large rebel supply

Clemente Vergara's exhumed body was returned to Laredo on March 8, 1914, for official identification and autopsy by both the Webb County coroner and representative of the Texas Attorney General's Office. It was determined Vergara was shot and hung. Source: Papers of Governor Colquitt, Texas State Archives, Austin.

group planned to cross the river into Mexico after midnight. Once the Federalists were distracted, the ranch hands and family crossed and recovered Vergara's remains and brought them back to the Texas side, four weeks after the kidnapping and murder.[55]

The body was first turned over to Captain Sanders and Consul Garrett on the Texas side of the border for transport to Laredo for autopsy. A hasty, misworded telegram to Governor Colquitt, ostensibly from Sanders, but in haste written by Garrett, stated: "Have just returned from Hidalgo, have Vergara's body on Texas soil." It was implied the Texas Rangers had crossed the Mexican border to recover the body. The source of the confusion about the so-called misworded telegram may never be known, yet the official report was the Texas Rangers had not crossed the river. Regardless, headlines across newspapers worldwide read; "Texas Rangers Invade Mexico and Recover Vergara's Body" as retractions and denials were swiftly issued to correct the record. Texas Adjutant General Hutchings arrived in Laredo with Texas state coroner Dr. O. C. Cook and Texas Ranger Captain Hughes to work with the Webb County coroner to oversee and document the autopsy. The body was positively identified by the family and on March 10, 1914, buried in the Laredo Catholic Cemetery, with the ceremony officiated by both the church and the fraternal organization, Woodmen of the World.[56]

No other foreign individual killed or kidnapped during the Mexican Revolution received more attention at the highest echelons of the US and Mexican governments than Vergara. The news media coverage was not just across the United States but also worldwide. Over two hundred newspapers carried details of the Vergara affair for over a month. Presidents Wilson and Huerta were separately in contact with Governor Colquitt, who also received cabinet-level attention from the Secretaries of Labor and War, the State Department, and the attorney general, which is reflected in a rare document of March 10, 1914, from Secretary of War Lindley M. Garrison sent to Secretary of State Bryan, who then briefed the president:

> Replying telegram Chief of Staff this morning relative recovery body of Vergara following just received, quote: Laredo March ninth, investigation shows Vergara taken from Hidalgo cemetery Saturday night by relatives of Vergara and hired Mexicans. Captain Sanders states positively no Texas Rangers crossed border. He met body at land-

> ing opposite San Enrique with undertaker Convery Sunday morning. Convery brought the body to Laredo seven thirty P.M. Sunday. He states no signs of burns in body. Found four bullet holes: neck chafed but not broken; body decomposed but pants on body match coat left at home by Vergara; identification seems reliable. Recovery of body said to have cost S. T. Hill, brother-in-law of Vergara, four hundred dollars. Body being held at request of Adjutant General Hutchings, expected tomorrow. No excitement.[57]

As the Vergara family and South Texas waited for a resolution to the tragic incident, Governor Colquitt continued his attack on the lack of action from Washington and basked in the media attention from across the country. Official Washington was greeted by a headline in the *Washington Post*: "TEXAS TO ACT ALONE: Gov. Colquitt Will Deal Direct with Mexican Officers," and *New York American*, a Hearst newspaper, reported, "Your [the governor] splendid attitude is very pleasing to [our] readers." And one admirer penned a poem:

> If Colquitt was in the White House
> and Wilson teaching school,
> I fear the tyrant Huerta
> would have short time to rule;
> For he would let our Rangers
> just cross the Rio Grande
> And wallop up old Mexico
> and put over them a man.[58]

"Go after Them"

Governor Colquitt used the nationwide attention on the violence on the border and in Mexico to urge an aggressive policy of armed intervention to halt the murders and property damage. Border leaders and US senators, such as Albert Fall of New Mexico, supported him. Colquitt's saber rattling continued as he "demanded" of the White House, "I want Washington to send me only three words—'Go after them'—with that authority I promise to keep the Mexican raiders out of Texas." President Wilson, after additional claims by the governor that given one hundred Texas Rangers he could do more toward keeping law and order in Texas than could ten thousand troops, warned against any hasty action and responded to the governor's demands that the recent incidents "will not cause him to deviate from the course marked out." He stated further, "to send armed forces of any kind into Mexico without the consent of the governing authorities there would be *an act of war*."[59] Responding to the "apparent laxity in not having taken decisive actions for protection of Texans," Colquitt captured the feelings of those in Texas and along the border:

> I would not be entirely candid if I did not express the opinion that now, since our government has dabbled into the local affairs of Mexico she will never be able to withdraw her hand from the controversy except in blood. Revolutions will continue until from sheer necessity either some friendly or angry force from without will have to temper and curb the furies raging within the Republic of Mexico.[60]

How many others citizens along the border were caught up in espionage and violence during the revolution will likely never be known, as Europe erupted into the Great War in August 1914—thus drawing attention away from events in Mexico. A list was maintained by the National Association for the Protection of American Rights in Mexico, a nonprofit organization located in New York City, of the US citizens killed during the revolution. This association presented their data numerous times to the news media and at US congressional hearings: the total was over 550 deaths. Senator Albert Fall, under protest from the White House, vigorously attacked Wilson's policy and read on the floor of the Senate the list of Americans killed in Mexico—highlighting the recent murder of Clemente Vergara. The friction and intrigue on the border would long be a mystery to both Washington and Mexico City. To this day *la frontera* is a region unto itself. In the aftermath of the Vergara affair, a sick and ailing President Wilson would be overwhelmed by events both near and far. The toll taken on Mexicans, Tejanos, and Texans was great, and the rise of Mexico out of a decade of revolution would forever shape and influence the destiny of the border region and the Mexican people.[61]

6
Only the River Knows

Every teller of the tale [of Clemente Vergara] is convinced that the episode, which occurred at a time when relations were strained, came near causing trouble between the United States and Mexico. Perhaps the river knows, the river that conceals its mysteries more effectually that the graves along its banks conceal the bones of men.

—Walter Prescott Webb
The Texas Rangers

The events surrounding the death of South Texan Clemente Vergara in February 1914 heightened worldwide attention on the US-Mexico border. The resolve of the Wilson administration to conduct foreign affairs in Mexico was viewed as a seemingly drifting policy toward the revolution and US intervention. Since the first day Woodrow Wilson entered the White House, his administration interfered with the internal affairs of Mexico. After a vacillating first year in office and the landing at Veracruz, General Huerta was deposed, with Wilson boasting at a press conference: "We Got Huerta." Inconsistent, dogmatic, and idealist goals only aggravated an early resolution to the civil war in Mexico. US Senate Foreign Relations hearings in 1919–20 on American involvement in Mexico during the revolution, while very politicized in the wake of the fight over the Wilson's handling of the League of Nations following World War I, revealed strong opinions on a decade of misdirection, unchecked violence, and meddling by US foreign policy advisers in Mexican affairs.[1]

American business investment interests in Mexico continued to be vocal against Wilson's confused foreign policy. For example, Edward L.

Doheny, president of the Mexican Petroleum Company, testified that the first clear misstep in determining Mexico's future was the recall of Ambassador Henry L. Wilson and the dispatch of novice "agent" John Lind on a delicate mission to Mexico. This mission was leaked to the press and resulted in demanding Mexico to hold new national elections and General Huerta to step down. "This was the first step of American intervention in Mexico," according to Doheny—not the Tampico incident or its response in Veracruz. The international media coverage of the Vergara affair only heightened the view that the White House perpetuated a weak-opportunist policy toward Mexico and appeared to be more concerned about long-range British reactions and relations than border violence and the protection of American citizens and property in Mexico.[2]

Also vocal during the weeks following the events of February 1914 was Governor Oscar Colquitt, who there is little doubt used the situation and attacks on the White House as a means to foster his political career and silence attacks from Texas opponents. Colquitt decided not to make the Texas Rangers by any means a scapegoat regardless of claims from Washington, and in fact fully and publicly accepted the version of events regarding Vergara presented by Ranger Captain J. J. Sanders. Colquitt further kept the controversy alive with a $1,000 cash reward for the capture and return to Texas soil of Clemente Vergara's murderers. The highly publicized blanket reward caused added concern in Washington of vigilantes that might incite new cross-border incidents. Unconcerned about repercussions, in dramatic fashion the governor addressed the Texas Cattle Raisers' Association annual meeting in Fort Worth on March 10, 1914, attacking both President Wilson and Texas Senator Morris Sheppard, declaring he would place the rights of Texans above the old failed policies of Wilson, and he concluded: "I'll never kiss anybody's toe in Washington."[3]

Those who took part in the death of Clemente Vergara were never brought to justice. There was little desire among the competing factions in northern Mexico or Huerta in Mexico City to resolve this or any other border issue. The Federalist commanders in the field and particularly in the border region were under added pressure to survive and defend their own area of concern. The lifting of the arms embargo in early February 1914 had indeed allowed the rebels to gain not only needed arms and supplies but also much needed momentum. Given the fact there was little or no quarter for those captured or wounded, all the fighting factions in Mexico could not be bogged down with one particular kidnapping case or death. One El Paso attorney who represented dozens of border violence cases "from homicide to plain cow stealing" reminded the Texas governor: "all the Mexican Chiefs during this Revolution were indifferent to the rights of foreigners, and would do anything that their interests or passions dictated."[4]

Adjutant General Hutchings and the Texas Rangers on the border continued a manhunt for those involved with the murder of Vergara; they also continued efforts to recover the stolen horses for return to the family. Hutchings encouraged assistance from the Mexican consuls in the Texas border towns and Mexican commanders across the river in an effort to clear this incident, pointedly informing Consul Gonzalo de A. Fernandez in Eagle Pass, Texas: "His Excellency, the Governor [of Texas], directs me to invite your attention to the fact that the President of Mexico personally directed the return of this stock, and the Governor expresses a desire that the matter may be speedily closed up."[5]

Governor Colquitt offered an additional reward for the return of Vergara's eleven horses, realizing there was little chance of Mexican authorities turning over either the perpetrators or the horses. He authorized Adjutant General Hutchings to "employ the necessary number of men on this side of the Rio Grande to cross and kidnap" the Mexicans responsible in the Vergara crime. This was a planned invasion. The US Army learned of the plan and was ordered to disband any group or expedition. No such Texas force is known to have crossed the border. While Colquitt's tough talk and schemes died down following the US landing at Veracruz, tension along the border remained high. The Huerta regime by late March and early April displayed clear signs of crumbling.[6]

Wilson's health throughout this period was at best frail. The president's private physician, Dr. Grayson, informed Colonel House in March 1914 that "Wilson's medical problems were serious." The stress of the cascading events as well as his wife's lingering illness—she died in the White House in August 1914—diminished the president's ability to put his full attention toward events in Mexico in general and border violence in particular. as the president also faced mounting pressure from Europe as war clouds developed on the horizon. Oddly, in response to the Vergara affair and Colquitt's demands, additional regular army troops were sent to Texas, bringing the total to over twenty thousand, while at the same time increasing arms and munitions shipments to revolutionary factions increased hostilities in Mexico.[7]

There was the saber rattling by Governor Colquitt, but otherwise there seems to have been no pretext by the White House to directly use the Vergara incident as a reason for intervention. Yet the Vergara murder and the extensive media coverage across the country set the stage in the minds of the American public in advance of the incident and the US protest at Tampico, Mexico. In Wilson's mind the events rose to the level of an "incident."

The inability or refusal of the Wilson administration to fully and clearly recognize any of the contending factions in Mexico only exasperated border policy to protect American citizens and property and dealings with other nations who contended they had a vested interest in the outcome. John Dos Passos notes, "Wilson's Mexico policy consisted of trying to find American style reformers in the Democratic tradition among warring bands" that seldom practiced democratic government. On the border as well as in the Mexican port cities, federal-state friction and jurisdictional disputes were magnified by the warring parties. For example, questions persisted: who was allowed access to the oil terminals in Tampico; who was the governing authority for extradition; and who would police the landing of arms and supplies from German and Japanese sympathizers? The US Navy was ordered not to engage in any altercations on the high seas, and the US Army on the border was ordered not to fire, unless fired upon, and then only in self-defense. It was becoming apparent, as one observer noted, that "Wilson often showed himself philosophically and temperamentally ill-suited to cope with international problems, whether it was border policy or submarine warfare with Germany."[8]

Wilson's crafting of an idealistic-righteous policy toward Mexico and the Huerta regime not only encouraged the revolutionaries but also eventually led to armed intervention by the United States at Veracruz in April 1914 and northern Mexico in 1916. Lofty claims by the president that the United States would never intervene in Mexico were soon dashed; a fully exaggerated US Naval landing-party incident at the Port of Tampico occurred when a few American sailors were temporarily detained, quickly released, and the commander of the Tampico federal garrison (as well as Huerta in Mexico City) publicly apologized. The White House allowed the incident to escalate into what was termed an "insult on the American flag"—which it was not. One contemporary observer of the Tampico incident noted it was "a screaming farce." This further was wrongly embellished by a combination of additional claims involving the rumored harassment of American diplomatic couriers and accelerated excuses for intervention.[9]

Detailed war plans for the invasion of Mexico—known in the War Department as War Plan Green—had been in the works for months. President Wilson ordered the US Atlantic Fleet to the coast of Mexico—the largest US flotilla of American warships to date—forty-six ships carrying over twenty thousand men. In the words of Wilson's archrival, Theodore Roosevelt, the president abandoned "watchful waiting" and chose what he felt was "righteousness" over peace. And soon the invasion timetable was accelerated (following a week-long delay for annual observance of *Semana Santa*—Easter Holy Week) with a landing party in force of some nine hundred US Marines and Navy "blue jackets" at Veracruz on April 21, 1914. The final pretext was to occupy the Mexican Customhouse to prevent the unloading of contraband arms by a German munition broker aboard the *Ypiranga*—which also carried American arms, explosives, and munitions under contract.[10]

The US landing at Veracruz came very close to uniting, if only temporarily, the many hostile factions in the Mexican civil war against the American invasion. The landing, under international law by any measure an "act of war'"—was one that former President William Taft characterized as an "act of war to punish the government of Mexico." Mexican diplomat, jurist, and historian José Isidro Pedro Fabela, in his classic *Historia diplomática de la revolución mexicana, 1912–1917*, strongly concluded the invasion at Veracruz was a violation of Mexican sovereignty regardless of the purpose. Nothing in international law sanctioned Wilson's actions. Carranza demanded the immediate withdrawal of US Marines and threatened to declare war. It is a certainty this would have occurred if American troops had marched on Mexico City—which was part of the original War Department invasion plan. Wilson expressed bewilderment and shock and felt a personal responsibility at the reports and pictures of both the US and Mexican casualties during the invasion of the Port of Veracruz. In response, the president "at all times was scrupulous" to place full responsibility for the revolution, the intervention, and deaths upon the shoulders of General Huerta. The US Navy, in order to avoid a repeat of events at Tampico, changed its official policy in 1916 on how and whom would officially address such future incidents.[11]

Within hours of the US landing at Veracruz, the Huerta government immediately ordered the US embassy closed on April 22, 1914, with chargé d'affaires Nelson O'Shaughnessy leaving Mexico at once for Veracruz and Washington. On departing, the embassy turned over all American diplomatic affairs and representation to Sir Lionel Carden. In the hours after the landing, rioting broke out in the streets of Mexico City; the statue of George Washington that had been dedicated only one year earlier was torn down by an angry mob and dragged through the streets. There was a fear and rumors across the city that the US Marines would march on Mexico City. Huerta was faced as well with new pressures from the north. By late April, Huerta ordered a "modified scorched earth policy" in northern Mexico as the beaten Federalist garrisons were evacuated from Piedras Negras, Nuevo Laredo, Saltillo, and Zacatecas. Nuevo Laredo was put to the torch, causing massive damage to the central business and residential district areas as well as creating a mass exodus of citizens across the Rio Grande to safety in Laredo. Departing federal troops exchanged gunfire with US troops at Fort McIntosh and attempted but failed to burn both the rail and pedestrian bridges across the Rio Grande.[12]

Special agent John Lind returned to his home in Minnesota. Former ambassador Henry Lane Wilson never returned to formal diplomatic service. During World War I, he served on the Commission for Relief of

Shortly after the recovery and burial of Clemente Vergara, Nuevo Laredo came under extended attack by the Constitutionalists to drive federal troops from the town. In the battles that followed, massive fires destroyed the central part of the town and threatened to damage the international bridge connecting Nuevo Laredo to Laredo, Texas, in the foreground. Courtesy Armengol Guerra III.

Belgium and opened an active law practice as counsel for US oil interests in Latin America. Constantly on the defensive against allegations against him by President Wilson, he published his memoirs, *Diplomatic Episodes in Mexico, Belgium, and Chile*, in 1927.[13]

Following General Huerta's fall in July 1914, he escaped to exile in Barcelona, Spain, and was soon enticed by German agents, eager to embroil the United States in a war with Mexico, to plan a counterrevolu-

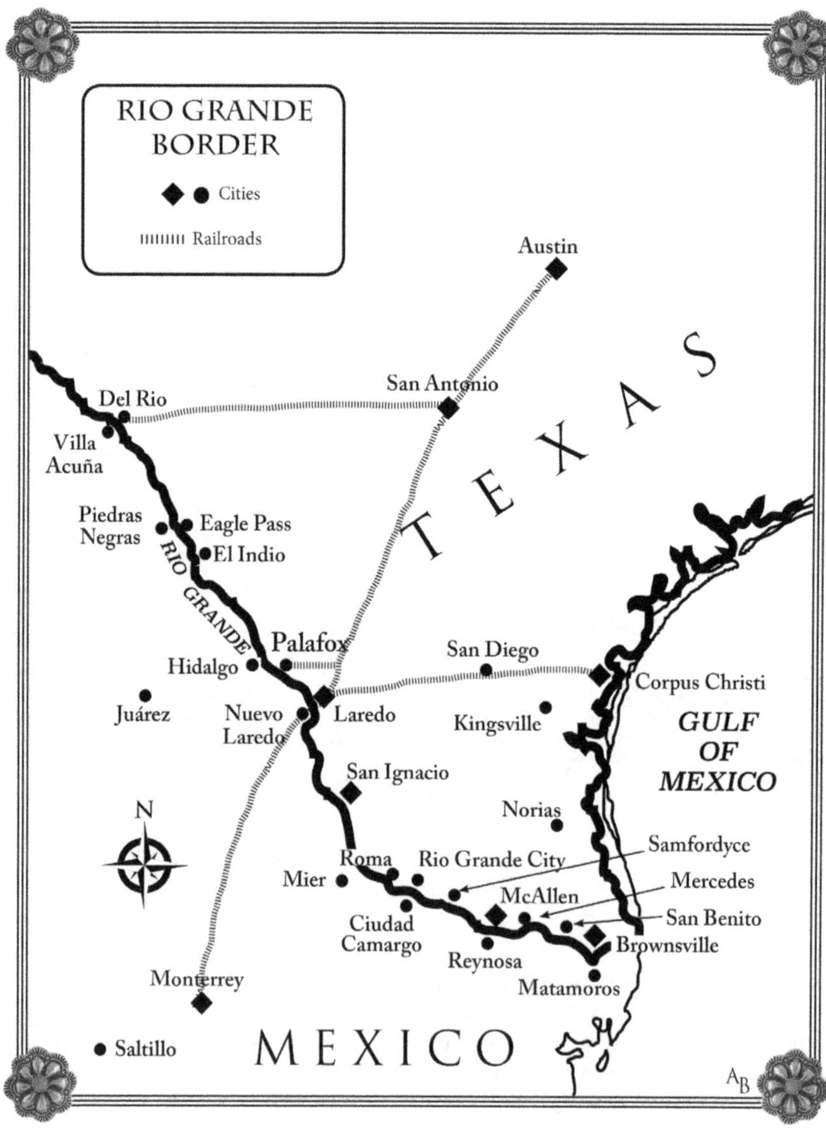

tion staged in Texas. The Germans offered arms and copious funding to assist Huerta and his friends in getting reinstated to the Mexican presidency. He returned to New York City in April 1915, to the center of anti-Constitutionalist activity in the United States. In June, Huerta traveled to the border and was detained near El Paso by US Marshals on charges of conspiracy to violate US neutrality laws. After being detained he sent an urgent telegram to German agents in Washington for assistance, yet received no reply. Huerta lived out his last years under house arrest in El Paso, Texas, at Fort Bliss, where he died from health complications in June 1916.[14]

While the US Marines spent only six months in Veracruz, the southern US-Mexico border remained in chaos. In the north on the border, Villa's March 1916 sacking and murder spree of seventeen Americans in Columbus, New Mexico, instigated a response. President Wilson would launch a second intervention into Mexico with General John "Blackjack" Pershing's "Punitive Expedition," for the sole purpose of capturing Pancho Villa—the renegade rebel general in whom Wilson had once expressed high confidence. The American troops under Pershing languished for weeks under the hot sun, crisscrossing arid northern Mexico, and never came close to corralling Villa. With the outbreak of war in Europe the "Mexican problem," as it was referred to in Washington, took second place in the attention of Americans and the president.[15]

El Jefe V. Carranza would soon consolidate both his political and military power, defeating Villa in the north and the Zapatistas in southern Mexico. Following the capture of Mexico City in August 1915, he rose to power as the thirty-seventh president. Violence remained an ever-present element in the waning years of the revolution. Emiliano Zapata was assassinated in April 1919, followed by the assassination of Carranza in May 1920. Pancho Villa, after retiring to his ranch in Parral, was ambushed and assassinated in June 1923.

In a footnote to history, William F. Buckley Sr., in a letter to former Ambassador Henry Lane Wilson in March 1928, put the use of political assassination in revolutionary Mexico politics in perspective:

> A point might be made in connection with the assassination of Madero that I do not think has been made in any book on this revolutionary period. The assassination of Madero did not shock Mexicans of any class or political affiliation. The enemies admitted

> it was good politics, and that it was what they would have done to Huerta if conditions had been reversed. It was only when the Madero partisans found out to their surprise that the American people were shocked and that President Wilson was disposed to take a hand, that they decided to make political capital out of the normal Mexican political expedient.[16]

In Laredo, Sheriff Sánchez would not stand for another term and was soon indicted on a number of charges that ended his career. Shortly after Clemente Vergara's funeral, rumors surfaced that he was assisting Félix Díaz in "spearheading" a new rebellion against the Mexican government. Quick to issue a rebuttal, the sheriff stated: "I shall be vigilant at all times to prevent disorder and shall not hesitate to use quickly all the power in me to prevent any effort to foment trouble." US Consul Garrett remained in Nuevo Laredo until 1919, and after a brief vacation was posted as Amer-

The grave of Clemente Vergara in Laredo, Texas. Author's collection.

ican consul to the sleepy uneventful community of Saint Stephen, New Brunswick, Canada, from 1920 to 1924. Texas Ranger Captain Sanders was reappointed to duty by incoming Governor James E. Ferguson in January 1915, yet came under harsh investigation in 1919 and retired. In a 1929 article in the popular tabloid *Frontier Times*, the editors wonder if in fact Captain Sanders led the Rangers into Mexico to recover Vergara and speculated that possibly on his deathbed in February 1924 the "indomitable Texas Ranger would have grinned and replied, 'Well they say I dug up Vergara's body, but I ain't a-saying.'" Only the river knows.[17]

Oscar Colquitt finished his term as governor in January 1915 and ran for the US Senate, losing in a close race to incumbent and former Texas governor, Charles Culberson. An obstinate man who prided himself on being self-made, Colquitt continued to criticize the Wilson administration. Colquitt returned to Dallas to be the president of an oil firm and stayed active in politics until his death in March 1940.

Colonel House would remain President Wilson's chief "special agent," strategist, and confidant—for the balance of the president's life. The British, who quietly recalled Washington Ambassador Spring Rice, were fully aware of House's power in the formulation of the Wilson administration's foreign policy. House was further critical in bridging relations with the new David Lloyd George government that replaced Prime Minister Asquith and Foreign Secretary Sir Edward Grey in December 1916. The rocky relationship between Wilson and Secretary of State William J. Bryan during the Mexico crisis and Bryan's opposition in support of Great Britain, helped hasten the secretary of state's resignation and departure in June 1915; he was replaced by Robert Lansing.

And Woodrow Wilson, overwhelmed with the coming military tensions in Europe, recalled General Pershing from Mexico in advance of American plans to assist the European allied powers "over there." The violence on the border continued until 1920, and the president's poor health persisted and continued throughout the balance of his administration. Following the Armistice in Europe on November 11, 1918, Wilson engaged in a personal crusade in the postwar peace process to encourage the European nations to form the League of Nations as a forum to prevent future horrific wars.

Any such accord involving the United States would require approval by two-thirds of the US Senate, thus Wilson return from the peace talks to take his message to the American people. His appeal to the citizens did not impress the Senate. After crisscrossing the county during mid-1919, he returned to the White House a tired and sick man. Sometime in the evening of October 1, 1919, he suffered a massive thrombosis—a clot in the blood vessels—which resulted in a stroke, partial spams, and paralysis on his left side. The reoccurrence of what he passed off as "neuritis" (arteriosclerosis) confined the president to his bed for months. Edith Wilson and Dr. Grayson completely shielded Wilson from any visits, which raised increasing rumors as to the health of the president. The only other person who knew the true nature of the situation was Colonel House, who had remained in Europe to insure support among the Allies for the League.[18]

As the Senate vote on the League approached, a diplomatic crisis not in Europe, but in Mexico, resulted in the members of the Committee on Foreign Relations demanding an audience with the president. Wilson's problems south of the border once again surfaced with the alleged kidnapping of US consular agent William O. Jenkins, reported by the *New York Times* as more than "a scathing condemnation of unfriendly behavior" on the part of the Mexican government, which was slow to respond to Washington's demands for release. In a meeting closely monitored by Dr. Grayson and Mrs. Wilson, the president's arch adversary Senator Fall was allowed to speak to the president with his case for immediate intervention, telling Wilson, "four-fifths of the Mexican people would welcome it." It seemed public opinion and a large standing army fresh from the fields of France posed a different scenario than the circumstance following the Tampico incident in March 1914. Before any rush to judgment, Consular Agent Jenkins was released from a Mexican jail and an armed intervention was averted. And the vote on the US ratification of the League of Nations failed in the Senate. The president completed his term as his illness lingered on until his death on February 3, 1921.

Except for the brief mention by Walter P. Webb in the 1935 volume on the *Texas Rangers*, Clemente Vergara's murder would have been long forgotten, along with hundreds of other victims of the Mexican revolutionary-era violence. In the months after his death, the Vergara family, with the assistance of brother-in-law S. J. Hill and Consul Garrett, sold the ranch, horses, and cattle at Palafox and joined relatives in Mexico City. Today, Vergara is remembered only by a ten-foot-high obelisk topped with a cross in the Laredo Catholic Cemetery.

Clemente Vergara and his son, Jesús Vergara, in early 1913. Vergara family collection.

Appendix A

Mexican Policy Statements and Milestones, President Woodrow Wilson, March 1913–March 1914

date	location	policy
March 4, 1913	Washington, DC	Wilson Inauguration
March 11	White House	neutrality: no special interest[1]
March 21	Amb. H. L. Wilson to DC	report on "*Decena Trágica*"
July 4	Gettysburg address	"righteousness and humanity"[2]
July 14	Wilson's inst. to H. L. Wilson	"Good offices for armistice"[3]
July 17	White House	"Huerta refuses to resign"
July 29	WW inst. to John Lind	"Mexico's nearest friend"[4]
August 4	WH: Ambassador recalled	"resignation accepted"[5]
August 15	Mexico City: John Lind	"Huerta refuses to resign"
August 27	Joint Session of Congress	Mexican Affairs Status[6]
October 17	Mobile, Alabama	"not one more foot"[7]
November 1	WW orders to O'Shaughnessy	"serious practical measures"[8]
November 7	Sec. Bryan announcement	"means to retire Huerta"
November 24	White House: circular note	"use of less peaceful means"[9]
December 2	1st Annual Address to Congress	"watchful waiting cont."[10]
February 3, 1914	White House Proclamation	"Lifting arms embargo"[11]
February 12–13	Clemente Vergara	kidnapped & murdered[12]
February 26	Cong. Julius Kahn	"Deadly drifting"
March 9, 1914	funeral for Vergara	Laredo, Texas[13]

Appendix B

Henry L. Wilson Telegrams

CIPHER
From: Mexico City
Dated: Feb. 9, 1913
Rec'd 11:58 P.M.
SECRETARY OF STATE
WASHINGTON, D.C.
February 9, 2 P.M. [sent]

Revolt against government started in this city early this morning. Felix Diaz and Reyes and other prisoners released. Reyes killed while attacking National Palace which is still in control of Madero, who is now holding cabinet meeting there. The President is said to have support of entire police, both foot and mounted, and of Chapultepec cadets. Severe fighting in cathedral square [Zócalo] in front of National Palace for half an hour beginning at eight thirty. Madero led his troops in person from Chapultepec down San Francisco Street to palace. Diaz is said to have three thousand troops including Tlalpam cadets, Twentieth Infantry and First Artillery.

Impossible to obtain accurate details at present since the innumerable rumors are unreliable. Schuyler has just returned from automobile trip through city and reports large but perfectly orderly crowds in main streets and heavy patrols of mounted police. (People crying Viva Diaz and Death to Madero.) Killed and wounded still in palace square. Hard attack being made on arsenal and barracks near [US] embassy. Have just been telephoning to Minister for Foreign Affairs, who is with president in National

Palace, at the request of diplomatic body. I asked for adequate guard for all diplomatic agents, all of which have been entirely without protection, and also that all saloons and pulque shops be closed indefinitely. He promised to take immediate action.

No Americans injured as far as known.

[Henry L.] Wilson
TELEGRAM RECEIVED
(Via Galveston) CIPHER
From: Mexico City, Mex.
Dated Mar. 3, 1913
Rec'd Mar. 4, 3:30 A.M.
SECRETARY OF STATE
Washington, D.C.
SEVENTY-FOUR
Mar. 3, 7 P.M.

Prior to the meeting of the announced reception of the diplomatic corps (*) Mr. De la Barra this morning I had a consultation with British and German colleagues and it was agreed with the approval of the entire diplomatic corps that at the conclusion of the reception I should hand him the following communication.

Quote. The diplomatic corps has entered into communication with the provisional government without committing themselves in any way as regards formal recognition which is left to their respective governments to determine when such recognition shall be afforded. End Quote.

This was done in order that no misinterpretation of our attitude towards this government should be made and our attitude evidences that such was the case and department will (*) that it is worded in such a way as not to offend the sensibilities of this government. It is understood between the diplomatic corps and Mr. De la Barra that this action was taken solely for our protection and not to be made public. The Brazilian, Norwegian, Chilean and Austrian diplomatic representatives formally informed me this morning that all matters of recognition of this government their actions would accord with those of this embassy. The other Latin American representatives concur but have not formally stated their concurrence. The German and British ministers also concur in this as in everything else.

The Spanish minister advises me that he intend to recommend the immediate formal recognition of this government to his but after learning the views of all his colleagues he informed me that he would await the embassy's action he however thinks that the government should be immediately recognized the moment it has clearly demonstrate its ability to maintain practical order and has satisfied the department as to its intension to deal promptly and justly in the matter of our complaints.

[Henry L.] Wilson

Appendix C

Medical Examination of Clemente Vergara: March 10, 1914, Laredo, Texas

At the request of General Henry Hutchings, Adjutant General Texas National Guard, we, the undersigned physicians, on the forenoon of Tuesday, March 10, 1914, went to the cemetery at Laredo, Texas, and there examined the body of a dead man which had been brought to Laredo from Palafox, Texas, by John Convery, undertaker, and which body was claimed to be that of Clemente Vergara.

Upon careful examination, we found that the body had been pierced by four bullets, the location of which hereinafter to be described, two depressions of the skull unquestionably inflicted by the same blunt instrument.

There was no evidence of fire having been applied to the body, this being absolutely certain and positive since the cloths which were on the body when found were neither scorched nor burned, neither were there blisters upon the surface of the body nor was the hair singed.

Entrance—The location of the bullet wounds: One just above the inner third or sternal end of the right clavicle; two through the middle third of the stream, the exits of there were respectively,

Exit—Just above the brim of the pelvis near the junction of the illium [*sic*] and sacrum, one through the spine almost in the middle about level of the twelfth lumbar vertebra, the other being at the same level slightly to the left.

The one [bullet wound] inflicted to the head did not show point of exit and evidently ranged down through the neck and into the body.

There were two large oval depressions in the skull. The bones of the forearms and the arms were not broken and showed no evidence of having been burned. The lower extremities showed no evidence of violence.

Respectively submitted,

O. J. Cook, M.D. City Health Office

W. W. MacGregor County Health Officer

Appendix D

American Controlled or Owned Petroleum Operations in Mexico Established before 1914

Name	Organized	Capital	Comments
Union Oil of California	1890	26,786 acres	owns: Union Oil of Mexico, Compania Mexicana de Petroles, Compania la Macarena
Mexican Petroleum Company	1902	1 million barrel storage, tank cars, refineries	
Tuxpam Petroleum Company	1906	$1,000,000	
Tamihua Petroleum Company	1906	$1,000,000	
Tuxpan Oil Company	1907	600 shares at $100 par value	8,000 acres in Vera Cruz (originated in Delaware)
Hausteca Petroleum Co.	1907	$15 million	1 million acres, pipe lines, railroad, wharfage, terminal
International Petroleum Co.	1910	60,000 shares	1.4 million acres: Tamaulipas subsidiary: Mexican Seaboard Oil Co. at $10 par value
Gulf Coast Corporation	1910	200,000 shares at $5 par value	Virginia Corp.

Name	Organized	Capital	Comments
Tal-Vez Oil Company	1910	100 shares at 1,000 pesos par value	produces 10,000 barrels/day (originated in Mexico)
Kern River Oil Fields, Ltd.	1910	28,500 acres in Panuco	
New England Fuel Oil Co.	1911	25,000 shares at $10 par value	produces 750 barrels/day (originated in Maine)
Continental Mexican Petro Co.	1911	5,000 shares at $100 par value	transit site Tampico 87,000 acres Panuco and Nuevo Leon
Southern Fuel & Refining Co.	1911	99,500 shares at $10 par value	441,000 acres owned (originated in Delaware)
Compania Transcontinental	1912	400,000 shares at 10 peso par value	subsidiary: Standard Oil de Petroleo, company of N. J.
Lagunita Oil Company	1912	7,000 shares at $100 par value	owns: Tampascas Oil Company (originated in West Virginia)
Mexican Gulf Oil Co.	1912	8,000 shares at $25 par value	operations in Panuco/Topila (originated in Delaware)
Penn Mex Fuel Company	1912	400,000 shares at $25 par value	160,000 acres in the state of Veracruz (originated in Delaware)
Tampascas Oil Company	1912	200 shares at $100 par value	produces 95 barrels/day (originated in West Virginia) subsidiary: Lagunita Oil Company
Penn-Mex Fuel Company	1912	400,000 shares at $25 par value	150,000 acres in Vera Cruz
The Cortez-Aguada	1913	1,500 shares	subsidiary: Atlantic Lobos Oil Co.

Source: *The Mexican Year Book*, 1920–1921.

Notes

Introduction

1. Testimony of Henry L. Wilson, April 16, 1920, US Senate, *Investigation of Mexican Affairs*, 66th Cong., 2d sess., Doc. No. 285, Vol. 2, Washington, DC, 1920, 2252 (hereafter: *Investigation of Mexican Affairs*); Frank Tannenbaum, *Peace by Revolution*, New York, 1933, pp. 172–73; Jules Davids, *American Political and Economic Penetration of Mexico, 1877–1920* (New York: Arno Press, 1976), 224–29; Taft to Knox, November 10, 1910, Taft Papers, Letter Book, Vol. 20, no. 12, seen in Evans Library, College Station.

2. Walter Prescott Webb, *The Texas Rangers* (Boston: Houghton Mifflin, 1935), 486–95. Note: Other mentions of Clemente Vergara since Webb include, Charles H. Harris and Louis R. Sadler, *The Texas Rangers and the Mexican Revolution* (Albuquerque: University of New Mexico Press, 2004), 162–86. Note: The serial publication *Frontier Times Magazine*, August 1929, also carried a story on Vergara.

Chapter 1

1. Alan Knight, *The Mexican Revolution: Porfirians, Liberals, and Peasants* (Cambridge: Cambridge University Press, 1986), 1: 30–36; Paul Garner, *Porfirio Diaz* (Harlow, UK: Pearson Education, 2001), 76–80.

2. Friedrich Katz, *The Secret War in Mexico* (Chicago: University of Chicago Press, 1981), 41–46; Enrique Krauze, *Mexico: Biography of Power* (New York: Harper Collins, 1997), 253–61; John Womack Jr. *Zapata and the Mexican Revolution* (New York: Vintage Books, 1968), 106–12.

3. *New York Times*, February 10, 1913; Investigation of Mexican Affairs, 2258; Lazaro Gutierrez de Lara and Edgcumb Pinchon: *The Mexican People: Their Struggle for Freedom* (Garden City, NY: Doubleday, Page, 1917), 348–50; Jose R. Del Castillo, *Historia de la Revolution Social de Mexico* (Mexico, 1915), 178–263; Rafael de Zayas Enriquez, *The Case of Mexico and the Policy of President Wilson* (New York: Albert and Charles Boni, 1914), 53–59, 119–20; Edith O'Shaughnessy, *Intimate Pages of Mexican History* (New York: George Doran, 1920), 66; Manuel Calero, *The Mexican Policy of President Woodrow Wilson as It Appears to a Mexican* (New York: Smith and Thompson, 1916), 1–12; Dolores Butterfield, "The Conspiracy Against Madero," *The*

Forum, September 1913, 464–82; Krauze, *Mexico: Biography of Power*, 261; Wilford H. Callcott, *Liberalism in Mexico, 1857*–1929 (Hamden, CT: Archon Books, 1965), 232; Rodolfo Rocha, "The Influence of the Mexican Revolution on the Mexico-Texas Border, 1910–1916" (PhD diss., Texas Tech University, 1981), 49–86; Edward Beatty, "The Impact of Foreign Trade on the Mexican Economy: Term of Trade and the Rise of Industry 1880–1923," *Journal of Latin American Studies* (May 2000): 399–433. Note: Madero, wealthy landowner in northern Mexico, had in 1908 penned the best seller *The Presidential Succession in 1910* on the prospects for political change. This resulted in the formation of the national Anti-reelectionist Party and the eventual declaration of his candidacy. Owner of one of the largest cattle ranches in Mexico, Madero was a vegetarian.

4. US National Archives, General Records of the Department of State, Record Group 59, Internal Affairs of Mexico, 1910–1919, H. L. Wilson to Secretary of State, September 22, 1911, 812.00/2384 (hereafter: State RG 59); W. Dirk Raat, *Revoltosos: Mexico's Rebels in the United States, 1903–1923* (College Station: Texas A&M University Press, 1981), 227–50; Michael C. Meyer, *Mexican Rebel: Pascual Orozco and the Mexican Revolution, 1910–1915* (Lincoln: University of Nebraska Press, 1967), 71–74; P. Edward Haley, *Revolution and Intervention: The Diplomacy of Taft and Wilson with Mexico, 1910–1017* (Cambridge, MA: MIT Press, 1970), 35; Edward J. Berbusse, "Neutrality-Diplomacy of the United States and Mexico," *The Americas* (January 1956): 265–83; William W. Johnson, *Heroic Mexico* (New York: Harcourt Brace, 1984), 108–9.

5. H. L. Wilson to Secretary of State, August 28, 1912, 812.00/4899; John S. D. Eisenhower, *Intervention* (New York: W. W. Norton, 1993), 19–22; Edith O'Shaughnessy, *A Diplomat's Wife in Mexico* (New York: Harper and Brothers, 1916), 189–210; Luz María Hernández Sáenz, "Smuggling for the Revolution: Illegal Traffic of Arms on the Arizona-Sonora Border, 1912–1914," *Journal of the Southwest* (Winter 1986): 358–60; Meyer, *Mexican Rebel*, 57–58. See also Camilo Cantreras Delgado and Moises Gamez, *Procesos y Espacios Mineros* (Tijuana: El Colegio de la Frontera Norte, 2004), and Marvin Bernstein, *The Mexican Mining Industry, 1890–1950* (Albany: State University of New York Press, 1965), 36–39, 50–56, for discussion of Madero family business and industrial holdings.

6. Colquitt campaigned in the 1910 governor's race to reduce the size and cost of state government and to include reduction of both the Texas Rangers and the Texas State Guard. In June 1913, the total number of Texas Rangers was sixteen, though authorized at a strength of eighty-five.

7. O. B. Colquitt to President F. I. Madero, November 21, 1912, and O. B. Colquitt to B. F. Bonner, December 4, 1912, Oscar Branch Colquitt Papers, American History Center, Austin, Texas (hereafter: Colquitt Papers); Don M. Coerver and Linda B. Hall, *Texas and the Mexican Revolution* (San Antonio: Trinity University Press, 1984), 20–30; Harris and Sadler, *Texas Rangers and the Mexican Revolution*, 70–76.

8. Garrett to Knox, November 2, 1911, Mexican Dispatches, XI, 812.0/2472; Davids, *American Political and Economic Penetration of Mexico*, 274–76; Krauze, *Mexico: Biography of Power*, 264–65; Beatriz de la Garza, *A Law for the Lion* (Austin: University of Texas Press, 2003), 71–76; Harris and Sadler, *Texas Rangers*, 77–85. See also Peter V. N. Henderson, *Mexican Exiles in the Borderlands, 1910–1913* (El Paso: Texas Western Press, 1979), 33–46, and Rocha, "Influence of the Mexican Revolution on the Mexico-Texas Border," 115–18.

9. Coerver and Hall, *Texas and the Mexican Revolution*, 31–54; Charles H. Harris and Louis R. Sadler, "The 1911 Reyes Conspiracy: The Texas Side," *Southwestern Historical Quarterly* (April 1980): 325–48; Harris and Sadler, *Texas Rangers*, 86–113; Hutchings to Colquitt, July 7, 1912, Governors Papers: Oscar B. Colquitt, Texas State Archives, Austin (hereafter: Colquitt Texas State Archives Papers). Note: President Taft (R) gave both men, Democratic operatives, a full pardon in February 1913! Chapa, who was also editor of *El Imparcial de Texas*, an anti-Wilson administration paper, and an active party organizer, remained under BOI observation throughout the Revolution; see BOI reports "In Re F. A. Chapa: Mexican Revolutionary Matters," May 1, 1914, May 9, 1914, August 11, 1915, and June 25, 1917, US Justice Department, US Bureau of Investigation (BOI), NARA M 1085, Mexican Files, 1909–1912 (hereafter "Mexican Files BOI"); and Chapa, "A Furious Tempest in a Glass of Water," *El Imparcial de Texas*, April 23, 1914.

10. Knox to American Ambassador, February 17, 1913, 812.00/6223a; Dolores Butterfield, "The Conspiracy against Madero," *The Forum* (October 1913): 464–82; Friedrich E. Schuler, ed., *Murder and Counterrevolution in Mexico: The Eyewitness Account of German Ambassador Paul von Hintze, 1912–1914* (Lincoln: University of Nebraska Press, 2015), 15–60. Note: A complete report of the coup against Madero and the rise of Huerta is found at: H. L. Wilson to Bryan, March 12, 1913, 812.00/6840 [No. 1901], *Papers Relating to the Foreign Relations of the United States*, Washington, DC: GPO, 1920, pp. 768–76. In this document Ambassador Wilson comments, "I anticipated that a mild form of *coup d'état*, which would lead to the resignation of Madero." And of the new Huerta government he noted, "The new administration is not popular, but it is respected." As ex-ambassador, Wilson gave a presentation to the University Club in Brooklyn in January 1914, defending his actions: "General Huerta is not my type of man, but he is the man for Mexico." "H. L. Wilson Blames Prida's Audience," *New York Times*, January 11, 1914.

11. "Chronological Statement of Events in Mexico City: February 9th to February 18th, 1913," William F. Buckley Sr. Papers, Benton Latin American Collection, Austin, Box 34, February 1913; "Madero Gratified by Reply," *New York Times*, February 18, 1913; "Madero," London *Pall Mall Gazette*, February 19, 1913; "Pacto de la Ciudadela," Foreign Relations, pp. 722–23; "The Problem in Mexico," *The Economist*, October 11, 1913, 696–97; Roberto D. Fernandez, *Los Gobernantes de Mexico* (Sabinas, Coahuila: Editorial Cuauhtémoc, 1931), 35–37; Wilson, *Diplomatic Episodes*, 279–88, 390; Thomas H. Russell, *Mexico in Peace and War* (Chicago: Reilly and Britton Syndicate, 1914), 79–80; Stanley R. Ross, *Francisco I. Madero: Apostle of Mexican Democracy* (New York: Columbia University Press, 1955), 276–93. For a contemporary view from a nongovernment official, see Henry Morris, *Our Mexican Muddle* (Chicago: Laird and Lee, 1916), 91–102, and "President Wilson and Mexico," *American Review of Reviews* (September 1913): 280–83. Note: The exact role of Ambassador Wilson will never be fully known. The ambassador's actions are further complicated by a memo from "no. 16" to William F. Buckley on January 19, 1920, reviewing the wisdom of allowing the former ambassador to testify to the Special Senate Committee of Mexican Affairs, due to the fact there was a spy in the American embassy, "It seems that Luis d'Antin, confidential clerk at the American Embassy gave the Mexican government a copy of every telegram, even those in code, sent by H. L. Wilson to the State Department and to the president . . . information from d'Antin was used by R. H. Murray for the attacks on H. L. Wilson and for

the articles in the *Harper's Weekly*, entitled 'the Two Wilsons and Huerta,'" see No. 16 to Buckley, Buckley Papers.

12. "Huerta Wires Story of Madero Deaths," *New York Times*, March 13, 1913; Testimony of H. L. Wilson, April 16, 1920, *Investigation of Mexican Affairs*, 2262, 2268–69; H. L. Wilson to Secretary of State, February 9, 18, 19, 20, 1913, 812.00/6058, 6246, 6264, 8287; Frederick Starr, *Mexico and the United States: A Story of Revolution, Intervention, and War* (Chicago: Bible House, 1914), 386; P. Edward Haley, *Revolution and Intervention* (Cambridge, MA: MIT Press, 1970), 62–64. Note: From the time it was known that Porfirio Díaz would not run for reelection in 1910, there rose a call for "intervention," not necessarily by the military, to protect the commercial interests of not only the United States, but also of Britain, Germany, France, and Spain. While the Taft administration downplayed such actions, planning for intervention, occupation, and/or annexation of Mexico was contemplated. The debate would drag on for two years on the formal recognition of Mexico as a government de jure as well as de facto. John B. Moore at the State Department advised the White House to no avail, supporting a claim for recognition based on the president, such as the quote from President Franklin Pierce, "It is the established policy of the United States to recognize all governments without question of their source or organization, or of the means by which the governing persons attained their power." See Editorial, *El Paso Herald*, February 24, 1912; "Fallacies about 'Recognition,'" *The Nation*, July 24, 1913, 70–77; Wilson, *Diplomatic Episodes in Mexico*, 210; Meyer, *Mexican Rebel*, 94–104; and F. A. Balmaseda-Napoles, "Mexico and the United States, 1912–1917" (PhD diss., Case Western Reserve, 1974), 35–36.

13. "The Problem in Mexico," *The Economist*, October 11, 1913, 696–97; Edith O'Shaughnessy, *Diplomatic Days* (New York: Harper and Brothers, 1917), 219; O'Shaughnessy, *Intimate Pages of Mexican History*, 133–36. See also Lowell L. Blaisdell, "Henry Lane Wilson and the Overthrow of Madero," *Southwestern Social Science Quarterly* (September 1962): 126–35.

14. Henry B. Parkes, *A History of Mexico* (Boston: Houghton Mifflin, 1950), 332; Joseph H. L. Schlarman, *Mexico* (Milwaukee: Bruce Publishing, 1950), 426. Note: The so-called sinister appearance could be attributed to first appearances of the aging general: "At fifty-nine, Huerta was bald, stocky in build, and had an oval, high cheek boned face that revealed his Indian ancestry. A consumer of legendary quantities of cognac, he was plagued by cataracts and usually wore smoked glasses. When he appeared without the glasses he squinted, which gave him a sinister appearance." As seen in Larry Hill, *Emissaries to a Revolution*, 8. See also O'Shaughnessy, *Intimate Papers of Mexican History*, 227.

15. Parkes, *History of Mexico*, 332–37; "Garrison Revolts, Seizes Matamoras," *New York Times*, February 18, 1913; Testimony of H. L. Wilson, Investigation of Mexican Affairs, April 16, 1920, 2267–77: Calvert, *Mexican Revolution*, 153–56; "Our Call to Recognize Villa," *Literary Digest*, July 26, 1913, 120; Michael Meyer, *Huerta: A Political Portrait* (Lincoln: University of Nebraska Press, 1972), 92–96, 140–43, 185–87. Note: Calvert presents a compelling argument that Huerta was not directly involved or responsible for the murders yet was clearly an accessory after the fact in the cover-up. Furthermore, in November 1914, US Vice President Thomas R. Marshall said, "it was no secret in Mexico that Madero was to be killed. And in spite of waiting three days before his death and an extensive appeal from "many high [level] Masons . . . I could do nothing." See "Knew Madero Was to Die," *New York*

Times, November 2, 1914. Also, when General Antonio Lopez de Santa Anna was captured after the Battle of San Jacinto on April 21, 1836, according to common belief he gave the Masonic distress signal, which was recognized by J. A. Wharton and Sam Houston who in turn spared the prisoner's life; see Winfred H. Callcott *Santa Anna* (Norman: University of Oklahoma Press, 1936), 139.

16. "Mexican Foothold Sought for Japan," *New York Times*, July 20, 1913, and "Mexico Embarrasses Japan," *New York Times*, July 21, 1913; "De la Barra," *New York Times*, December 27, 1913; "De la Barra Decorated," *New York Times*, December 25, 1913; "Japan's Cold Shoulder to Mexico," *Literary Digest*, September 27, 1913, 518; Luis Licéaga, *Félix Díaz* (Mexico City: Editorial Jus, 1958), 232–60; Johnson, *Heroic Mexico*, 133; Friedrich E. Schuler, *Secret Wars and Secret Policies in the Americas* (Albuquerque: University of New Mexico Press, 2010), 73–77; Meyer, *Mexican Rebel*, 109. Note: General Díaz was never received by the Yamamoto Cabinet in Tokyo, suggesting that, "The cabinet was obliged to take this course for fear that the cordial reception might hurt the feelings of the United States."

17. "Plan of Guadalupe [March 26, 1913]," US Congress, Senate, Affairs of Mexico, 64 Cong., 1st sess., Doc. No. 324, February 17, 1919, p. 24; *Adiciones al Plan de Guadalupe y Decretos Dictados Comforme a las Mismas* (Veracruz: Secretaría de Instrucción Pública y Bellas Artes, 1915); Charles C. Cumberland, *Mexican Revolution: The Constitutionalist Years* (Austin: University of Texas Press, 1972), 70–83; Friedrich Katz, *The Secret War in Mexico* (Chicago: University of Chicago Press, 1981), 125–45; Enrique Krauze, *Mexico* (New York: Harper Collins, 1997), 241; Hill, *Emissaries to a Revolution*, 15–19; Laura Mendez de Cuenca, *Alvaro Obregon*, n.p., n.d., circa 1918, seen in Texas and Borderlands Collection, Cushing Library, College Station, Texas. Note: Carranza refused to take the title of "provisional president" since it could make him ineligible to be elected president; however, his full revolutionary title was "Primer Jefe de la Revolución Constitucionalista y Encargado del Poder Ejecutivo de la República."

18. Henry L. Stimson, Sec. of War to Sec. of Commerce and Labor, Washington, DC, February 25, 1913, National Archives Record Group 85 as seen in Records of Immigration and Nationalization Service, Part 2: Mexican Immigration, 1906–1930, Reel 4, Bethesda: University Publications of America, 1994 (hereafter: Records of Immigration, RG 85); *Austin Statesman*, February 20, 25, 1913. See also George P. Huckaby, "Oscar Branch Colquitt: A Political Biography" (PhD diss., University of Texas at Austin, 1946), 383–95.

19. H. L. Wilson to Secretary of State, February 10, 18, 1913, 8120.00/6076, 6245c; Knox to Secretary of the Navy, February 25 and 28, 1913, 812.00/6274; Colquitt to S. B. Colquitt, March 3, 1913, Colquitt Papers; Harris and Sadler, *Texas Rangers*, 104, 118–20. Note: In addition to the troop movements, six American warships were dispatched to the water off Mexico, four to the Veracruz-Tampico area: the *Georgia*, *Vermont*, *Nebraska*, and *Virginia*; and on the Pacific Coast the *South Dakota* was dispatched to Acapulco, and the *Colorado* along the coast between Mazatlán and Manzanillo; Haley, *Revolution and Intervention*, 64–65.

20. Ray S. Baker, *Woodrow Wilson*, vol. 4 (New York: Greenwood, 1968), 61 (reprint of 1931 first edition); Henry Lane Wilson, *Diplomatic Episodes in Mexico, Belgium, and Chile* (Port Washington, NY: Kennikat Press, 1971), 296–99; Arthur S. Link, *Woodrow Wilson and the Progressive Era* (New York: Harper Torchbooks, 1963), 108. Note: Ambassador Wilson notes that "some years after" the fall of Madero, former

Secretary Knox told him, "if the Huerta government had conceded our demands in full he would, even as late as ten o'clock on the morning of March 4th [1913]," he would have recommended to President Taft that "full recognition be accorded." See also P. C. Knox to H. L Wilson, February 20 and 25, 1913, *Foreign Affairs of the United States*, 1913, 725, 738, and "Why [Henry Lane] Wilson Aids Huerta," *New York Times*, March 8, 1913.

21. As seen in William Diamond, *The Economic Thought of Woodrow Wilson* (Baltimore: Johns Hopkins Press, 1943), 131.

22. *De Como Vino Huerta y Como se Fue*, [no author], Mexico, 1914, p. 178–79; Baker, *Woodrow Wilson*, 4: 61–66, 237–39; "The Problem in Mexico," *The Economist*, October 11, 1913, 696–97; Harley Notter, *The Origins of the Foreign Policy of Woodrow Wilson* (Baltimore: Johns Hopkins Press, 1937), 289–90. Note: Other pressing issues in the early weeks of the administration included the "Six Power Loan" arrangements for China being proposed, a domestic issue in which California had pending legislation regarding land ownership by Japanese—a major affront to Tokyo, and a dispute over islands in the Philippines.

23. Link, *Wilson the Diplomatist*, 9–10. See also Diamond, *Economic Thought of Woodrow Wilson*, 143–52, and David Milne, *Worldmaking: The Art and Science of American Diplomacy* (New York: Farrar, Straus and Giroux, 2015), 84–85.

24. Lodge to Spring Rice, March 10, 1913, Stephen Gwynn, ed., *The Letters and Friendships of Sir Cecil Spring Rice*, 2 vols. (Boston: Houghton Mifflin, 1929), 1: 189; Josephus Daniels [Secretary of the Navy 1913–1921], *The Wilson Era* (Chapel Hill: University of North Carolina Press, 1944), 180–82; Calvert, *Mexican Revolution*, 167–74. See also William H. Taft, "The Powers of the President," *Yale Review* (August 1914): 25–42.

25. *New York World*, March 7–13, 1913; Testimony of H. L. Wilson, April 16, 1920, *Investigation of Mexican Affairs*, 2287; "Chronological Statement of Events in Mexico City: February 9 to February 18, 1913, n.d., Buckley Papers. Note: These articles, written by Richard H. Murray, were later published in *Harper's Weekly* under the title "The Two Wilsons." Since, according to Ambassador Wilson, Murray was an "utterly worthless man with no moral or financial standing," he brought suit against Norman Hopgood, the editor, in the District Court of Columbia and obtained a judgment for slander.

26, Howard F. Cline, *The United States and Mexico* (Cambridge, MA: Harvard University Press, 1963), 141–45; Notter, *Origins of the Foreign Policy of Woodrow Wilson*, 193–99; *The Times* (London), "The Rising in Mexico," February 12, 1913, 5; *New York World*, March 7–13, 1913; Link, *Woodrow Wilson and the Progressive Era*, 25–32; Lindsay Rogers, "President Wilson's Theory of His Office," *The Forum*, February 1914, 174–186. Note: President Madero in early 1913, disgruntled with Ambassador Lane Wilson, bypassed Taft and secretly contacted president-elect Wilson to request he recall the compulsive ambassador as soon as he takes office in March 1913. See also Samuel G. Inman, *Intervention in Mexico* (New York: Association Press, 1919).

27. Colquitt to W. G. McAdoo, Chairman DNC, September 28, 1912; Colquitt to Henry Morgenthau, Treasure DNC, October 16, 17, 1912; Colquitt to J. F. Wolters, October 22, 1912, Colquitt Papers.

28. Colquitt to Governor Woodrow Wilson, December 27, 1912, and January 7, 1913, Colquitt Papers; Arthur Walworth, *Woodrow Wilson* (New York: W. W. Norton, 1978), V1: 342–57.

29. Colquitt to Wilson, December 27, 1912; Wilson to Colquitt, January 3, 1913; Colquitt to Wilson, January 7, 1913, Colquitt Papers, University of Texas, Austin; "President Wilson's Cabinet," *New York Times*, March 6, 1913.

30. Robert C. Hilderbrand, "Edward M. House," in *Profiles in Power*, ed. Kenneth E. Hendrickson and Michael L. Collins (Austin: University of Texas Press, 2004), 2–5; Governor L. S. Ross to Holmes, April 20, 1892, Governor Lawrence S. Ross Papers, Cushing Library, College Station, Texas; Joe B. Franz, *Texas* (New York: W. W. Norton, 1976), 157; Charles E. Neu, "In Search of Colonel Edward M. House: The Texas Years, 1858–1912," *Southwestern Historical Quarterly* (July 1989): 25–29; *The Industrial Advantages of Houston, Texas and Environs* (1977; Houston: Akehurst Publishing, 1984), 15, 18. Note: Governor Ross was encouraged to run against Hogg in 1892, but declined in favor of supporting George Clark of Waco, who had served as campaign manager for the former governor's 1886 and 1888 elections. The House family beginning in the early 1890s had extensive banking, cotton brokerage, barge shipping operations, and agricultural activities.

31. Baker, *Woodrow Wilson*, 4: 64; George S. Viereck, *The Strangest Friendship in History: Woodrow Wilson and Colonel House* (New York: Liveright Publishers, 1932),1–10, 18, 27; Anne W. Lane and Louise H. Wall, eds., *The Letters of Franklin K. Lane* (Boston: Houghton Mifflin, 1922), 118–21, 129–30. Also see James Bryce to Sir Edward Grey, April 19, 1913, in Kenneth Bourne, ed., *British Documents on Foreign Affairs: Foreign Office Confidential Print; North American Affairs, 1911–1914*, Part 1, Vol. 15, n.p.: University Publications of America, 1987, Doc. 75, pp. 203–6 (hereafter: British Foreign Documents: 1911–1914). Note: Colonel House referred to the siege of office seekers as the "hungry horde."

32. Godfrey Hodgson, *Woodrow Wilson's Right Hand: The Life of Colonel Edward M. House* (New Haven, CT: Yale University Press, 2006), 54–67; Viereck, *Strangest Friendship in History*, 11, 21. Note: While some, like Arthur Link, decades later minimized the role of Colonel House in carrying Texas, the fact remains he was a key factor in securing the vote of the swing state at a critical time of the election. This negative view of House was possible fueled by the disgruntled comments of William F. McCombs, a former Wilson campaign manager, expressed in L. J. Lang, ed., *Making Woodrow Wilson President* (New York: Fairview, 1921). See also Arthur S. Link, "The Wilson Movement in Texas, 1910–1912," *Southwestern Historical Quarterly* 48 (1945): 169–85.

33. David Houston, *Eight Years with Wilson's Cabinet* (New York: Doubleday, Page, 1926), 21–22; Viereck, *Strangest Friendship in History*, 37–41, 48; Robert C. Cotner, *James Stephen Hogg* (Austin: University of Texas Press, 1959), 298–99, 307, 318–20, 413–15, 480; Alexander L. George and Juliett L. George, *Woodrow Wilson and Colonel House* (New York: John Day, 1956), 92; Lane and Wall, *Letters of Franklin K. Lane*, 134; Adrian Anderson, "President Wilson's Politician: Albert Sidney Burleson," *Southwestern Historical Quarterly* (January 1974): 339–54; Franz, *Texas*, 157–58; Lewis C. Gould, *Progressives and Prohibitionists: Texas Democrats in the Wilson Era* (Austin: University of Texas Press, 1973), 100–106; Hodgson, *Woodrow Wilson's Right Hand*, 69–80; "Wilson to Fill 1,400 Jobs," *New York Times*, March 4, 1913, and "Senate Confirms Wilson Cabinet," *New York Times*,, March 6, 1913. Note: Incoming Secretary Franklin K. Lane of the Interior did not meet Wilson for the first time in person until March 3, 1913, on the eve of the inauguration. Colonel House's first choice for Interior was Walter H. Page; when he called Page, he was out on vacation so House called and confirmed Lane and later recommended Page as ambassador to England.

34. "The Mexican Difficulty," *The Nation*, July 31, 1913, 92; Rose Gregory, "To Do Good in the World: Woodrow Wilson," in *Makers of American Diplomacy*, ed. Frank Merli and Theodore Wilson (New York: Scribner's Sons, 1974), 62; Hill, *Emissaries to a Revolution*, 4. Note: Arthur S. Link notes: "To Wilson the issue was plain as daylight, and he refused on moral grounds to recognize Huerta—even if he controlled most of Mexico and was constitutional in form." See Link, *Diplomatist*, 19. While one contemporary source notes: "The French, German, English, and Spanish daily and weekly sneered at what they dubbed the moral policy of a puritan school teacher"; Carlo de Fornaro, *Carranza and Mexico* (New York: Mitchell Kennerley, 1915), 205.

35. President Wilson to Amb. Wilson, June 12, 1913, 812.00/7743, US Department of State Papers; Houston, *Eight Years with Wilson Cabinet*, 9–13; Arthur S. Link, *Wilson the Diplomatist* (Baltimore: Johns Hopkins Press, 1957), 25; Cotner, *James Stephen Hogg*, 320; Arthur D. Link, "The Wilson Movement in Texas, 1910–1912," *Southwestern Historical Quarterly* 48 (October 1944), 169–85; Charles Seymour, *The Intimate Papers of Colonel House*, vol. 1 (Boston: Houghton Mifflin, 1926), 63–66; Hodgson, *Woodrow Wilson's Right Hand: The Life of Edward M. House*, 69–80; Baker, *Woodrow Wilson*, 4: 66. Note: By the mid-nineteenth century the United States had a policy (defined in 1848 by Secretary of State James Buchanan) to recognize de facto governments, without questioning the legitimacy of the government, as long as the new government complied with international norms and protected foreign interests. See Cline, *The US and Mexico*, 141.

36. Arthur Walworth, *Woodrow Wilson*, 3rd ed. (New York: Norton, 1978), 356–57. Note: Winner of the 1959 Pulitzer Prize for biography.

37. David Cronon, ed., *The Cabinet Diaries of Josephus Daniels, 1913–1921* (Lincoln: University of Nebraska Press, 1963), 29–30.

38. Cronon, *Cabinet Diaries of Josephus Daniels*, 42.

39. Arnoldo De León, ed., *War along the Border: The Mexican Revolution and Tejano Communities* (College Station: Texas A&M University Press, 2012); Oscar J. Martinez, *Troublesome Border* (Tucson: University of Arizona Press, 1988); and S. C. Gwynne, *Empire of the Summer Moon* (New York: Scribner, 2010).

40. Cronon, *Cabinet Diaries*, 43. See also "British Foreign Policy," *The Economist*, November 15, 1913, 1054, and Arthur D. H. Smith, *Mr. House of Texas* (New York: Funk and Wagnalls, 1940), 81–83.

41. Doctor Atl, "The Mexican Revolution and the Nationalization of the Land: The Foreign Interests and Reaction," New York: n.p., 1915, 8–10. Note: The Germans and the French were fully aware of the British recognition, and they too assisted Huerta to protect their investment interests in Mexico.

42. Testimony of Michael J. Slattery, April 1, 1920, Investigation of Mexican Affairs, pp. 1998–2006; James Middleton, "Mexico, The Land of Concessions," *The World's Work*, January 1914, 289–98; De León, *War along the Border*, 12–14; Alex M. Saragoza, *The Monterrey Elite and the Mexican State, 1880–1940* (Austin: University of Texas Press, 1988), 102–5. See also "Our Call to Recognize Huerta," *Literary Digest*, July 26, 1913, 120.

43. O. B. Colquitt to Secretary of State, May 19, 1913, *U.S. Foreign Relations*, File No. 812.00/7577, p. 880; "The Civil War in Mexico," *The Economist*, December 27, 1913; Katz, *Secret War in Mexico*, 127–28; Harris and Sadler, *Texas Rangers*, 118–19; Raat, *Revoltosos*, 253–62. See also Ethan A. Nadelmann, *Cops Across Borders* (University Park: Pennsylvania State University Press, 1993), 68–75.

44. Cronon, *Cabinet Diaries*, 44; Calvert, *Mexican Revolution*, 169–70. Note: Surveyors were some of the most detested and murdered people on the frontier of Texas and Mexico, as in most cases they signaled the opening and occupation of tribal lands to outsiders. See also Gwynne, *Empire*, 130–41.

45. Houston, *Eight Years with Wilson's Cabinet*, 69; Daniels, *Wilson Era*, 181.

Chapter 2

1. Determining the exact amount of foreign direct investment (FDI) in Mexico in 1913–14 is difficult but not impossible. Most sources have tended to underestimate the full investment, placing all foreign capital for this period in the range of $1.7 to $2 billion, which I believe is a low estimate. Low because, in spite of the Madero revolution in 1910, FDI was still flowing into Mexico until early 1913. The most cited estimate of FDI was the "Letcher Report" of 1912, which was challenged by Senator Albert Fall in a US Senate investigation of Mexican affairs in 1919–20. One reason for the underestimate, primarily for the United States, Great Britain, France, Germany, and the Netherlands, is that few account for the boom in oil products, railroad expansion, mining, investments in Mexican bank stocks of the period, and seaport-terminal enhancements—not to mention a robust agriculture and light manufacturing sector. One expert noted for example, "French investments have been made in such fashion they elude pursuit [identification]." Furthermore, due to the Mexican government changes between 1910 to 1914, accurate data was not collected or analyzed.

American Investment in Mexico—1913 (estimate)

Type	amount $ millions	percentage
Railroads	$653.2	58.1
Mining	281.5	24.4
Govt. bonds	52.3	4.3
Oil and Refining	43.2	3.6
Banking	35.7	3.2
Real estate	28.7	2.2
Rubber	18.3	1.5
Manufacturing	15.1	1.3
Misc.	17.8	1.4

Note: Estimates do not include all oil, mining, and real estate held in secret or foreign ownership. Total value of some fifty US owned oil production and refining operations are likely undervalued. The silver, gold, and agricultural commodities markets constantly vary. See also the table in chapter 4.

However, by mid-1914 there is a clear point of change. There was a drop in mining production as facilities were destroyed by the revolutionist, railroad failed to pay investors due to troop and supply use (as well as rail destruction), the closing of seaports, and most damaging was the massive capital flight of patrimony to the US (primarily Texas) banks. One clear event: Mexican public debt extensively held abroad was in default and credit worthiness from July 1914 until an international consortium of banks could reissue bonds in 1925; full recovery did not occur until 1942! See Marion Letcher, "Wealth of Mexico," Bureau of Foreign and Domestic Commerce, Dept. of Commerce and Labor, *Daily Consular and Trade Reports*, 15th year, III, No. 168, July 18, 1912; "Concessions in Mexico," *New York Times*, November 10, 1913; Wallace Thompson, *Trading with Mexico* (New York: Dodd, Mead, 1921); Max Winkler, *Investments of United States Capital in Latin America* (Boston: World Peace Foundation, 1929); Senate, *Investigation of Mexican Affairs*, 66th Cong., 2 sess., No. 285, 2 Vols., 1920, pp. 759–66, and Senate Report, No. 645, 1920, p. 2005 ($1 bill), p. 2252 ($1.2 bill). See also Page, *The Life and Letters of Walter H. Page*, 1: 178; Marvin D. Bernstein, *The Mexican Mining Industry, 1890–1950* (Albany: State University of New York, 1964); Robert S. Smith, *The United States and Revolutionary Nationalism in Mexico, 1916–1932* (Chicago: University of Chicago Press, 1972); Lorenzo Meyer, *Mexico and the United States in the Oil Controversy, 1917–1942* (Austin: University of Texas Press, 1972), 1–41; O'Shaughnessy, *Diplomatic Days*, 261; and John A. Adams Jr., *Mexican Banking and Investment in Transition* (Westport, CT: Quorum, 1997), 69.

2. David M. Plecther, *Rails, Mines, and Progress: Seven American Promoters in Mexico, 1867–1922* (Ithaca, NY: Cornell University Press, 1958), 3, 313–15; Sandra Kuntz Ficker and Paolo Riguzzi, *Ferrocarriles y vida económica en México, 1850–1950* (Mexico City: UNAM, 1996), 223–356; Fehrenbach, *Fire and Blood*, 502; Katz, *Secret War in Mexico*, 21–27, 71–76, 156–83; Peter Calvert, *The Mexican Revolution, 1910–1914* (Cambridge: Cambridge University Press, 1968), 19–20; Bernstein, *Mexican Mining Industry*, 49–77. See also Russell, M*exico in Peace and War*, 292, 306–7; Beatty, "Impact of Foreign Trade on the Mexican Economy," 403, 406–10; Louis M. Teitelbaum, *Woodrow Wilson and the Mexican Revolution, 1913–1916* (New York: Exposition Press, 1967), 13–16; and Camilo Contreras Delgado and Moises Gamez, *Procesos y Espacios Mineros* (Tijuana: El Colegio de la Frontera Norte, 2004).

3. Link, *Woodrow Wilson and the Progressive Era*, 22–24. Note: Of the 14.8 million votes cast, Wilson received 43 percent, Roosevelt 27 percent, Taft 24 percent, and Debs, 6 percent; in the electoral college count, Wilson won forty-one states, Roosevelt six, and Taft two.

4. Katz, *Secret War in Mexico*, 156.

5. US Foreign Relations, 1913, 838–41; Secretaría de Hacienda y Crédito Público, *La Deuda Externa de Mexico* (Mexico City, 1926), 9–19; Edgar Turlington, *Mexico and Her Foreign Creditors* (New York: Columbia University Press, 1930), 244–59. Note: The capitalization or bonding of foreign governments by multinationals, especially in Latin America, is an extensive and complicated web of loans, pledges, trade agreements, and "gentlemen's agreements." The loan mentioned here is but one of many the Huerta government inherited. Mexico had experienced this same financial dynamics and international debt pressure in the early 1860s, when European governments did intervene to collect debt.

6. Cecil Spring-Rice to Sir Edward Grey, May 19, 1913, British Foreign Documents, 1911–1914, Doc. 96, 216–17; Baker, *Woodrow Wilson*, 4: 245; Katz, *Secret War in Mexico*, 166. Note: Foreign investor concerns were fueled by double-digit inflation in Mexico. While Mexico was legally a bimetallist country, gold slowly disappeared from circulation and the value of the peso was based on the price of silver—while the value of the US dollar was pegged to the value of gold. See Edwin Kemmerer, *Inflation and Revolution: Mexico's Experience 1912–1917* (Princeton, NJ: Princeton University Press, 1940).

7. "The Greene-Cananea Consolidation," *Engineering and Mining Journal*, December 22, 1906, 1183; "The Mexican Crisis and the Railroads of Mexico," *The Economist*, November 8, 1913, 998–1000; Link, *Woodrow Wilson and the Progressive Era*, 108; Hart, *Revolutionary Mexico*, 146–55, 284–86.

8. Baker, *Woodrow Wilson*,4: 245–49. See also C. L. Sonnichsen, *Colonel Greene and the Copper Skyrocket* (Tucson: University of Arizona Press, 1974), and "British Naval Base Here," *New York Times*, August 4, 1913; O'Shaughnessy, *Diplomatic Days*, 261. Note: One contemporary noted, Doheny was a "man of genius . . . he appears on the scene of the future [Mexican] oil drama . . . and oil gushed."

9. Memorandum, Counselor John B. Moore to Sec. of State, August 22, 1913, 812.00/10499, US Department of State Papers; Baker, *Woodrow Wilson*, 4: 249–53; Houston, *Eight Years with Wilson's Cabinet*, 1: 69; Seymour, *Intimate Papers*, 1: 215. Note: Shortly following this briefing Moore resigned from the State Department.

10. James B. Moore, "Memorandum on the Mexican Situation," May 14, 1913, US Foreign Relations; "Our Call to recognize Huerta," *Literacy Digest* July 16, 1913, 120; Louis C. Simonds, "Mexico as It Is," *Atlantic Monthly* (October 1913): 564; Calvert, *Mexican Revolution*, 19–20. Note: The Monroe Doctrine was the umbrella by which the United States did exactly this in sending USMC, for example, to Nicaragua to run customhouses and collect duties to pay debt obligations.

11. Hodgson, *Woodrow Wilson's Right Hand*, 88; Katz, *Secret War in Mexico*, 167; Walworth, *Woodrow Wilson*, 365: J. Fred Rippy, *Latin America in World Politics* (New York: Alfred A. Knopf, 1928), 230–34. See also Samuel F. Bemis, *The Latin American Policy of the United States* (New York: W. W. Norton, 1943).

12. "Mexicans Insist Fall Aided Rebels," *New York Times*, July 2, 1913; "A Free-Gun Policy for Mexico," *Literary Digest*, July 12, 1913, 42–43. See also Clifford W. Trow, "Woodrow Wilson and the Mexican Interventionist of 1919," *Journal of American History* (June 1971): 46–72.

13. Hodgson, *Woodrow Wilson's Right Hand*; Hill, *Emissaries to a Revolution*, ix–x; US Congressional Record, Vol. 51, p. 4527.

14. Baker, *Woodrow Wilson*, 4: 218. See also "Wilson Suggest Plan to Mexico," *New York Times*, August 5, 1913.

15. Cronon, *Cabinet Dairies of Josephus Daniels*, 43; Larry D. Hill, *Emissaries to a Revolution: Woodrow Wilson's Executive Agents in Mexico* (Baton Rouge: Louisiana State University Press, 1973), 3–20. See also H. M. Wriston, "Presidential Special Agents in Diplomacy," *American Political Science Review* 10 (August 1916): 481 99. Note: The Minister of External Relations and Foreign Affairs, Gamboa, on May 10 issues a statement that the Mexican government would no longer negotiate with the US embassy except on routine matters—in effect reducing the ambassador to a mere charge or staff role. Special agent reports were sent to third-party addresses and then forwarded to the White House.

16. Testimony of H. L. Wilson, Investigation of Mexican Affairs, April 16, 1920, 2290; Hill, *Emissaries to a Revolution*, 21–39; "Monroe Doctrine Safe," *New York Times*, August 5, 1913. See also Kenneth J. Grieb, "Reginald del Valle: A California Diplomat's Sojourn in Mexico," *California Historical Quarterly* (December 1968): 315–28. Note: William Hale edited Wilson's campaign addresses during 1912 and published a compilation as *New Freedom* in 1913.

17. Testimony of H. L. Wilson, Investigation of Mexican Affairs, April 16, 1920, 2290–99; H. L Wilson to W. J. Bryan, June 9, 1913, and June 29, 1913; Woodrow Wilson to W. J. Bryan, July 1, 1913, FR of the US, 1913, 807; Wilson, *Diplomatic*

Episodes, 310–13; Link, *Wilson: The New Freedom* (Princeton, NJ: Princeton University Press, 1956), 67–70; Link, *Wilson the Diplomatist*, 24–24; Baker, *Woodrow Wilson*, 4: 243–4; "Hurry Call Sent to Envoy Wilson," *New York Times*, August 4, 1913.

18. Hart, *Revolutionary Mexico*, 285–86; Kenneth J. Grieb, "The Lind Mission to Mexico," *Caribbean Studies* (January 1968): 25–43; Kendrick A. Clements, "Woodrow Wilson's Mexican Policy, 1913–15," *Journal of Diplomatic History* (Spring 1980): 118–36.

19. Testimony of John Lind, April 27, 1920, Investigation of Mexican Affairs, 2318–24; US Foreign Relations, 1913, 819–20; Stephenson, *John Lind of Minnesota*, 208; "Mr. John Lind," *The Nation*, August 7, 1913, 112; "Huerta to Insure Safety for Lind," and "Mexicans Criticize Wilson," *New York Times*, August 9, 1913; "Mr. Lind Should Be Cautious," *New York Times*, November 8, 1913; "Mr. Lind's Mission to Mexico," *Literary Digest*, August 16, 1913, 235 (pix); Link, *Woodrow Wilson*, 113–15.

20. Testimony of M. J. Slattery, April 1, 1920, Investigation of Mexican Affairs, 2007. See also "Says H. L. Wilson Guilty with Huerta," *New York Times*, January 10, 1914. Note: Luis Lara Pardo in *Matchs de Dictadores* (1942) noted in his chapter "The Tragic Farce of John Lind" that "Wilson scraped the bottom of boorish nothingness to pick the most incompetent man," p. 57.

21. Larry D. Hill, "The Progressive Politician as a Diplomat: The Case of John Lind in Mexico," *The Americas*, April 1971, 355–72; Haley, *Revolution and Intervention*, 97–108; Testimony of John Lind, April 27, 1920, Investigation of Mexican Affairs, 2241. Note: In Lind's testimony to Congress he was a bit unsure of the Huerta agent's role, commenting: "Huerta sent down spies [to Veracruz]. Whether they were sent down to spy on me or to guard me against any accident or any incident that might cause friction, I cannot say."

22. Sir Edward Grey to Sir C. Spring-Rice, May 21, 1913, British Foreign Document, 1911–14, Doc. 93, p. 215; Calvert, *Mexican Revolution*, 190–96; Hodgson, *Wilson's Right Hand*, 95. Note: Also joining Grey and House were US Ambassador Page and the Earl of Crewe, Secretary of State for India.

23. "A Rival Isthmian Canal," *The Nation*, July 31, 1913, 92–93; Viereck, *Strangest Friendship in History*, 50; Katz, *Secret War in Mexico*, 174–75; Seymour, *Intimate Papers of Colonel House*, 195–97; August Heckscher, *Woodrow Wilson* (New York: Charles Scribner's Sons, 1991), 325–27; Baker, *Woodrow Wilson*, 4: 287; British Foreign Documents, Doc. 139, p. 247; Notter, *Origins of the Foreign Policy of Woodrow Wilson*, 252; William S. Coker, "The Panama Canal Tolls Controversy: A Different Perspective," *Journal of American History* (December 1968): 555–64. Note: The US and British disagreement centered on the interpretation of Art. 111, No. 1 of the Hay-Pauncefote Treaty signed by US Secretary of State John Hay and UK Ambassador to the US Lord Pauncefote on November 18, 1901, and ratified by the US Senate on December 16, 1901. Further complicating diplomatic matters were both the British and German strategic interest in developing a second canal in Nicaragua absent American approval and participation. With Europe on the brink of all-out war, the US Senate, as House had promised the British, on June 15, 1914, repealed the Panama Canal Tolls exemption clause. See also "Says Canal Means American Empire," *New York Times*, November 2, 1913; "Mr. Wilson 'Point of Honor,'" *New York Times*, February 8, 1914; "Wilson Accused of British Deal," *New York Times*, March 29, 1914; and Williams, *Anglo-American Isthmian Diplomacy*, 313n.

24. Stock Certificate No. 003593, Series B, "La Compañía Mexicana de Petróleo—El Águila, S.A.," Enero 1912, author's collection; N. A. Jennings to William R. Hearst, March 23, 1914, Buckley Papers, Austin; N. A. Jennings to William R. Hearst, March 23, 1914, Buckley Papers, Benson History Center, Austin, Texas. Note: Edith O'Shaughnessy, in *Intimate Pages of Mexican History* (1920), in her blunt observations on "Mexican oil," noted that "prior to the advent of the foreign oil-devils the Mexican either completely ignored their petroleum fields, or had the oozing, horrid indications fenced off so that man nor beast could fall into them and lose his life."

25. Z. A. B. Zeman, *The Gentlemen Negotiators: A Diplomatic History of World War I* (New York: Macmillan, 1971), 164–65, 318–22; Kenneth J. Grieb, "Standard Oil and the Financing of the Mexican Revolution," *California Historical Quarterly* (March 1971): 60; Jonathan C. Brown, *Oil and Revolution in Mexico* (Berkeley: University of California Press, 1993), 171–95. See also "The Navy and the Future," *Edinburgh Review* (April 1914): 448–68, and Archibald Hurd, "The Whole-World Needs of the Navy," *Quarterly Review* (October 1913): 493–508, and Hew Strachan *The First World War* (New York: Viking, 2004), 7–22.

26. Gwynn, *Letters and Friendships of Sir Cecil Spring Rice*, 1: 179; "Mr. Churchill's Failure to Stop Naval Rivalry," *Literary Digest*, November 15, 1913, 936; "British Oil Precautions," *New York Times*, December 21, 1913; "The German Navy," *The Economist*, March 30, 1912, 689, and "Our Dreadnought Superiority," *The Economist*, November 8, 1913, 1017; Calvert, *Mexican Revolution*, 173–77; Cooper, *Walter Hines Page*, 262–63; Grieb, "Lind Mission to Mexico," 36–37. See also Winston L. S. Churchill, *The World Crisis, 1911–1918* (London, 1931), 89–93, and "A Naval Revolution Through Oil-Fuel," *Literary Digest*, November 8, 1913, 868. Note: Oil for the Admiralty sourced in Mexico was modified after June 1915 to purchase fuel from the Standard Oil Company, driven by fear in the British financial circles to invest in the expansion of Pearson's El Águila oil operations. Katz, *Secret War in Mexico*, 179–80; Robert K. Massie, *Castles of Steel* (New York: Ballantine Books, 2003), 73, 92–95; "Wilson for Two-Ship Plan," *New York Times*, January 30, 1914; and David Milne, "On American Foreign Policy," *Wall Street Journal*, December 22, 2015.

27. Sir Cecil Spring Rice to Senator Henry C. Lodge, August 2, 1913, in Gwynn, *Letters and Friendships of Sir Cecil Spring-Rice*, 1: 191. Note: Such slang was apparently a part of British communiqués as is noted in Sir Spring Rice's June 1, 1914, annual report to White Hall: "In last year's report, Lord Bryce [former ambassador to Washington] writing from personal experience, points out that North Americans will be always to the South American a 'gringo,' and the Latin American to the North American a 'greaser,' and that this is the fundamental fact in the situation," as seen in British Foreign Affairs, 270.

28. Seymour, *Intimate Papers of Colonel House*, 194–97; Sir C. Spring Rice to Sir Edward Grey, July 21, 1913, British Foreign Documents, Doc. 127, 232–33; Katz, *Secret War in Mexico*, 161; Baker, *Woodrow Wilson*, 4: 259–61. Note: American chief of the general staff, General Leonard Wood, noted: "Cowdrays' oil concession alone thus exceeds that of Russia, while oil wealth of Mexico as a whole probably exceeds that of the United States." In a few short years, Mexico, by 1913, had moved from seventh to third place in world oil production.

29. Sir C. Spring Rice to Sir Edward Grey, August 15, 1913, British Foreign Documents, 1911–14, 233; David H. Burton, *Cecil Spring Rice: A Diplomat's Life* (Rutherford, NJ: Fairleigh Dickinson University Press, 1990), 151; Cooper, *Walter Hines Page*, 265–66; Calvert, *Mexican Revolution*, 168. See also "The End of Wilson," *The*

Globe and Commercial Advertiser (New York), August 5, 1913. See also "The End of Wilson," *The Globe and Commercial Advertiser* (New York), August 5, 1913.

30. Baker, *Woodrow Wilson*, 4: 273.

31. Testimony of H. L. Wilson, April 16, 1920, Investigation of Mexican Affairs, 2289; Sir C. Spring Rice to Sir Edward Grey, August 14, 1913, British Foreign Documents, 1911–114, 234; Baker, *Woodrow Wilson*, 4: 73–75; Walworth, *Woodrow Wilson*, 349–52, 367–68. Note: Wilson's recognition of the Chinese government in May 1913 was followed shortly by a counterrevolution in China in which Yuan has the opposition leader, Song Jia Oren, assassinated, with Secretary Bryan writing to Wilson, who notes, the Yuan regime has "adapted something of Huerta's methods and given the same reasons."

32. Sir Edward Grey to Sir C. Spring Rice July 11, 1913, and July 25, 1913, and Spring Rice to Grey, July 12, 1913, and July 21, 1913, British Foreign Documents, 1911–14, 230–33.

33. Spring Rice to Grey, July 21, 1913, British Foreign Documents, 1911–14, 232–33.

34. Spring Rice to Grey, August 19, 1913, British Foreign Documents, 1911–14, 235. See also Hill, *Emissaries*, 95

35. Spring Rice to Grey, August 19, 1913, British Foreign Documents, 1911–14, 235. See also "Mr. Lind's Mission to Mexico," *Literary Digest*, August 16, 1913, 235.

36. Spring Rice to Grey, August 19, 1913, British Foreign Documents, 1911–14, 235.

37. Calvert, *Mexican Revolution*, 202.

38. Spring Rice to Grey, August 19, 1913, British Foreign Documents, 235; May 19, 1913, 217; Lt. Col. M. F. Gage, "Report on the United States Army, 1912–13," April 29, 1914, British Foreign Documents, 311–12; "500,000 Soldiers Available for War," *New York Times*, November 4, 1913, and "Mexico and Mobilization," *New York Times*, November 6, 1913. Note: Total active strength of combat arms on November 5, 1913 (infantry, cavalry, and field artillery), was between 32,000 and 38,000 men.

39. Memorandum by Sir L. Carden, n.d., Doc. 132, British Foreign Documents, 236–38. Note: Senator Lodge wrote Ambassador Spring Rice on August 13, 1913: "in the existing situation in Mexico something like blowing up the 'Maine' may happen at any moment and then this country would flame up." Gwynn, *Letters and Friendships of Sir Cecil Spring Rice*, 1: 192. See also "Free-Gun Policy for Mexico," *Literary Digest*, July 12, 1913, 42–43.

40. Spring Rice to Grey, June 23, 1913, Doc. 122, British Foreign Documents, 227–29; Viscount [Sir Edward] Grey of Fallodon, *Twenty-Five Years, 1892–1916*, vol. 2 (New York: Frederick A. Stokes, 1925), 96–97; Gwynn, *Letters and Friendships of Sir Cecil Spring Rice*, 1: 178; Viereck, *Strangest Friendship in History*, 50; Burton, *Cecil Spring Rice*, 148. See also Baker, *Woodrow Wilson*, 4: 394–418; Seymour, *Intimate Papers of Colonel House*, 199–207; Massie, *Castles of Steel*, 2003.

Note 1: To seal the vote for the nullification of the Taft 1912 law exempting tolls for certain US ships, Colonel House arranged to have the Senate Foreign Relations Committee, Republicans and Democrats, come to the White House to explain the sensitive situation with Mexico and Great Britain. The bill was brought to the attention of the Congress in January 1914, and in June Congress passed the repeal into law in time for the grand opening of the canal in August 1914. Assisting on Capitol Hill to line up votes were Secretaries McAdoo and Burleson, in the Senate and House of Representatives respectively.

Note 2: Ambassador Sir Cecil Spring Rice worked closely with Colonel House to insure the British did not interfere with or release any harmful statements that would sidetrack the Panama Canal tolls reconsideration in Congress. The major obstacle in the Senate was a Tammany-backed Irish senator, James Aloysios O'Gorman. Spring Rice noted, he was the son of parents evicted from Ireland forty years before, and "he hates England." The ambassador advised Colonel House he had an uphill battle, "You know that an Irishman would refuse to go to Heaven if St. Peter were an Englishman!"

41. "An Address on Mexican Affairs to a Joint Session of Congress," August 27, 1913, *Papers of Woodrow Wilson*, vol. 27, 1978, 227–31; "After Huerta, Who?" *North American Review* (January 1914): 17–22.

42. "Wants All American out of Mexico: Lind Returning, Mission a Failure," *New York Times*, August 26, 1913, 1, and "Wilson Triumphs with Message," *New York Times*, December 3, 1913, 1; *Foreign Relations*, 1913, 820–27; Scott, *President Wilson's Foreign Policy*, 1–10; "The American Exodus from Mexico," *Literary Digest*, September 13, 1913, 405–6. See also Eugene C. Brooks, *Woodrow Wilson as President* (Chicago: Row, Peterson, 1916), 209–15, and British Foreign Documents, 230–49. Note: Wilson would continue his development of a Latin American policy with comments at the Southern Commercial Congress at Mobile, Alabama, on October 27, 1913, and again in his first annual message to Congress on December 2, 1913.

43. O'Shaughnessy to Secretary of State, August 27, 1913, 9:00 p.m., Wilson Papers, Ser. 2; "Mexico Will Yield to Moral Force," *New York Times*, August 28, 1913, 1, and "Gamboa's Reply to Lind," *New York Times*, August 28, 1913, 2.; "President Warns American to Leave Mexico," *Daily Reporter-Star* (Orlando), August 28, 1913, 1.

44. "New Notes Passed in Mexican Crisis," *New York Times*, August 29, 1913, 1, and "London Sees Little Hope in Wilson's Policy toward Mexico," August 2, 1913, 2; and "Germans Assail Wilson's 'Delirium,'" *New York Times*, November 1, 1913, 1; "'Flee Mexico' Orders Americans," *Philadelphia Inquirer*, August 28, 1913, 1; British Foreign Documents, p230–34. Note: Editorials in Berlin following Wilson's October address in Mobile expressed skepticism, calling the president's high-minded ideas of Latin America "impractical" and a "colossal arrogance," and intimating "the American procedure in Mexico is a hypocritical, free booting policy, concealed mainly in the interest of the Standard Oil Company . . . a policy veiled to impose a protectorate over the republic." See also Baker, *Woodrow Wilson*, 4: 286, and "Germans Denounce Mexico Policy," *New York Times*, November 5, 1913.

45. Colquitt to E. M. House, March 24, 1913, and Colquitt to Attorney General James C. McReynolds, March 24, 1913, Colquitt Papers; "Mexico Viewed from Texas," *Literary Digest*, March 14, 1914, 535. See also Harris and Sadler, *Texas Rangers*, 114–36.

46. "I Would Protect Americans," *Daily Reporter-Star* (Orlando Florida), August 30, 1913. Note: Not surprisingly, these comments by Governor Colquitt were in marked contrast to those given in Interior Secretary Franklin's presentation, who praised Wilson and his Mexico policies.

Chapter 3

1. Testimony of Edward R. Sartwell, December 29, 1919, Investigation of Mexican Affairs, 845–53. Note: In addition to the State Department maintaining an unofficial list of killings and murders of Americans in Mexico, a private watch group in New

York City, the National Association for the Protection of American Rights in Mexico, maintained detailed records of all incidents from 1910 to 1920 and created for submission to Congress the "Murder Map of Mexico." The champion of constantly reporting updates was Senator Albert B. Fall of New Mexico, who submitted the first list of Americans killed to the Senate on March 9, 1914, and published in the *New York Times*, March 10, 1914. See also Senate Doc. No. 324, 66th Cong., 1st sess. February 17, 1916; Senate Doc. No. 67, 66th Cong., 1st sess., July 31, 1919; the Fletcher List in House Rules Committee document, July 22, 1919; "Mexico's American Victims," *Indianapolis News*, February 18, 1916, and in Thomas E. Gibbon murder list in *Mexico under Carranza*, 1919.

2. Parkes, *A History of Mexico*, 344; "Mediation as a Remedy for Mexico," *Literary Digest*, August 9, 1913, 193–95; "President Firm in Attitude of Non-Recognition," *Mexican Herald*, August 1, 1913; F. Gamboa, Secretary of Foreign Affairs to Lind, August 26, 1913, *U.S. Foreign Affairs*, File no. 812.00/9069, 832–35.

3. Testimony of John Lind, April 27, 1920, 2318–23, and Edward J. Doheny, September 11, 1919, 774–78, Investigation of Mexican Affairs; Larry D. Hill, "The Progressive Politician as a Diplomat: The Case of John Lind in Mexico," *Americas*, April 1971, 355–72; Calero, *Mexican Policy of Woodrow Wilson*, 15–8; Davids, *American Political and Economic Penetration of Mexico*, 332–37; Bernstein, *Mexican Mining Industry*, 95–104; Meyer, *Mexico and the United States in the Oil Controversy*, 3–38.

4. Commissioner General to Inspector, El Paso, Doc. 53108/71H, November 6, 1913; W. J. Bryan to Sec. of Labor, Doc. 108, August 26, 1913; "The American Exodus from Mexico," *London Daily*, September 13, 1913, 406; Letcher, Consul, Chihuahua, to Department of State, December 11, 1913, all seen in Records of Immigration, RG 85. Note: Exact totals on the citizens from any given country at any period are at best estimates. Even countries that purport to register all incoming foreigners do not have exact counts. In the case of Mexico in 1913–44, total American ex-pats numbering 55,000 as well as Spain, which had between 65,000 and 75,000, followed by the British (8,000), Germans (6,000), and Italians (5,000). The most undercounted and most abused foreigners in Mexico during the revolution period were the Chinese, of which there are no known estimates. See Investigation of Mexican Affairs, 776, 2253; Robert Chao Ramero, *The Chinese in Mexico 1882–1940* (Tucson: University of Arizona Press, 2010), 145–56; and Julian Lim, "Chinos and Paisanos: Chinese Mexican Relations in the Borderlands," *Pacific Historical Review* (February 2010): 50–85.

5. John Mason Hart, *Empire and Revolution: The American in Mexico since the Civil War* (Berkeley: University of California Press, 2002), 161–63, 179–234, 260, 306; Spring Rice to Grey, British Foreign Documents, Doc. 127, July 12, 1913, 232; Amb. Wilson to the Sec. of State, May 15, 1913, 812.00/7652, US Department of State Papers.

6. See Deborah J. Baldwin, *Protestants and the Mexican Revolution: Missionaries, Ministers, and Social Change* (Urbana: University of Illinois Press, 1990).

7. Testimony of Michael J. Slattery, Investigation of Mexican Affairs, April 1, 1920, 2006–11; "The American Exodus of Mexico," *Literary Digest*, September 13, 1913, 405–6, and "Idealism as a Mexican Policy," *Literary Digest*, November 8, 1913, 855–57; *Mexican Herald*, August 29, 1913; "Mexican Refugees Bring Millions," *New York Times*, December 3, 1913; James C. Chastain, *Thirty Years in Mexico* (El Paso: Baptist Publishing House, 1922), 146. Note: The Hartford *Courant* called the exodus order "ill-considered"; the New Orleans *Picayune*, "cowardly, inhuman, and cold

blooded"; and the *Times Democrat* called it "Washington's Thumb-Twiddling Policy . . . a Harm to National Prestige." See also Hart, *Empire and Revolution*, 238–43.

8. Telegram C. F. Z. Canacristi to Governor Colquitt, June 19, 1913; Paul Mason to Colquitt, August 5, 1913, A. B. Crosthwaite to Colquitt, August 21, 1913, Austin: Texas State Archives (TSA), Governor Colquitt Papers; Coerver and Hall, *Texas and the Mexican Revolution*, 61; Zoraida and Meyer, *United States and Mexico*, 100–101; "Rebels Kill an American," *New York Times*, November 7, 1913.

9. Colquitt to Underwood, May 5, 1913, and Colquitt to Wilson, July 16 and 21, 1913, and W. A. Carpenter to Colquitt, September 9, 1913, TSA, Colquitt Papers; Hernández Sáenz, "Smuggling for the Revolution," 371–374. See also George T. Díaz, *Border Contraband: A History of Smuggling across the Rio Grande* (Austin: University of Texas Press, 2015), 65–90.

10. "Proceedings of the Joint Committee of the Senate and the House in the Investigation of the Texas State Rangers Force," Austin, January 1919, TSA, 1219–25, 1422–27; Harris and Sadler, *Texas Rangers*, 118–36; Dorothy P. Kerig, *Luther T. Ellsworth: U.S. Consul on the Border during the Mexican Revolution* (El Paso: Texas Western Press, 1975).

11. Link, *Wilson: The New Freedom*, 364. See also "Dollarless Diplomacy for Mexico," *Literary Digest*, November 22, 1922, 987–89. Note: At the time of the revolution Baja was known as the "Northern Territory" and was administered as a federal jurisdiction territory prior statehood in January 16, 1952. Hill, *Emissaries*, 96–98; Jessie S. Lyon, "Huerta and Adachi: An Interpretation of Japanese-Mexican Relations, 1913–1914," *Americas* (April 1978): 476–89; "Mediation as a Remedy for Mexico," *Literary Digest*, August 9, 1913, 193; Katz, *Secret War in Mexico*, 168–69

12. Hill, *Emissaries to a Revolution*, 96–98; Eisenhower, *Intervention*, 62–64; Link, *New Freedom*, 364; "The Week," *The Nation*, August 14, 1913; Berta Ulloa, *La revolución intervenida* (Mexico City: El Colegio de Mexico, 1976) as seen in Zoraida and Meyer, *The United States and Mexico*, 101–3.

13. Grey to Spring Rice, July 11, 1913, Doc. 124, and July 25, 1913, Doc. 126, British Foreign Documents, 230–31; "The Week," *The Nation*, November 13, 1913, 447; Haley, *Diplomacy of Taft and Wilson in Mexico*, 103–4.

14. Bliss letter, Sec. of War to Sec. of State, August 14, 1913, RDS-IA, 812.00/9122; Sec. of War to State, August 18, 1913, RDS-IA, 812.00/8679; *Texas and the Mexican Revolution*, 64–66. Note: USMC Major Smedley Butler, plan for Mexico occupation, sent to US Army War College for study.

15. Katz, *Secret War in Mexico*, 171 83; Coker, "The Panama Canal Tolls Controversy," 555–64. See also Mark E. Benbow, "Intelligence in Another Era—All the Brains I Can Borrow: Woodrow Wilson and Intelligence Gathering in Mexico, 1913–15," last updated June 25, 2008, Central Intelligence Agency, at www.cia.gov/center-for-the-study-of-intelligence.

16. Katz, *Secret War in Mexico*, 84–85, 210–31; John P. Jones, *The German Secret Service in America, 1914–1918* (Boston: Small, Maynard, 1918). See also Adolf Carlson, *Joint U.S. Army-Navy War Planning on the Eve of the First World War: Its Origins and Its Legacy* (Carlisle, PA: Army War College, 1998), and David P. Mowry, "German Clandestine Activities in South America in World War II," National Security Agency, 1989, NSA/CSSM 123–2, declassified April 13, 2009.

17. Lyon, "Huerta and Adachi," 476–89; *New York Times*, August 27, 1913; Chester H. Rowell, "The Japanese in California," *World's Work* (June 1913): 195–201; Rippy,

Latin America in World Politics, 230–34. See also Iyo Iimura Kunimoto, "Japan and Mexico, 1886–1917" (PhD diss., University of Texas at Austin, 1975).

18. Governor O. B. Colquitt to Sec. of State, April 3, 1913, 812.00/7056, US Department of State Papers; Raat, *Revoltosos*, 194–99; Michael D. Carmen, *U.S. Customs and the Mexico Revolution* (El Paso: Texas Western Press, 1976), 16–47.

19. Charles Harris and Louis Sadler, "The 'Underside' of the Mexican Revolution: El Paso, 1912," *The Americas* (July 1982): 72, 76–77; Michael C. Meyer, "Villa, Sommerfeld, Columbus y los alemanes," *Historia Mexicana* (April 1979): 546–66; Charles C. Cumberland, "Border Raids in the Rio Grande Valley—1915," *Southwestern Historical Quarterly* (January 1954): 286; Holcombe, "U.S. Arms Control and the Mexican Revolution, 1910–1924," 53; Baker, *Wilson*, 4: 290.

20. U.S. vs. Phelps Dodge Co. and Douglas Hardware Co., December 5, 1913, 812.00/8571 and U.S. vs. W. C. Schwamm, I. Ilitzky et al., Phoenix, December 3, 1913, 812.00/10246; Hernández Sáenz, "Smuggling for the Revolution," 361–75; Raat, *Revoltosos*, 244–6; Díaz, *Border Contraband*, 74–77.

21. Grey to Spring Rice, July 11, 1913, Doc. 124, and Spring Rice to Grey, July 12, 1913, Doc. 125; July 21, 1913, Doc. 127, and January 25, 1914, *British Foreign Documents*.

22. Lord Carden to Grey, September 25, 1913, Doc. 132, *British Foreign Documents*. See also Cooper, *Walter Hines Page*, 262–63.

23. Gwynn, *Letters and Friendships of Sir Cecil Spring Rice*, 1: 179. See also "German Official Quarters," *The Nation*, October 13, 1913, 375; "Bryan Evasive of Mexico Note," *New York Times*, November 5, 1913; "Mr. Churchill's Failure to Stop Naval Rivalry," *Literary Digest*, November 15, 1913, 936. Note: *The Nation* reported, "Mr. Churchill has bluntly stated what everybody knows to be the fact—that Great Britain and Germany are building against each other!" Furthermore, the Germans were in a massive expansion of the Zeppelin dirigible fleet as well as "heavier-than-air machines"—i.e., fighter planes—many, many months before August 1914.

24. War planning has been a part of military practice for centuries, in the case of the United States, war planning became more formalized during the Spanish-American War and was supported by the Naval War College (founded in 1884) and the Army War College (founded in 1901). Detailed military plans on the invasion of Mexico were code named "War Plan Green." Acrimonious service rivalry between the navy and the army on the means to do joint planning resulted in President Wilson assigning the Army War College in Carlisle to draw up plans for Mexico. See "Mexico as a Military Problem," *World's* Work (January 1914): 306–7; Army War College, *America War Plans Special Text* (Carlisle, PA: US Army War College, 2001); Alan C. Lowe, *The Development of War Plan Green: The U.S. Army and Mexico* (Carlisle, PA: Army War College, n.d.); and Henry G. Gole, *The Road to Rainbow: Army Planning for Global War, 1934–1940* (Annapolis, MD: Naval Institute Press, 2003).

25. Testimony of Leroy H. Ault, April 10, 1920, Investigation of Mexican Affairs, p. 2246; Frederick S. Calhoun, *Power and Principle: Armed Intervention in Wilsonian Foreign Policy* (Kent, OH: Kent State University Press, 1986), 41–46; Richard H. Heindel, *The American Impact on Great Britain, 1898–1914* (New York: Octagon Books, 1968), 98–118. Note: The 265,000 troop estimate is over half of the number the War Department stated would be needed to guard foreign property in Mexico; see "Mexico and Mobilization," *New York Times*, November 6, 1913, and "Nicaragua Plan Alarms Republics," *New York Times*, December 8, 1913.

26. "Idealism as a Mexican Policy," *Literary Digest*, November 8, 1913, 855–57; Katz, *Secret War in Mexico*, 164–66, 171–78, 224–27; Haley, *Diplomacy of Taft and Wilson in Mexico*, 111; Hans Schmidt, *Maverick Marine: General Smedley D. Butler* (Lexington: University of Kentucky Press, 1987), 63–70. See also Adolf Carlson, *Joint U.S. Army-Navy War Planning on the Eve of the First World War: Its Origins and Legacy* (Carlisle, PA: Army War College, 1998), 16, 22–26, and Michel Gobat, *Confronting the American Dream: Nicaragua Under U.S. Imperial Rule* (Durham, NC: Duke University Press, 2005), 1–4.

27. Nelson O'Shaughnessy to Secretary of State, October 11, 1913, Wilson Papers, Ser. 2; Johnson, *Heroic Mexico*, 138; "Army on Border Prepares to Stay," *New York Times*, December 3, 1913; Katz, *Secret War in Mexico*, 182. Note: Edith O'Shaughnessy, *A Diplomats Wife in Mexico*, penned a firsthand account of her days in Mexico City, noting that upon the release of the Mexican Congress, General Huerta was bold in assuming the role as dictator; writing in her diary: "Only by the hand of iron can this passionate, tenacious, mysterious, gifted, undisciplined race, composed of countless unlike elements, be kept in order. In the States . . . this isn't quite understood."

28. Lind to Secretary of State, September 1, 1913, Foreign Affairs, 812.00/8635; "Warships Reach Veracruz," *New York Times*, November 5, 1913; "Troops for Fort Bliss," *New York Times*, November 5, 1913; "Navy Orders Significant," *New York Times*, November 6, 1913; "Want No Foreign Pressure," *New York Times*, November 9, 1913; Schmidt, *Maverick Marine*, 63–70. Note: The leading battleship class ships of the era were dispatched to Mexico to include, for example, the USS *Rhode Island, New Jersey, Virginia, Nebraska, Florida, and New Hampshire* as well as cruisers USS *Chester*, *California*, and *Pittsburgh*, and supply ships USS *Culgoa* and *Celtic*; the German dispatched the SMS *Bremen*, *Hertha*, and *Nurnberg*; the Japanese the *Izimo*; and a dozen British and French vessels.

29. O'Shaughnessy, *Diplomat's Wife in Mexico*, 17.

30. Bryan to Charge d'Affaires, October 13, 1913, *U.S. Foreign Relations*, File No. 812.00/9180a, 838; "Secrecy in Mexico City," *New York Times*, November 5, 1913; "Congress Annuals Mexico Election," *New York Times*, December 10, 1913; "To Stop Mining in Mexico," *New York Times*, December 3, 1913; "Huerta as a Dictator," *Literary Digest*, October 25, 1913, 737–38; Hill, *Emissaries to a Revolution*, 96–97, 106–8; Russell, *Mexico in War and Peace*, 94–96; Eisenhower, *Intervention*, 62–65.

31. Spring Rice to Grey, August 19, 1913, *British Foreign Documents*, Doc. 131, 235–36; "Huerta Seeks a Paris Loan," *New York Times*, December 10, 1913, and "Huerta Congress Adjourns Till April," *New York Times*, December 16, 1013; O'Shaughnessy, *Diplomat's Wife in Mexico*, 107.

32. "President Calls Members of Foreign Relations Committee," *New York Times*, November 10, 1913; "Say Lind Upset Situation," *New York Times*, November 8, 1913; "Mexican Finance," *The Economist*, November 22, 1913, 1182; Edgar Turlington, *Mexico and Her Foreign Creditors* (New York: Columbia University Press, 1939), 248–58. See also Andrew Godley, "Weetman Pearson in Mexico and the Emergence of a British Oil Major, 1901–1919," unpublished manuscript. Reading: University of Reading, 2007.

33. "Oil Co. Employees Leaving," *New York Times*, November 13, 1913; "Dollarless Diplomacy for Mexico," *Literary Digest*, November 23, 1913, 987; Testimony of William B. Mitchell, November 1, 1919, Investigation of Mexican Affairs, 685–87; O'Shaughnessy, *Diplomats Wife in Mexico*, 46; John Coatsworth and Alan Taylor,

eds., *Latin America and the World Economy since 1800* (Cambridge, MA: Harvard University Press, 1999), 355.

34. *Daily Mail* quote seen in "Huerta Worries British," *New York Times*, November 7, 1913. See also "Huerta Defiant, but Might Yield If Europe Asked," *New York Times*, November 8, 1913, and "Mexican Oil Down," *New York Times*, November 4, 1913; "London Market Unsettled by the Mexican Situation," *New York Times*, November 9, 1913; "Nervousness in London," *New York Times*, November 10, 1913; "Berlin Again Unsettled—Acute Mexican Situation," and "Paris Markets Gloomy," *New York Times*, November 10, 1913; Noel Maurer, *The Power and the Money: The Mexican Financial System* (Stanford, CA: Stanford University Press, 2002), 141–45.

35. Lind to Secretary of State, October 25, 1913, Wilson Papers, Ser. 2; "Rival Oil Giants in Mexican Broils," *New York Times*, November 9, 1913; "Suspense in Mexico," *The Economist*, November 22, 1913, 1125; "Carden Removed from Mexican Post," *New York Times*, January 6, 1914; Link, *Wilson*, 372–75; "'Big Business' behind the Mexican Muddle," *Literary Digest*, November 14, 1913, 935–36; Walter V. Scholes and Marie Scholes, "Wilson, Grey, and Huerta," *Pacific Historical Review* (May 1968): 151–58. Note: Again, in November 1913, there were charges (rumors) that Wilson and the British had made a "deal" on the Panama Canal tolls issue in exchange for the support of US policy in Mexico. Gold 50-peso Mexican coins were called "*centenario*,' and silver coins were referred to as "*onzas*."

36. Katz, *Secret War in Mexico*, 169–79; Haley, *Diplomacy of Taft and Wilson*, 108–11; "As France Sees Our Mexican Policy," *Literary Digest*, November 29, 1913, 1055, and "Why We Heckle Huerta," *Literary Digest*, November 22, 1913; "Arms to Huerta Indirectly," *New York Times*, December 24, 1913; "Japanese Arms for Huerta," *New York Times*, December 22, 1913; "Japanese Again Resentful," *New York Times*, December 19, 1913; Bailey, *Great Power Strategy in Asia*, 67; Gwynn, *Letters and Friendships of Sir Cecil Spring Rice*, 1: 200. Note: See also "Warn Ojinaga Combatants," *New York Times*, December 28, 1913, which states that prior to the Battle of Ojinaga starting on January 1, 1914, Japanese agents and diplomatic representatives feared Villa would kill all Japanese given their support of Huerta, but the British vice consul in Chihuahua assured their protection, and Villa agreed there would be no harm done.

37. Schuler, *Murder and Counterrevolution*, 71–75; Hiram Bingham, "The Monroe Doctrine: An Obsolete Shibboleth," *Atlantic Monthly* (June 1913): 732; "German Jingoes Warned," *New York Times*, November 10, 1913; "Wilson Holds Japan Blameless," *New York Times*, January 30, 1914.

38. "Mexico Wants to Borrow," *New York Times*, November 1, 1913; "Huerta Must Go, Europe Is Told" *New York Times*, November 3, 1913; "Lind Advised It," and "Anglo-American Harmony," *New York Times*, November 4, 1914; "Huerta Aided with Money from England," *New York Times*, November 9, 1913; "Getting War Materials Here," *New York Times*, November 6, 1913; "German Squadron to Sail," *New York Times*, November 7, 1913; "XXX," *Mexican Herald*, November 4, 1913; "Mexico and the New Monroe Doctrine in South and Central America," *The Economist*, December 13, 1913, 1282–83; Page, *Life and Letters of Walter H. Page*, 194–208. Note: The Germans deployed the super dreadnoughts *Kaiser* and *Konig Albert* along with the cruisers *Strasbourg*, *Bremen*, and *Hertha*—sent accordingly to the German Admiralty to South America so German residents could "again see a piece of the German Fatherland as a visible indication of her power and greatness."

39. "Rebels Repulse Reported," *New York Times*, November 9, 1913; "Rebels Kill an American," *New York Times*, November 7, 1913; "Wilson Summons Senators," *New York Times*, November 9, 1913; Calhoun, *Power and Principle*, 27–33, 41–42.

40. Letcher, American Consul at Chihuahua, to Secretary of State, November 30, 1913, *U.S. Foreign Relations 1913*, File no. 812.00/10054, 856, 864; Katz, *Secret War in Mexico*, 181–84.

41. "Rebels Expect Recognition," *New York Times*, November 9, 1913; Michael M. Smith, "Carrancista Propaganda and the Print Media in the United States," *Americas* (October 1995): 155–74. See also a sample of public relations in the full-page story, "With Gen. Venustiano Carranza's Army in Mexico," *New York Times*, November 9, 1913.

42. "Carranza Not Pleased," *New York Times*, November 5, 1913; "Carranza Expects Dr. Hale," *New York Times*, November 6, 1913; "Lift the Embargo, Carranza's Plea," *New York Times*, November 7, 1913; "Carranza Denies Deal with Huerta, Ibid, November 8, 1913. See also Houston, *Eight Years with Wilson's Cabinet*, 78–79; Hill, *Emissaries*, 107–; Katz, *Secret War in Mexico*, 181–83; Angle, *Crosssroads:1913*, 196–99.

43. Bryan to W. H. Page, November 19, 1913, 812.00/9817a; Grieb, "Reginald del Valle: A California Diplomate Sojourn in Mexico," 315–28.

44. Katz, *Secret War in Mexico*, 222–31; Schmidt, *Maverick Marine*, 63–70.

45 "Public and Financial Disorders in Mexico," *The Economist*, December 6, 1913, 1229.

46. Quote as seen in "How the President's Message Is Received," *Literary Digest*, December 13, 1913, 1155. See also "The State of the Union," *New York Times*, December 3, 1913, and "Mexico and the New Monroe Doctrine," *The Economist*, December 13, 1913, 1282.

47. *Commerce and Financial Chronicle*, December 27, 1913, and January 17, 1914; *New York Times*, December 31, 1913; "Suspense in Mexico," *The Economist*, November 22, 1913, 1125; Turlington, *Mexico and Her Foreign Creditors*, 246–48; James B. Scott, ed. *President Wilson's Foreign Policy* (New York: Oxford University Press, 1918), 27–30. Note: Wilson bluntly stated, "Mexico has no government."

48. "Rebels Won't Halt Till Huerta Leaves," *New York Times*, December 29, 1913; "The Mexican Loan," *New York Times*, January 7, 1913; *Washington Post*, November 17, 1913, 1; *New York Sun*, November 23, 1913; Hart, *Empire and Revolution*, 306–7; Cox, "'An Enemy Closer to Us Than Any European Power': The Impact of Mexico on Texan Public Opinion before World War I," *Southwestern Historical Quarterly* (July 2001): 42.

Chapter 4

1. Supervising Inspector to Commissioner General, Doc. 5012/92, January 5, 1914, Records of Immigration, RG 85; Charles C. Cumberland, *Mexican Revolution: The Constitutionalist Years* (Austin: University of Texas Press, 1972), 11–14; "Nuevo Laredo Balks Rebels," *New York Times*, January 4, 1914, and "'Move on Ojinaga; Give no Quarter,'" *New York Times*, December 25, 1913; Adams, *Conflict and Commerce on the Rio Grande*, 73–74, 112–13; J. Gilberto Quezada, *Border Boss: Manuel B. Bravo and Zapata County* (College Station: Texas A&M University Press, 1999), 17. See also "Hammond's Railroad Map of Mexico," New York, C. S. Hammond, 1913;

Tracy H. Lewis, *Along the Rio Grande* (New York: Lewis Publishing, 1916), 115–17, 128–34; Cumberland, "Border Raids in the Lower Rio Grande Valley—1015," 285–93; Levario, *Militarizing the Border*, 39–42, 78–79; and Frederick Turner, Anti-Americanism in Mexico, 1910–1913," *Hispanic American Historical Review* (November 1967): 512–17. Note: Rebel forces were also dispatched to the Gulf of Mexico port of Tampico to take control, see "1,500 Rebels in Tamaulipas," *New York Times*, December 28, 1913. In addition to the Mexican National Railroad, Laredo had terminals for the International and Great Northern (I&GN), the Texas-Mexican Railroad, and the Rio Grande Eagle Pass Railroad. At El Paso the principle railroads were the Santa Fe Railway, Mexican Northwestern Railroad, Mexican Central Railroad, and Southern Pacific and Texas Pacific Railroads. See also map of I&GN across Texas connecting with the Mexican National to Mexico City at D. J. Price, I&GN Agent to General Henry Hutchings, April 10, 1914, Texas Adjutant General Correspondence, Texas State Archives, Austin.

2. "Rebel Forces Attack N. Laredo and Repulsed with Heavy," *Laredo Daily Times*, January 1, 1914; "Rebels Checked at New Laredo and at Ojinaga," *Austin American Statesman*, January 3, 1914; "Intrenching [*sic*] at Laredo," *New York Times*, January 4, 1914; "Ojinaga Falls under Arrack Led by Villa," and "Scene of Battle Near the Mexican Border," *New York Times*, January 11, 1914. See also "Federals Still Hold Fort, Fighting Hard," *El Paso Herald*, January 5, 1914, and Glenn Justice, *Revolution on the Rio Grande* (El Paso: Texas Western Press, 1992), 3–5, and "The Rise of Villa's Star," *Literary Digest*, April 18, 1914, 889; and Carlos Zuniga Garcia, "The Fire in Nuevo Laredo: 100 Years Ago," *El Mañana*, April 24, 2014.

3. "Rebel Forces Still Threating Nuevo Laredo and Retain Ground," *Laredo Daily Times*, January 2, 1914; Captain Hiram A. Philips, "Report of One Hundred Wounds Received in Battle of Nuevo Laredo, January 1st and 2nd 1914," *Journal of the Association of Military Surgeons*, May 1914, 445. See also Leanor Villega de Magón, *The Rebel*, ed. Clara Lomas (Houston: Arte Público Press, 1994), 93–106.

4. Lindley M. Garrison, Secretary of War to Sec. of State, January 3, 1914, and Inspector to Sec. of State, January 5, 1914, Records of Immigration, RG 85; Jerry Thompson, *Laredo: A Pictorial History* (Norfolk, VA: Donning, 1986), 272–79.

5. "Rebel Drop Back and Are Now Fifteen Miles Down the River," *Laredo Daily Times*, January 3, 1914; "Acts of Barbarism," *Austin American Statesman*, January 3, 1914; "Nuevo Laredo Federals Incinerate Their Dead," *Austin American Statesman*, January 5, 1914; "Stampede from Ojinaga: Two Thousand Mexicans Cross Border into Texas," *Austin American Statesman*, January 4, 1914; Lt. Bruse P. Disque, "The Battle of Laredo—Mexico: January 1–2, 1914," *U.S. Cavalry Journal* (May 1914): 892–907.

6. Charles Morris, *The Story of Mexico* (N.p.: L. T. Myers, 1914), 294. Note: Increased hostilities in northern Mexico along the border and the flood of combatants and civilians into Texas border towns raised concerns and prompted mobilization plans by both the Texas Adjutant Generals (TAG) office and the US War Department; Texas law enforcement officers across the state offered volunteers and supplies, and border mayors called for additional protection from the TAG, see Biennial Report of Adjutant General of Texas, 1913–14, 7; C. R. Moore to General Henry Hutchings, February 27, 1914; and "Joint Maneuvers—1914," The Adjutant General, War department to Commanding General, Fort Sam Houston, Texas, seen in Texas Adjutant General's Correspondence, Texas State Archives.

7. "Wilson Joins Lind on Scout," *Austin American Statesman*, January 3, 1914, 1; "Lind Is Coming to See Wilson," *New York Times*, December 31, 1913, 1.

8. "Anglo-American Relations," *The Times* (London), January 2, 1914; Calhoun, *Power and Principle*, 41–46; "Lind Returns to Mexico: President Says Conference Merely Get-Together Talk," *Austin Statesman*, January 4, 1914.

9. Bryan to Lind, January 17, 1914, US Foreign Relations, 812.00/10580a; "Mexico Short of Change," *New York Times*, January 6, 1914; "Mexican Northern Power," *The Times* (London), January 3, 1914. Note: The Huerta government in late 1913 had a monthly income from import and export duties collected at the ports of $4.2 million per month; see "Mexican Custom Receipts," *The Times* (London), January 2, 1914.

10. Hale to Wilson, January 13, 1914, Wilson Papers, Ser. 2, and Wilson to McAdoo, January 15, 1914, Wilson Papers, Ser. 2; Hill, "The Progressive Politician as a Diplomat," 359–70; Haley, *Diplomacy of Taft and Wilson in Mexico*, 125; Hernández Sáenz, "Smuggling for the Revolution," 357–77. Note: Wilson sent what amounted to a direct order to Secretary McAdoo on January 15, 1914, "that in some confidential way the arrangements" would be made to allowed arms and munitions to skirt US Custom inspection and federal agents and sent to Mexico.

11. Woodrow Wilson to Secretary of Treasury, December 15, 1913, Records of Immigration, RG 85.

12. Wilson to Sec. of Treasury, December 15 and 19, 1914, Records of Immigration, RG 85.

13. John Reed, *Insurgent Mexico* (Middlesex, England: Penguin, 1983 [first published in 1914]), 114–15; Gwynn, *Letters and Friendships of Sir Cecil Spring Rice*; Spring Rice to Tyrrell, January 27, 1914, 1: 199: Spring Rice to Grey, February 7, 1914, Doc. 176.

14. "Villa to Adopt Civilized Warfare," *New York Times*, January 31, 1914, and "Villa to Execute Bandits," *New York Times*, January 29, 1914; "Villa, Bandit and Brute, May Be Mexican President," *New York Times*, December 14, 1913. See also Morris, *Story of Mexico*, 298, and Edward I. Bell, *The Political Shame of Mexico* (New York: McBride, Nast, 1914), 376–77.

15. Krauze, *Mexico*, 311; "Quiet in Mexico," *New York Times*, January 10, 1914; "The Villa Movies Shock Aged Madero," *New York Times*, January 23, 1914; Hill, *Emissaries*, 129–32; Robert E. Quirk, *The Mexican Revolution, 1914–1915* (Bloomington: Indiana University Press, 1960), 16–18; Hart, *Revolutionary Mexico*, 267–68; Katz, *Secret War in Mexico*, 139–40, 145–52. Note: From the thousands of feet of film shot by Mutual, a movie, *The Life of General Villa*, was released in May 1914. See also Margarita de Orellana, *Filming Pancho: How Hollywood Shaped the Mexican Revolution* (London: Verso, 2009).

16. Supervising Inspector to Commissioner General of Immigration, Doc. 5012/92, December 13, 1913, Records of Immigration, RG 85; Hill, "The Progressive Politician as a Diplomat," 359–70; Douglas W. Richmond, "Confrontation and Reconciliation: Mexicans and Spaniards during the Mexican Revolution, 1910–1920," *The Americans* (October 1984): 215–28. Note: Some five hundred Spaniards, merchants, families, priests, and nuns were deported to El Paso, and most, if not all, of their property was seized for Villa's plan to redistribute the wealth to "widows and orphans."

17. "Republic of Sierra Madre," *New York Times*, October 1 and 3, 1851; "Mexico —Zuloaga's Fall Probable—Vidaurri and the Republic of Sierra Madre," *New York Times*, April 21, 1858; Hart, *Revolutionary Mexico*, 288. Note: A grandiose grand plan,

first attempted by filibuster José María Carvajal in 1851 (armed and bankrolled by Charles Stillman and Richard King) during the unrest over the failed Republic of the Rio Grande, attempted to establish the "Republic of the Sierra Madre" and was promoted a second time in 1858 by Monterrey, Mexico, industrialist (and father-in-law to Patricio Milmo) Santiago Vidaurri; the plan was harbored by a group of large landowners in the late 1870s through 1910—James Stillman, Randolph Hearst, William F. Buckley, John Kirby, and others—in northern Mexico, to promote the outright annexation of the region under the name of the "Republic of the Sierra Madre." See also David M. Vigness, "Relations of the Republic of Texas and the Republic of the Rio Grande," *Southwestern Historical Quarterly* (January 1954): 312–21.

18. Haley, *Diplomacy of Taft and Wilson in Mexico*, 128; "Villa Says Huerta Will Soon Collapse," *New York Times*, January 22, 1914; "Has No Change in Policy," *Austin Statesman*, January 4, 1914.

19. "Arms for Mexico," *The Times* (London), February 4, 1914; Hill, *Emissaries*, 134–43; Katz, *Secret War in Mexico*, 182–84.

20. Hart, *Revolutionary Mexico*, 148–49. See also William F. Buckley Sr. Papers, Benson Latin American Collection, University of Texas, Austin, boxes 32 and 34.

21. Hart, *Revolutionary Mexico*, 148–56, 281–91; House Diary, May 14, 1913; Hodgson, *Woodrow Wilson's Right Hand*, 87; Hart, *Empire and Revolution*, 303–7.

22. Anna Burr, *The Portrait of a Banker: James Stillman* (New York: Duffiel, 1927), 223–39; Hart, *Revolutionary Mexico*, 96–128, 134–37; S. G. A. Reed, *A History of the Texas Railroad* (Houston: St. Clair Publishing, 1941), 404; David Pletcher, "Mexico Opens the Door to American Capital, 1977–1880," *The Americas* (July 1959): 1–14; Robert F. Bruner and Sean D. Carr, *The Panic of 1907* (Hoboken, NJ: Wiley and Sons, 2007), 143. See also S. G. A. Reed, *A History of the Land Grants and Other Aids to the Texas Railroads by the State of Texas* (Kingsport, TN: Kingsport Press, 1942); Phillip Hastings, "Tex-Mex: An International Switching Line," *Railroad* (June 1951): 56–61; Maury Klein, *The Life and Legend of Jay Gould* (Baltimore: Johns Hopkins University Press, 1977), and John Kennedy Winkler, *The First Billion: The Stillmans and the National City Bank* (New York: Vanguard Press, 1934).

23. Hart, *Revolutionary Mexico*, 145–49, 288–89; Godley, "Weetman Pearson in Mexico," 8–25.

24. Hart, *Empire and Revolution*, 303–7; Godley, "Weetman Pearson in Mexico," 1–30.

25. Bernstein, *Mexican Mining Industry*, 36–39, 50–56, 60, 66, 158.

26. Hart, *Empire and Revolution*, 139–41; "Mexican War Hurt Smelters' Earnings," *New York Times*, March 25, 1914, and "Mexico City Banks Are Near a Crisis," *New York Times*, December 19, 1913; "Mexican Rebels Take Copper Camp," *New York Times*, January 23, 1914; "Mexican Railways Are in a Bad Way," *New York Times*, December 11, 1913.

27. Carlo de Fornado, *Carranza and Mexico* (New York: Mitchell Kennerley, 1915), 99–105.

28. Luis Cabrera, *The Mexican Situation from a Mexican Point of View* (Washington, DC: Confidential Agency of the Constitutional Government of Mexico, 1914). See also, "An Agrarian Policy Mexico's Only Hope," *New York Times*, February 15, 1914, and Walter and Marie Scholes, "Wilson, Grey, and Huerta," *Pacific Historical Review* (May 1968): 154–55.

29. Spring Rice to Grey, February 7, 1914, Doc. 176.

30. Hart, *Revolutionary Mexico*, 103; Patrick L. Cox, "An Enemy Closer to Us Than Any European Power: The Impact of Mexico on Texas Public Opinion before World War I," *Southwestern Historical Quarterly* (July 2001): 63–64. See also "An Agrarian Policy Mexico's Only Hope," *New York Times*, February 15, 1914.

31. William C. Redfield, "What Underwood Tariff Really Accomplished," *New York Times*, October 1, 1916; O. M. W. Sprague, "The Federal Reserve Act of 1913," *Quarterly Journal of Economics* (February 1914): 213–54; Gould, *Progressives and Prohibitionist*, 283; Marquis James, *Mr. Garner of Texas* (New York: Bobbs-Merrill, 1939), 66–69; see also Bruner and Carr, *Panic of 1907*, 141–48.

32. Houston, *Eight Years with the Wilson Cabinet*, 80–109; "5,007 Banks Join Regional System, *New York Times*, January 24, 1914.

33. Quote seen in Hart, *Empire and Revolution*, 307; Mark E. Benbow, "Intelligence in Another Era: All the Brains I Can Borrow," CIA, 1–12.

34. Spring Rice to Grey, January 23, 1914, Doc. 167; "Carranza Is Firm: No Peace Till the Constitutionalist Army Triumphs, He Declares," *New York Times*, January 26, 1914; Hill, "John Lind in Mexico," 362–73.

35. Baker, Wilson, 4: 309.

36. Coerver and Hall, *Texas and the Mexican Revolution*, 64–65; Calhoun, *Power and Principle*, 42–45.

37. Edith O'Shaughnessy, quoted in *The Wind That Swept Mexico*, 41.

38. Spring Rice to Grey, British Foreign Documents, January 23, 1914, Doc. 167; "Marines for Veracruz," *New York Times*, January 11, 1914, and "Mexican Crisis a Wilson Success," *New York Times*, January 12, 1914; "Wilson for Two Ship Plan," *New York Times*, January 30, 1914. Note: The British fortified and armed their Mexico City embassy in the event of an uprising following the lifting of the arms embargo; "British Bluejackets with Machine Guns Sent to Mexico City," *Austin American Statesman*, February 14, 1914.

39. Baker, *Wilson*, 4: 304–7; "Wilson Is Vilified," *Austin American Statesman*, February 15, 1914; "Huerta Sees Hope of Checking Rebels: Undaunted by Northern Defeat, He Fits Out Army to Check Advance to Capital," *New York Times*, January 26, 1914.

40. Spring Rice to Grey, February 7, 1914, FO 414/239, 53–54, 64–65; "New Wilson Policy Alarms Mexicans," *New York Times*, January 28, 1914; "Villa's Gain Greatest," *New York Times*, February 4, 1914; "The Mexico Move," *New York Times*, February 5, 1914; Hill, *Emissaries to a Revolution*, 139–40.

41. Clements, "Woodrow Wilson's Mexican Policy, 1913–15," 122; Hugh G. Miller and Joseph C. Freehoff, *The Panama Toll Controversy* (Boston: Chappie Publishing, 1914), 21–90; "Letting the Guns into Mexico," *Literary Digest*, February 14, 1914, 303–4; "Where the U.S.A. Face Turbulent Mexico," *London News*, November 22, 1913, 1; "President Wilson and the Mexican Embargo," *Outlook*, February 14, 1914, 330.

42. O'Shaughnessy, *Intimate Pages of Mexican History*, 275.

43. "New Wilson Policy Alarms Mexican," *New York Times*, January 28, 1914; N. A. Jennings, INS to William R. Hearst, March 23, 1914, Buckley Papers.

44. "Wilson on Peru Case," *Washington Post*, February 17, 1914; Morris, *Story of Mexico*, 315–17. Note: Bold headlines in the Mexico City *El Imparcial* noted, "The Word on Wilson Lacks Honor, as Does He Himself," as seen in *Austin Statesman*, February 15, 1914. Note: Wilson noted the revolt in Peru was a change in government

"in an effort to maintain constitutional government" and thus "differs entirely from Huerta in Mexico."

45. "Huerta to Degree Huge Fiat Issue," *New York Times*, February 17, 1914; "Huerta's Sovereign Power," *New York Times*, December 13, 1913; "Arrests in Plot to Oust Huerta," *New York Times*, February 1, 1014; Bemis, *Latin American Policy of the United States*, 177; *Wall Street Journal*, January 15, 1914, 5. Note: Both Japan and Germany were active in shipping arms and munitions to Huerta through February and March, with the full knowledge of the Wilson administration—they looked the other way and publicly stated, "no such shipment took place." Arms sales was an "international" endeavor as Japanese arms shipments were sent COD, brokered by a British syndicate, often shipped on German-flagged ships with bank drafts cleared through London and Paris banks.

46. "Wilson Lifts Embargo on Selling Arms to Mexican Rebels," *The World* (New York), February 4, 1914; "Report Is Interesting One," *Laredo Daily Times*, March 3, 1914; Raat, *Revoltosos*, 215–18, 230–33; Hernández Sáenz, "Smuggling for the Revolution," 357–77; Díaz, *Border Contraband*, 70–81.

47. "Guns Sent from Vera Cruz [*sic*]," *New York Times*, February 14, 1914; "Threatened Life of O'Shaughnessy," *New York Times*, February 15, 1914; "Say We Fear Huerta," *New York Times*, February 26, 1914.

48. "Says Huerta Is Beaten," *New York Times*, February 17, 1914; "Says Wilson Policy Is 'Deadly Drifting,'" *New York Times*, February 26, 1914; "Sees Intervention Looming before Us," *New York Times*, February 27, 1914.

49. "Army Appropriation Bill," HR 13453, *Congressional Record*, House, February 26, 1914, 3969–76; "American Citizens Killed and Murdered by Mexican," Investigation of Mexican Affairs, 848–53; "List of American Victims of Barbarous Mexico," *Austin Statesman*, March 10, 1914.

50. Coerver and Hall, *Texas and Mexican Revolution*, 24–27; "Mexico's Darkening Outlook," *Literary Digest*, March 7, 1914, 473–75.

51. Reed, *Insurgent Mexico*, 131. See also Tamara Hovey, *John Reed: Witness to Revolution* (New York: Crown Publishers, 1975).

52. "Bandits Seize Americans," *New York Times*, February 7, 1914; "El Paso Hearings on Mexico Begin," *New York Times*, February 4, 1920; "Mexican Outlaw Who Burned Train and Its Fifty Odd Passengers," *Austin Statesman*, February 21, 1914; "Castillo Prisoner of Ninth Cavalry," *Houston Post*, February 18, 1914.

53. "Record of Benton Trail Made Public," *Houston Post*, February 22, 1914; "Benton Executed by General Villa," *Houston Post*, February 21, 1914; "Venustiano Carranza Defies Washington in Benton Case," *Mexico Herald*, March 1, 1914.

54. O'Shaughnessy, *Diplomat's Wife in Mexico*, 200; "Alvarez Will Avenge Death of C. Vergara," *Houston Post*, February 26, 1914; "Call on Huerta to Avenge the Vergara Murder," *New York Times*, February 28, 1914.

Chapter 5

1. Walter P. Webb, *The Texas Rangers* (Austin: University of Texas Press, 1991), 486; Indianapolis *News*, "Mexico's American Victims," February 18, 1916. Note: According to the list maintained by the National Association for the Protection of American Rights in Mexico and presented to Congress, Clemente Vergara was the 137th documented death of an American citizen in Mexico or on the border since the start of the revolution in November 20, 1910, to October 1919. See also, a special "Murder

Map of Mexico" with 550 deaths indicated and presented to the Senate Foreign Affairs Committee; Testimony of Edward R. Sartwell, December 29, 1919, Investigation of Mexican Affairs, 845.

2. *Daily Chronicle* seen in "Villa's Gain Greatest," *New York Times*, February 4, 1914; "Finance: Mexico and the Markets," *The Nation*, March 19, 1914, 313; Turlington, *Mexico and Her Foreign Creditors*, 255–58; Spring Rice to Grey, February 7, 1914, British Foreign Documents, 346; Edwin W. Kemmerer, *Inflation and Revolution: Mexico's Experience of 1912–1917* (Princeton, NJ: Princeton University Press, 1940), 10–35. See also, editorial "The Mexican Move," *New York Times*, February 5, 1914; Katz, *Secret War in Mexico*, 184–86; Krauze, *Mexico*, 244–47; Harris and Sadler, *Texas Rangers*, 172. Note: Steps to the monetary destabilization of the Mexican economy and Huerta government included: (1) departure from the gold standard on July 1, 1913; (2) an era of depreciated paper money; (3) Huerta demands on Mexican banks to provide unsecured loans to the government; (4) all complicated by the fact that silver coins (already in short supply) were melted down and exported as "bullion" despite stringent laws; and (5) the combination of these actions ushered in inflation.

3. As seen in "German Praise of Huerta," *New York Times*, January 31, 1914.

4. Schuler, *Murder and Counterrevolution*, 78–81; Scholes and Scholes, "Wilson, Grey, and Huerta," 151–58; Katz, *Secret War in Mexico*, 186–89; "Transcendental Foreign Politics," *The Nation*, January 8, 1914, 26; Godley, "Weetman Pearson in Mexico," 11–23; "Envoys See Wilson," *Washington Post*, March 9, 1914; "Canal Tolls Crisis," *Washington Post*, February 18, 1914. See also "Mr. Wilson's 'Point of Honor,'" *New York Times*, February 8, 1914, and "'Big Business' behind the Mexican Muddle," *Literary Digest*, November 15, 1913, 935–36.

5. O'Shaughnessy, *Diplomat's Wife in Mexico*, 187–91; "Says Huerta Is Beaten," *New York Times*, February 17, 1014; "La palabra de Woodrow carece de honradez como el mismo," *El Imparcial*, February 14, 1914; "Insults to Wilson Stir O'Shaughnessy," *New York Times*, February 12, 1914; "Threatened Life of O'Shaughnessy," *New York Times*, February 15, 1914; "Arrest in Plot to Oust Huerta," *New York Times* February 1, 1914; "Huerta Seizes Times," *New York Times*, February 1, 1914; "'American Charge' in Mexico City Carries Gun for Self Defense," *Austin Statesman*, February 25, 1914. Note: To reduce the possible influence of the American media, Mexican authorities at Progresso, on the border in deep South Texas, confiscated all copies of the *New York Times* and the *San Antonio Light and Express News* bound for Mexico City on the grounds the publications were "injurious" to the Huerta regime. Secretary Bryan wired chargé d'affaires O'Shaughnessy on behalf of the president and confirmed that additional secret service agents and six marines would be sent from Veracruz to protect the chargé d'affaires.

6. "Death for Aiding Huerta," *New York Times*, February 3, 1914; "Villa Warns Spaniards," *New York Times*, February 4, 1914; "Orders Aliens Protected," *New York Times*, February 6, 1914; "AMERICAN Charge in Mexico Carries Gun for Protection," *Austin Statesman*, February 25, 1914; "British Bluecoats with Machine Gun Sent to Mexico City," *Austin Statesman*, February, n.d.; "Envoy Will Shoot," *Washington Post*, February 20, 1914; "Protect U.S. Charge," *Washington Post*, February 19, 1914; Turner, "Anti-Americanism in Mexico," 502–18. Note: Huerta, seizing on the propaganda opportunity, immediately issued a circular that all noncombatants were to be given as much protection as possible.

7. "Special: Laredo," *New York Times*, February 26, 1914.

8. "American Rancher Kidnapped," *Laredo Daily Times*, February 14, 1914; "Kidnap American Citizen," *Laredo Daily Times*, February 15, 1914; "American Citizen Kidnaped [*sic*]," *Austin Statesman*, February 15, 1914.

9. "Bryan and Wilson," *The Nation*, January 22, 1914, 74; Edwin A. Weinstein, *Woodrow Wilson: A Medical and Psychological Biography* (Princeton, NJ: Princeton University Press, 1981), 251; Margaret MacMillan, *Paris 1919* (New York: Random House, 2002), 200, 489–91; Baker, *Woodrow Wilson*, 2: 422, notes: Wilson, "suffered intensely from neuritis . . . the sight in one eye was defective," and "Dr. S. Weir Mitchell's exam about the time he entered the presidency, doubted whether he could service the overwhelming labour of the great office he was soon to fill."

10. Weinstein, *Woodrow Wilson*, 140–50; House Diary, April 13, 1913; Walworth, *Woodrow Wilson*, 72; Phyllis Lee Levin, *Edith and Woodrow: The Wilson White House* (New York: Scribner, 2001), 34, 48, 124, 295. Note: Weinstein's review of the records concluded: Woodrow Wilson suffered from very high blood pressure and his fundi (retinas) showed hypertensive vascular changes with advanced atherosclerosis (thickening of vessel walls), angiospasticity (spasm of retinal vessels), retinal hemorrhages, and exudates. Dr. Carl Grayson, who always maintained modesty and discretion concerning the president, wrote a book, *Woodrow Wilson: An Intimate Memoir* (1959), covering very little of his health status from late 1913 through April 1914, other than to note, "Neither she [Ellen Wilson] nor the president was entirely well when they moved into the White House."

11. Edward Weinstein, "Woodrow Wilson's Neurological Illness," *Journal of American History* (September 1970): 324–51; "President Has a Cold," *New York Times*, December 4, 1913; "Wilson Continues to Gain—Doctor Cancels Today's Engagements," *New York Times*, December 15, 1913; "Wilson Meets Cabinet," *New York Times*, December 17, 1913; "President off for a Rest," *New York Times*, December 24, 1913; "Wilson Health Mending," *New York Times*, December 30, 1913; "New Huerta Border Move: Villa Fears Flank Attack," *New York Times*, February 14, 1914; Callahan, *American Foreign Policy in Mexican Relations*, 543–45. Note: The second-floor meeting room was the location made historic by the signing of the Emancipation Proclamation.

12. "Wilson in Bed with a Cold," *New York Times*, February 13, 1914; "Wilson's Cold Improves," *New York Times*, February 16, 1914; "Wilson at Work Again," *New York Times*, February 17, 1914; "President Ill; Engagements Are Cancelled," *Austin Statesman*, February 13, 1914; "Wanton Reign of Murder and Robbery in Mexico Is Blamed on U.S. in Protest to Congress," *Washington Post*, February 21, 1914.

13. "New Huerta Border Move," *New York Times*, February 14, 1914; Odie Arambula, "Rebel Lucio Blanco Is of Local Interest," LMTonline, July 6, 2013; Odie Arambula, http://www.lmtonline.com/opinion/editorials/article/Rebel-Lucio-Blanco-is-of-local-interest-10103335.php. Cumberland, "Border Raids in the Lower Rio Grande Valley," 285–311; Raat, *Revoltosos*, 203–50; Coerver and Hall, *Texas and the Mexican Revolution*, 64–65. See also Hammond's, "Railroad Map of Mexico," New York: C. S. Hammond, 1913.

14. Adams, *Conflict and Commerce on the Rio Grande*, 144–54.

15. Rawlin M. Colquitt to Governor Colquitt, January 22, 1914, TSA, Colquitt Papers; Adams, *Conflict and Commerce on the Rio Grande*, 148–57; Coerver and Hall, *Texas and the Mexican Revolution*, 65–67.

16. Colquitt to Secretary of War, December 13, 1913, Records of Immigration, RG

85; John A. Valls, Webb District Attorney, to Colquitt, February 21, 1914, CP-AHC, Box 3P157.

17. Allan R. Millett, *The General: Robert L. Bullard and Officership in the United States Army, 1881–1917* (Westport, CT: Greenwood Press, 1975), 275–76. See also Matt M. Matthews, "The US Army on the Mexican Border: A Historical Perspective," Fort Leavenworth, Combat Studies Institute Press, n.d.; and Levario, *Militarizing the Border*, 38–52.

18. Gilberto Hinohosa, "Curse of Palafox," Laredo: n.d., Palafox File, Webb County Heritage Foundation, Laredo. Note: The township of San Jose de Palafox was established by the Spaniards in 1765, yet not occupied in number until the early 1880s, growing to a population of over three hundred supporting both the ranching and coal mining operations in the region.

19. US Federal Census, 1910, Webb County, Texas, p. 13A, RG 29; "Los Laborantes de Laredo," Mexico City *El Imparcial*, February 28, 1914. Italics in quote added for emphasis.

20. Statement of Marcelo Villarreal, March 9, 1927, Aldrich Papers; "The Vergara Case," *Laredo Daily Times*, March 1, 1914; "Vergara Ordered Released," *Laredo Daily Times*, February 17, 1914; Harris and Sadler, *Texas Rangers*, 166.

21. Statement of Dolores Vergara, March 11, 1914, Aldrich Papers; Harris and Sadler, *Texas Rangers*, 166. Note: Prior to 1910, Piedras Negras was known as Ciudad Porfirio Díaz, and continued to be referred to as such for years.

22. "Vergara Killing Stirs Up Colquitt," *Laredo Weekly Times*, March 1, 1914. See also, "An Exciting Border Incident," *Frontier Times*, August 1919, 441–43.

23. "Dr. Garrett, as U.S. Consul, Was in Thick of Activities on Border during 3 Revolutions," *Gallipolis Daily Tribune*, March 9 and 10, 1932, www.galliagenealogy.org.

24. "Benton Executed by General Villa," *Houston Post*, February 21, 1914; "Record of Benton Trail Made Public," *Houston Post*, February 22, 1914; "British Subject Is Executed by Villa: Indignation Great," *Austin Statesman*, February 21, 1914; "Villa Claims That Benton Was Armed and Wanted to Kill Him," *Austin Statesman*, February 22, 1914; "Villa's Defense Is Attack by Benton," *Laredo Weekly Times*, February 22, 1914. See also Eisenhower, *Intervention*, 72–78.

25. A sample of the worldwide media coverage: "Clemente Vergara Was Hanged," *Laredo Daily Times*, February 25, 1914; "La muerte de Vergara," *El Mundo* (Havana), February 26, 1914; "Vergara fur torturado antes de darle muerte los federales," *El Mundo* (Havana), March 5, 1914; "Mejico [*sic*] 28," *El Mercurio* (Valparaíso, Chile), March 1, 1914; "La Cuestion Mexicana," *La Prensa* (Buenos Aires, Argentina), February 26, 1914; "Texas Rangers Invade Mexico," *Democratic Banner* (Mount Vernon, Ohio), March 10, 1914; "American Policy in Mexico," *The Times* (London), March 2, 1914; "Body Not Taken by Texas Troops," *Suffolk County News* [Sayville, NY], March 13, 1914. Also, the future years' papers carried coverage and updates: "Fue aprehendido y llevado a Laredo, Texas, el matador de Clemente Vergara," *La Prensa* (San Antonio), September 21, 1915; "Chale 'No Entiende,'" *La Prensa* (San Antonio), July 2, 1933; "Guajardo Is Upheld by Foreign Office," *Mexican Herald*, March 23, 1914.

26. "Delicate Crisis Seems Near at Hand," *Austin American Statesman*, February 24, 1914; "Senate May Take Hand in the Case," *Laredo Weekly Times*, February 24, 1914; "England Will Never Recognize Carranza, So Carden Declares," *Austin*

Statesman, March 2, 1914. See also Alan Knight, *The Mexican Revolution* (Cambridge: Cambridge University Press, 1986), 108–12.

27. Hutchings to Captain E. M. Matson, February 26, 1914, Aldrich Papers. Note: Texas law in 1914 authorized a maximum strength of four Ranger companies, yet in February 1914 only three companies (A, B, C) were active. Company organization and monthly pay was one captain, $100; one sergeant, $50; and up to 20 privates, $40 each. On joining the Texas Rangers members were required to furnish their own horse, tack, and arms. *Biennial Report of the Adjutant General of Texas, 1913–1914*, 10.

28. Clemente Vergara Petition, File SF 9791, survey no. 2331, Texas General Land Office, Austin; "Vergara Did Not Own Island," *Houston Post*, February 26, 1914; "Austin, Texas," *New York Times*, February 26, 1914; "Status of Vergara Island," *Austin Statesman*, February 26, 1914. Note: Further confusing the investigation, the county surveyor in Webb advised Ranger Sanders (without confirming with Austin) that local records in late February 1914 indicated the island belonged to Texas. The legal status of the islands in the Rio Grande on the Texas-Mexico border from the Chamizal at El Paso to Boca Chica at the mouth of the river had been in dispute since 1848. Harris and Sadler, *Texas Rangers*, 165, incorrectly states, the "island was a part of Texas."

29. J. J. Sanders to Colquitt, February 26, 1914, Colquitt Papers. See also the statement of Marcelo Villarreal, March 9, 1914, Aldrich Papers. Note: Laredo surveyor Sam Foster advised Ranger Captain Sanders incorrectly: "that island referred to is on Texas side." Foster had only done the survey and the status of the island was determined by the Texas general land commissioner.

30. Colquitt to Wilson, February 26, 1914, Aldrich Papers; "Colquitt Insistent in Plea to Wilson," *New York Times*, February 26, 1914.

31. "Threat of Texas to Send Rangers into Mexico," and "Texas Wants to Use Force," *New York Times*, February 27, 1914; "Colquitt Is Warned against Hasty Action," *Austin American Statesman*, February 27, 1914: "Mexico Subject for the Cabinet," *El Paso Herald*, February 27, 1914. See also "War by Any Other Name," *The Nation*, March 5, 1914, 228–29.

32. Wilson to House, February 25, 1914, and Page to Wilson, February 24, 1914, seen in Baker, *Woodrow Wilson: Life and Letters*, 308–9; "Delicate Crisis Seems Near at Hand," *Austin American*, February 24, 1914; "The British Press on Benton," *Literary Digest*, March 7, 1914, 481; "British Protest Direct to London," *New York Times*, March 1, 1914. Note: Page wrote the president on February 28: "Kill an Englishman at home and there is no undue excitement. But kill one abroad and gunboats and armies and reparation are at once thought about."

33. United States Congress, House, Committee on Interstate and Foreign Commerce, "Panama Canal Tolls," Address by the President to a Joint Session of Congress, March 5, 1914, Washington, DC, 1914; "Toll Issue Vital to Our Relations with Whole World," *San Antonio Express*, March 9, 1914; Williams, *Anglo-American Isthmian Diplomacy*, 313; Baker, *Woodrow Wilson*, 310–14. Note: The United States paid Nicaragua $3 million for the canal rights in 1914, and kept options for the development of a canal active until 1970, when the treaty was mutually abrogated; see Ambassador [Kennedy] Crockett to Department of State, Doc. 486, Airgram A-115, June 9, 1969, RG 59, www.history.state.gov.

34. "Was Taken to Mexico City," *Laredo Weekly Times*, February 22, 1914. Note: There were in fact other kidnaping and murder cases of Americans under investiga-

tion. On February 20–21, Consul Garrett was involved with the negotiation of the release of two ranchers from Hebbronville, Texas, Inocento Benavidez and John Hinnant, both captured by Federalists near Hidalgo and retained on "trivial charges," jailed first in Saltillo, then moved to Mexico City. The final disposition is unknown. The only other individual case by name that attracted some attention was Gustavo Bauch, an American, with German parents, who was born in Louisiana and disappeared in northern Mexico in late February 1914; "Bauch Case Unsolved Mystery," *El Paso Herald*, March 7, 1914.

35. Rear Admiral Sir C. Cradock to Admiralty, Doc. 190, March 8, 1914, Diplomatic Relations Papers.

36. Rear Admiral Sir C. Cradock to Admiralty, Doc. 190, March 8, 1914, Diplomatic Relations Papers.

37. Rear Admiral Sir C. Cradock to Admiralty, Doc. 190, March 8, 1914, Diplomatic Relations Papers.

38. "Benton Shot in a Scuffle?" *New York Times*, February 28, 1914; "Texas Wants to Use Force," *New York Times*, February 27, 1914; "Vergara Reported Alive," *New York Times*, March 1, 1914; "Huerta Promises to Punish Slayers," *New York Times*, February 28, 1914; "Threat of Texas to Send Rangers into Mexico," *New York Times*, February 27, 1914; "Vergara Assassin Must Be Punished," *Laredo Daily Times*, February 27, 1914; "El gobierno de Washington y la muerte del Americano Clemente Vergara," *El Imparcial*, February 28, 1914. See also "Mexican Intervention," *Austin Statesman*, February 5, 1914; "Hanging of Texan by Huerta: Troops across Border," *Austin Statesman*, February 26, 1914.

39. O. B. Colquitt to B. F. Looney, Attorney General, February 26, 1914, Governor O. B. Colquitt Papers, Texas State Archives, Austin. See also "Slayers of Vergara to Be Speedily Punished," *Washington Post*, February 26, 1914, and "To Recover Body of Vergara," *Laredo Daily Times*, February 26, 1914.

40. Texas Attorney General, B. F. Looney to Governor Colquitt, February 27, 1914, Aldrich Papers; "The Vergara Case," *Laredo Daily Times*, February 27, 1914; "Developments Vergara Case," *Laredo Daily Times*, February 27, 1914; Harris and Sadler, *Texas Rangers*, 167–68.

41. Henry G. Gole, *The Road to Rainbow: Army Planning for Global War, 1934–1940* (Annapolis, MD: Naval Institute Press, 2003), 22–25; Alan C. Lowe, "The Development of War Plan Green: The U.S. Army and Mexico," 2002, www.carlisle.army.mil/usemhi; Harris and Sadler, *Texas Rangers*, 164–71; Matthews, "The US Army on the Mexican Border," pp. 59–61. Note: The color coded "Rainbow" war plans were established by General Tasker Bliss, developing, for example, the United States coded as the "Blue" country, and Germany—black, Japan—orange, Mexico—green, Brazil—purple, Russia—pink, and France—gold, etc. See also "American War Plans Special Text 2001," Carlisle Barracks, Army War College, 2000.

42. O. B. Colquitt to Secretary of State, February 27, 1914, Colquitt Papers; Texas Adjutant General, *Biennial Reports of the Adjutant General of Texas*, 1913–15 (Austin: Von Boeckmann-Jones, 1915), 10; "Neutrality Matters," March 28–31, 1914, and "In re Filibustering Expedition at Douglas, Arizona," April 2–4, 1014, Mexico Files BOI.

43. Adams, *Conflict and Commerce on the Rio Grande*, 123–25, 147–49; Jerry Thompson, *Warm Weather and Bad Whiskey* (El Paso: Texas Western Press, 1991), 100–144; C. L. Sonnichsen, "Boots and Sandals," in *Ten Texas Feuds* (Albuquerque: University of New Mexico Press, 1957), 159–66.

44. "Vergara Girl Tells of Capture of Her Father," *San Antonio Express*, March 14, 1914. Note: List of Federalist soldiers implicated in the murder of Vergara: Apolonio Rodriquez, Nito Sierra, Jesus Maria Castillon, Andres Rodriquez; "La pretendida ejecución de Clemente Vergara por soldados federales," *La Prensa*, March 5, 1914.

45. Garrett to Secretary of State, February 27, 1914, Aldrich Papers. Note: the San Antonio *La Prensa*, March 5, 1914, noted, "encontrar el cadáver de Vergara, que muchos vaqueros aseguran haber visto pendiente de un árbol."

46. Garrett to Secretary of State, February 27, 1914, Aldrich Papers. See also Sanders to Colquitt, February 26, 1914, Aldrich Papers, and "Says Vergara Joined Rebels: Absurd Report Sent Out by Mexican Federal Commander," *Laredo Daily Times*, March 2, 1914.

47. Garrett to Secretary of State, February 27, 1914, Aldrich Papers. See also "Vergara Escape Report Rendered by General Guajardo," *Mexico Herald*, March 1, 1914 (reprinted as "What Mexico Claims," *San Antonio* Express, March 16, 1914), and C. A. Z. Carracristi to Gov. Colquitt, September 25, 1913 and R. M. Colquitt [brother] to Gov. Colquitt, Jan. 22, 1914, TSA, Colquitt Papers.

48. Schuler, *Secret War and Secret Policies*, 82. See also "What Mexico Claims," *San Antonio Express*, March 16, 1914.

49. "What Mexico Claims," *San Antonio Express*, March 16, 1914. See also "Say Vergara Was Friends of Rebels," *Mexican Herald*, March 12, 1914; "Vergara Committee [in Mexico City] Summons Witnesses," *Mexican Herald*, April 6, 1914; "Daughter of Vergara Told of Capture," *Houston Post*, March 14, 1914; Testimony of John A. Valls, January 22, 1920, Investigation of Mexican Affairs, 1199–225; "Complaint Is Filed in Vergara Affair," *Galveston Daily News*, March 1, 1914; Rocha, "The Influence of the Mexican Revolution on the Texas-Mexican Border," 195–97.

50. Armando Sanchez to Colquitt, February 28, 1914, Aldrich Papers.

51. O. B. Colquitt to W. J. Bryan, March 26, 1914, Colquitt Papers; J. J. Sander to Colquitt, March 16, 1914, Colquitt Papers; Captain John R. Hughes to O. B. Colquitt, March 26, 1914, Colquitt Papers; "The Vergara Case," *Laredo Daily Times*, March 6, 1914.

52. "The Vergara Case," *Laredo Daily Times*, March 6, 1914; "Mexico—Viewed from Texas," *Literary Digest*, March 14, 1914, 535–36; "Threat of Texas to Send Rangers into Mexico," *New York Times*, February 27, 1914. Note: There is no doubt that the Vergara case was handled at the highest levels in the Wilson administration by cabinet secretaries as well as the White House. The following critical letter from Secretary of War Garrison to Secretary Bryan confirms the administration's actions:

WAR DEPARTMENT TELEGRAM

Washington

March 10, 1914

THE HONORABLE SECRETARY OF STATE:

March ninth commanding general, Southern Department, Fort Sam Houston, Texas, telegraphed:

QUOTE—Replying telegram Chief of Staff this morning relative recovery body of Vergara following just received. Quote: Laredo March ninth, investigation shows Vergara taken from Hidalgo cemetery Saturday night by relatives of Vergara and hired Mexicans. Captain Sanders states positively no Texas Ranger's crossed border. He met body at landing opposite San Enrique with undertaker Convery Sunday morning. Convery brought the body to Laredo seven thirty P.M. Sunday. He states no signs of burns in body. Found four bullet holes; neck chafed but not broken; body decomposed but pants on body match coat left at home by Vergara; identification seems reliable. Recovery of body said to have cost S. T. Hill, brother-in-law of Vergara, four hundred dollars. Body being held at request of Adjutant General Hutchins [Texas], expected tomorrow. No excitement Howard.—END QUOTE.

Lindsay M. Garrison
Secretary of War

53. Telegram, Amador Sanchez to Gov. O. B. Colquitt, April 1, 1914, Colquitt Papers.

54. Sir Edward Grey to Spring Rice, Doc. 177, February 23, 1914, and William J. Bryan to Spring Rice, Doc. 219, June 2, 1914, Diplomatic Relations Papers; US Congressional Record, 63rd Cong., 2nd sess., Vol. 51, pt. 5, March 9, 1914, 4532–33; "Say Vergara Not Tortured before Death," *El Paso Herald*, March 11, 1914; "Washington Gets Full Reports on Vergara Incident," *Mexican Herald*, March 11, 1914; Morris Sheppard, "The Mexican Situation," *American Review of Reviews* 49 (May 1914): 421–25.

55. Lindley Garrison, Secretary of War to the Secretary of State, March 10, 1914, Records of Immigration, RG 85; Webb, *Texas Rangers*, 492; "Vergara's Widow Financed Party Recovering Body," *Austin American*, March 11, 1914; "No Rangers Went Over into Mexico," *San Antonio Express*, March 10, 1914. "Wilson Wants Them to Clean Up Affair," *Laredo Weekly Times*, March 15, 1914.

56. "No Conflict with Texas," *Evening Post* (New York), March 10, 1914; "Mexico City Hears Body Was Given Up," *New York Times*, March 10, 1914; *Dallas News*, March 9, 10, 11, 1914; Post Card Collection, 1913–14, Vergara postmortem pictures, Laredo Public Library Archives. See articles, for example, printed on March 9 and 10, 1914, in *Austin Statesman, Detroit Free Press, San Antonio Express, New York American, Chicago Daily News, Washington Post, New York Times*, and *Los Angeles Daily Times* as well as *Estado de Sao Paulo, La Prensa* (Buenos Aires), and *El Pais* (Mexico City) along with the *El Diario* and the *Herald*.

57. Garrison, Secretary of War to the Secretary of State, March 10, 1914, Colquitt Papers. See also Sanders to Hutchings, March 9, 1914, Colquitt Papers. See also "Vergara's Widow Financed Party Recovering Body," *Austin Statesman*, March 11, 1914.

58. Cardiff to Colquitt, May 28, 1914, Colquitt Papers; "Colquitt Praised for Mexico Stand," *San Antonio Express*, March 11, 1914; "TEXAS TO ACT ALONE," *Washington Post*, March 11, 1914; Senator Albert Fall to O. B. Colquitt, March 13, 1814, Colquitt Papers.

59. "Colquitt Demands That Texas Citizens be Protected; Wants the Authority to Send Rangers into Mexico," "Sending of Marines Would Be Act of War," and "No Idea of Sending Marines," *Austin Statesman*, February 27, 1914; "'Go After Them' All Colquitt Wants," *San Antonio Express*, Match 14, 1914; "Colquitt Wants Hundred Rangers to Guard Border," *Austin Statesman*, March 13, 1914.

60. "Colquitt Unbraids Bryan," *Austin Statesman*, March 1, 1914; "Colquitt Defies U.S. Government: Calls Wilson Policy 'Namby Pamby,' Says He Will Protect Texans," *Rochester Herald*, March 13, 1914. See also William Anderson, "The Nature of the Mexican Revolution as Viewed from the United States, 1910–1917" (PhD diss., University of Texas at Austin, 1967), 128–53.

61. "The Mexican Situation," *Laredo Daily Times*, March 5, 1914; "Fall Gives List of Victims of Mexican," *San Antonio Express*, March 10, 1914; "Mexican Raiders

Kill at Tecate," *San Antonio Express*, March 15, 1914; "Mexican Tension Relaxes Somewhat: Villa Threatens to Kill Prisoner," *Austin Statesman*, March 6, 1914.

Chapter 6

1. Wilson Press Conference, November 14, 1914, *Papers of Woodrow Wilson*, 31: 351.

2. Testimony of William F. Buckley Sr., Investigation of Mexican Affairs, September 11, 1919, 773–75; Scholes, "Wilson, Grey, and Huerta," 151–58. Note: Buckley, a Mexico City oil and gas attorney, minced no words in detailing the atmosphere of "scurrilous rumors" attacking recalled Ambassador Henry Lane Wilson, the flood of misinformation and threats from the network of the Carranza propagandists, and their paid agent Robert H. Murray of the *New York World* that was given access to confidential files at the State Department. See also Fowler, *British American Relations*, 1969.

3. "No Complications over Recovery of Vergara's Body," *San Antonio Express*, March 11, 1914.

4. W. M. Coldwell to Governor O. B. Colquitt, March 14, 1914, TSA, Colquitt Papers. See also *Laredo Times*, March 18, 1914, and Robert M. Utley, *Lone Star Lawmen: The Second Century of the Texas Rangers* (Oxford: Oxford University Press, 2007), 23–24.

5. Letter, the Adjutant General to Consul Gonzalo de A. Fernandez, April 9, 17, and 18, 1914; Henry Hutchings to Governor Colquitt, April 17, 1914; and Captain Co. A Ranger Force John R. Hughes to General Henry Hutchings, April 22, 1914, Texas Adjutant General Correspondences, Texas State Archives.

6. Henry Hutchings to Governor Colquitt, April 17, 1915; Harris and Sadler, *Texas Rangers*, 169–72; Robert E. Quirk, *An Affair of Honor: Woodrow Wilson and the Occupation of Veracruz* (New York: W. W. Norton, 1962), 5.

7. Weinstein, *Woodrow Wilson: A Medical and Psychological Biography*, 258–59. Note: The author concludes, "Wilson's distress over his wife's illness may have been a factor in his bellicose actions which almost led to war between the United States and Mexico."

8. Charles E. Neu, "Woodrow Wilson and Colonel House," in *The Wilson Era*, ed. John Cooper and Charles Neu (Arlington Heights, IL: Harlan Davidson, 1991), 255; John Dos Passos, *Mr. Wilson's War* (New York: Skyhorse Publishing, 2013), 83.

9. Daniels to Flag Officer [USS] *Florida*, Veracruz, April 12, 1913, Buckley Papers, noted: "The statement by Huerta does not meet demand by Admiral Mayo. Insult was open and public"; Coerver and Hall, *Texas and the Mexican Revolution*, 60; O'Shaughnessy, IPMH, 306; Josephus Daniels, *The Wilson Era: Years of Peace, 1913–1917* (Chapel Hill: University of North Carolina Press, 1946), 191. Note: Secretary Daniels at the time of the Tampico incident felt "that Admiral Mayo, when apologies were promptly offered, should have accepted them." In September 1916, Daniel changed US Navy regulations to require the commanding officer in such a similar event to communicate with the Navy Department first before making demands of a foreign government.

10. Consular dispatch, Veracruz, April 20, 1914, *Foreign* Affairs, 1914, 477. In the note from O'Shaughnessy to Commander US Atlantic Fleet, USS *Florida* Flagship, April 12, 1914: "positive refusal of Mexican Government in writing to accede to de-

mands of Admiral Mayo relative to salute at Tampico," as seen in Buckley Papers; "U.S. Naval Deployment," in *Atlas of the Mexican Conflict* (Chicago: Rand McNally, 1914), 7–8; "Ordered Seizure of Veracruz without Waiting for Senate," *Laredo Daily Times*, April 21, 1914. See also Samuel G. Inman, *Intervention in Mexico* (New York: Association Press, 1919), 1–12, and Henry Baerlen, *Mexico: The Land of Unrest* (Philadelphia: J. B. Lippincott, 1914). Note: The *Ypirango*, which is often spelled *Ipirango*, was intercepted and given a no-landing order for Veracruz on April 20, 1914, and then sailed on to Tampico where it unloaded its arms and munitions for the Huerta army!

11. V. Carranza to President Wilson, April 22, 1914, 812.00/11618, US Department of State Papers; Admiral Badger to General Maas, Veracruz, 1:00 PM, April 21, 1914, "forces seized the Custom House . . . we do not wish to use our heavy guns of 12 inch caliber . . . therefore require you cease firing," Buckley Papers; "Wilson Sending Atlantic Fleet to Make Huerta Salute the Flag," *Atlanta Constitution*, April 15, 1914, 1; Isidro Fabela, ed., *Documentos hist6ricos de la revoluci6n mexicana*, 28 vols. (Mexico City, 1960–1976), 1: 331–32, 346–47, 365; Katz, *Secret War in Mexico*, 232–40; Mark E. Benbow, "Intelligence in Another Era: All the Brains I Can Borrow—Woodrow Wilson and Intelligence Gathering in Mexico, 1913–15," n.d. https://www.cia.gov/library/center-for-the-study-of-intelligence.

12. Knight, *Mexican Revolution*, 158–65; Schuler, *Murder and Counterrevolution in Mexico*, 97–99.

13. "Rioting Begins in Mexico City," *New York Herald*, April 24, 1914; "Pulled Down Washington Statue," *Laredo Daily Times*, April 25, 1914. See also Maurice Lord, "An Englishman's Review of President Wilson," *Houston Post*, 31–32, and Patrick Beesly, *Room 40: British Naval Intelligence 1914–1918* (London: Hamish Hamilton, 1982), 229–30.

14. O'Shaughnessy, IPMH, 341–51; Schuler, *Murder and Counterrevolution*, 253–60; George Rausch, "The Exile and Death of Victoriano Huerta," *Hispanic American Historical Review* (May 1962): 133–51; Michael C. Meyer, "The Mexican-German Conspiracy of 1915," *Americas* (July 1966): 76–89; Meyer, *Mexican Rebel*, 120–30; Clements, "Woodrow Wilson's Mexican Policy, 1913–15," *Journal of Diplomatic History* (Spring 1980): 136.

15. Vandiver, *Blackjack*, 2: 640–68; Quirk, *An Affair of Honor*, 5; Krauze, *Mexico*, 347; Friedrich Katz, "Alemania y Francisco Villa," *Historia Mexicana*, July 1962, 96–97; William W. Anderson, "The Nature of the Mexican Revolution as Viewed from the United States, 1910–1917" (PhD diss., University of Texas at Austin, 1967), 79.

16. Buckley to H. L. Wilson, March 24, 1928, Buckley Papers. Note: Buckley made the same comments at the US Congressional Hearings on Mexican Affairs in 1919.

17. Angel Algara, Secretary of Foreign Affairs to Washington, March 13, 1914, in Josefina E. de Fabela, *Historical Documents of the Mexican Revolution*, 3: 43–44; "Felix Diaz Seeks Aid of the United States to Start New Revolt," *Austin Statesman*, March 5, 1914; "Gen. Diaz has New Plan to End the Mexican Troubles," *San Antonio Express*, March 12, 1914; "A Model Address," *Crockett Courier*, May 14, 1914; "An Exciting Border Incident," *Frontier Times*, August 1929, 441–43.

18. "Demand on Mexico Still Unheeded," *New York Times*, November 23, 1919; "Why Jenkins Stay Jailed," *Herald Democrat*, November 28, 1919; Dimitri D. Lazo,

"Lansing, Wilson, and the Jenkins Incident," *Diplomatic History*, 1998, 177–98; David Gerber, "1919: William Jenkins, Robert Lansing, and the Mexican Interlude," *Southwestern Historical Quarterly* (January 1971): 337–56.

Appendix A

1. Hill, *Emissaries*, 63; *New York Times*, March 12, 1913,1.
2. Public Papers, III, 42.
3. Baker, *Wilson*, 4: 253–54.
4. Baker, *Wilson*, 4: 266–67.
5. Henry L. Wilson, Diplomatic Episodes, 317–18; *New York Times*, August 5, 1913.
6. James B. Scott, *President Wilson's Foreign Policy* (New York: Oxford University Press, 1918), 1–10.
7. Wilson, Presidential Messages, Addresses, and State Papers, 32–36.
8. P. M. Angle, *Crossroads*, 1913, 198.
9. British Foreign Documents, June 1, 1914, Doc. 147, 278–79.
10. Woodrow Wilson, Presidential, Messages, Addresses, and State Papers, 36–40.
11. Foreign Affairs, 1914, 447–48
12. Report of Consul Garrett, Nuevo Laredo, February 15, 1914.
13. *Laredo Morning Times*, March 10, 1914.

Selected Bibliography

Archival and Primary Material

Benson Latin American Collection, University of Texas, Austin.
William F. Buckley Sr. Papers
Lazara de la Garza Papers
Ferrocarril Noroeste de Mexico Papers
Papeles Varios Sobre la Revolución, 1910–1915, Garza 117, Papers
Briscoe (Baker) American History Center, Austin.
Papers of Oscar B. Colquitt
Papers of Walter P. Webb
T. W. House Papers
Roy Wilkinson Aldrich Papers
Albert S. Burleson Papers
Edward M. House Papers
James S. Hogg Papers
Deutsche Auswaertiges Amt, Mexico, Innere Zustande u. Allgemeine Angelegenheiten, University of California, Berkeley, microfilm
Laredo Public Library Archives
Photo Card Collection, 1910–15
Clippings, *Laredo Daily Times*, 1913–14
John E. Conner Museum, Texas A&M University, Kingsville, Texas
James L. Allhands Papers
Texas State Archives, Austin, Texas
Adjutant General. *Biennial Reports of the Adjutant General of Texas, 1913–1915.* Austin: Von Boeckmann-Jones, 1913–17.
Proceedings of the Joint Committee of the Senate and House in the Investigation of the Texas State Ranger Force, January 13, 1919.
Governors' Papers: Oscar B. Colquitt
Texas Ranger Papers
Texas A&M University, Evans and Cushing Library, College Station, Texas
Mexican Revolution Oral History
Mercurio Martinez Papers
Texas and Borderlands Collection
J. D. Wheelan Mexican Revolution Photographs (1913–14)

Jeff Dykes Collection
William A. Owens Papers
Anderson Alford van Patten Papers
Taft Papers, Letter Book
Texas Land Office
Survey and Petitions of Islands in the Rio Grande, 1910–14
Webb County Courthouse
Deeds and Probate Records: 1912–21
Webb County Heritage Foundation
Palafox File
Zimmermann Library, University of New Mexico
Albert B. Fall Papers

Government Documents

Great Britain. Parliament (5th) Parliamentary Debates, House of Commons, 1914, LVIII and LXII.

Mexico. Secretaria de Relaciones Exteriores. *Diplomatic Dealings of the Constitutionalist Revolution of Mexico*. Mexico City: Imprenta Nacional, 1919.

———. Secretaria de Hacienda y Crédito Público. *La Dueda Exterior de Mexico*. Mexico City: Editorial Cultura, 1926.

———. Secretaria de Gobernación. *Pasa a la Verdad: Causas de la revolución mexicana*. Mexico City: 1920.

———. Secretaria de Instrucción Pública y Bellas Artes. *Adiciones al Plan de Guadalupe y Descretos Dictados Conforme a las Mismas*. Veracruz: 1915.

"Panama Canal Tolls: Symposium of Views Protesting against a Surrender of American Rights." Congressional Record 1912–13, Washington, DC, 1913.

"Panama Canal Tolls: The Traditional Policy of the United States in Relation to Waterways." Hon. Theodore E. Burton of Ohio, Washington, DC: Government Printing Office, May 19, 1914.

US Congress. House. "Appointment of Committee for Investigation of Mexican Situation." Committee on Rules, 66th Cong., 1st sess., H.J. Res. 124, part 1, 1919.

———. "Conditions in Mexico." *Congressional Record.* Senate, March 9, 1914, 4510–22.

———. "Report of the Secretary of War." 35th Cong. 2nd sess., Ex. Doc. No. 2, October 19, 1858, 277–78.

———. Senate. "Affairs in Mexico." 64th Cong., 1st sess., Doc. No. 324, February 17, 1916.

———. "Claims against Mexico." 66th Cong., 1st sess., Doc. No. 67, July 31, 1919.

———. "Investigation of Mexican Affairs." Full Committee Report, 66th Cong., 2nd sess., Doc. No. 285, 2 vols., 1920.

US Bureau of Immigration. Records of the Immigration and Naturalization Service, Part 2: Mexican Immigration, 1906–1930. Bethesda: University Publications of America, 1994, Record Group 85.

US Central Intelligence Agency (CIA). Mark E. Benbow, *Intelligence in Another Era—All the Brains I Can Borrow: Woodrow Wilson and Intelligence Gathering in Mexico, 1913–1915*. Updated June 25, 2008, https://www.cia.gov/library/center-for-the-study-of-intelligence.

US Federal Census Records, 1910. Webb [County], Texas; Roll T624–1599, p. 13A, RG 29p.

US Department of State. *Papers Relating to the Foreign Relations of the United States, 1910–1920.*

———. *Papers Relating to the Foreign Relations of the United States, 1913–1915.* Washington, DC: Government Printing Office, 1920–24.

———. *Records of the Department of State Relating to Political Relations between the United States and Mexico, 1910–1929.*

———. *Records of the Department of State Relating to the Internal Affairs of Mexico, 1910–1920.*

US Department of Justice. Federal Bureau of Investigation. Record Group 65, Mexican File.

US Department of the Treasury. United States Secret Service. Daily Reports of Agents, 1875 thru 1936. Record Group 87.

US National Security Agency (NSA). David P. Mowry, *German Clandestine Activities in South America in World War II.* NSA/CSSM 123-2, 1989, declassified April 13, 2009.

US War Department. *Annual Reports, 1912–1915.* Washington, DC: GPO, 1912–15.

Newspapers, Periodicals and Serials

Atlanta Constitution
Atlantic Monthly
Auckland Star
Austin American Statesman
Crockett Courier
Daily Reporter-Star (Orlando)
Dallas Morning News
Del Rio Herald
El Diario (Mexico City)
The Economist (London)
El Paso Herald
El Paso Morning Times
La Estrella (Las Cruces)
Evening Post (New York)
Financial Age
Financial World
Forum
El Heraldo de Cuba
Houston Post
El Imparcial (Mexico City)
El Imparcial (San Antonio)
Independent
Indianapolis News
Laredo Morning Times
Laredo Weekly Times
Leslie's Illustrated Weekly Review
Light (San Antonio)

Literary Digest
London Daily Mail
London News (New York)
London Spector
El Mañana (Nuevo Laredo)
Mexican Herald (Mexico City)
The Nation
New York Sun
New York Times
New Outlook
News-Guide (Eagle Pass)
New York World
El Pais (Mexico City)
Pall Mall Gazette (London)
La Prensa (Mexico City)
La Prensa (San Antonio)
San Antonio Express-News
Texas Republic (San Antonio)
The Times (London)
Wall Street Journal
Washington Post

Contemporary Period Books and Articles: 1912–20

"After Huerta, Who?" *North American Review* (January 1914): 17–22.

"The American Exodus from Mexico." *Literary Digest*, September 13, 1913, 405–6.

Atl, Doctor. "The Mexican Revolution and the Nationalization of the Land: The Foreign Interests and Reaction." New York: n.p., 1915.

Atlas of the Mexican Conflict. Chicago: Rand McNally, 1914.

Baerlen, Henry. *Mexico: The Land of Unrest*. Philadelphia: J. B. Lippincott, 1914.

Batchelder, Roger. *Watching and Waiting in the Border*. New York: Houghton Mifflin, 1917.

Bell, Edward I. *The Political Shame of Mexico*. New York: McBride, Nast, 1914.

Blyth, S. G. "Mexico: Record of a Conversation with President Wilson." *Saturday Evening Post*, March 23, 1914, 2–4.

"The British Press on Benton's Fate." *Literary Digest*, March 7, 1914, 481.

Brooks, Eugene C. *Woodrow Wilson as President*. Chicago: Row, Peterson, 1916.

Bulnes, Francisco. *The Whole Truth about Mexico: Wilson's Responsibility*. New York: M. Bulnes Book, 1916.

Butterfield, Dolores. "The Conspiracy against Madero." *Forum*, October 1913, 464–82.

Cabrera, Luis. *The Mexican Situation from a Mexican Point of View*. Washington, DC: Confidential Agency of the Constitutionalist Government of Mexico, December 1, 1913. Reprinted in the *Journal of Race Development*, January 1914, 245–61.

Calero, Manuel. *The Mexican Policy of President Woodrow Wilson as It Appeared to a Mexican*. New York: Smith and Thompson, 1916.

———. *La politica mejicana del Presidente Woodrow Wilson*. Madrid, 1916.

———. *Un decenio de política mexicana*. New York, n.p., 1920.

"The Case of Vergara." *American Review of Reviews* (April 1914): 408–9.

Castillo, José R. del. *Historia de la Revolución Social de México*. Mexico: n.p., 1915.

Colquitt, O. B. "The Texas Ranger as He Is." *Leslie's Illustrated Weekly Newspaper*, April 16, 1914, 367.

De Como Vino Huerta y Como se Fue [no author]. Mexico: n.p., 1914.

Dillon, E. J. "The Mexican Mess." *Contemporary Review* 72 (1914): 575–79.

Disque, Brice P. "The Battle of Nuevo Laredo, Mexico (Jan. 1–2, 1914)." *Journal of the United States Cavalry* (May 1914) 892–907.

Everett, Marshall. *Exciting Experiences in the War in Mexico*. Chicago: Bible House, 1914.

Falvella, James W. *A Souvenir Album of Laredo, the Gateway to Mexico*. Laredo: n.p., 1916.

Flandrau, Charles M. *Viva Mexico*. New York: Appleton, 1912.

"For a Permanent Mexican Solution." *World's Work* (January 1914): 243–49.

Fernández Rojas, José. *La Revolución Mexicana: De Porfirio Díaz a Victoriano Huerta, 1910–1913*. Mexico City: F. P. Royas, 1913.

Fornaro, Carlo de. *Carranza and Mexico*. New York: Mitchell Kennerley, 1915.

"A Free-Gun Policy for Mexico," *Literary Digest*, July 12, 1913, 42–43.

Fyfe, Hamilton H. *The Real Mexico: A Study on the Spot*. New York: McBride, Nast, 1914.

"German Plots in Mexico: U.S. Invasion Planned Revelations by Spy." *Auckland Star*, November 17, 1919.

Gibbon, Thomas E. *Mexico under Carranza*. New York: Doubleday, Page, 1919.

Gutierrez de Lara, Lazaro, and Edgcumb Pinchon. *The Mexican People: Their Struggle for Freedom*. Garden City, NY: Doubleday, Page, 1917.

Hale, William B. *The Story of a Style*. New York, 1920.

"Hammonds Railroad Map of Mexico." New York: C. S. Hammond, 1913.

Hurd, Archibald. "The Whole World Needs of the Navy." *Quarterly Review* (October1913): 493–508.

Jones, John P., and Paul M. Hollister. *The German Secret Service in America: 1914–1918*. Boston: Small, Maynard, 1918.

"Letting the Guns into Mexico." *Literary Digest*, February 14, 1914, 303–5.

Lewis, Tracy Hammond. *Along the Rio Grande*. New York: Lewis Publishing, 1916.

Low, A. Maurice. "An Englishman's Review of President Wilson's First Year." *Century Magazine*, May 1914, 26–32.

———. "President Wilson's Latin-American Policy." *Contemporary Review* (January 1914): 21–29.

Lowry, Edward G. "What the President Is Trying to Do for Mexico." *World's Work* (January 1914): 261–66.

MacHugh, R. J. *Modern Mexico*. London: Methuen, 1914.

McLaren, Alice Day. "The Tragic Ten Days of Madero." *Scribner's Magazine*, January 1914, 97–111.

Mellado, Guillermo. *Tres etapas politicas de Don Venustino*. Mexico: n.p., 1916.

"Mexico's Darkening Outlook." *Literary Digest*, March 7, 1914, 473–75.

Middleton, James. "Mexico, the Land of Concessions." *World's Work* (January 1914): 289–298.

Miller, Hugh G., and Joseph C. Freehoff. *The Panama Canal Tolls Controversy*. Boston: Chapple Publishing, 1914.

Moore, John Bassett. "Law and Organization." *American Political Science Review* (February 1915): 1–15.

Morris, Charles. *The Story of Mexico*. N.p.: L. T. Myers, 1914.

Morris, Henry. *Our Mexican Muddle*. Chicago: Laird and Lee Publishers, 1916.

"Mr. Bryan Rides Behind." *North America Review* (March 1914): 321–35.

Nason, Frank L. "Political Mexico To-Day." *Yale Review* (April 1912): 586–99.

"The Navy and the Future." *Edinburgh Review* (April 1914): 448–68.

Oppenheim, Lassa. *The Panama Canal Conflict between Great Britain and the United States of America*. London: Cambridge University Press, 1913.

O'Shaughnessy, Edith. *Diplomatic Days*. New York: Harper and Brothers, 1917.

———. *A Diplomat's Wife in Mexico*. New York: Harper and Bros., 1916.

———. *Intimate Papers of Mexican History*. New York: George Doran, 1920.

Phillips, Hiram A. "Report of One Hundred Wounds Received, in the Battle of Nuevo Laredo, January 1st and 2nd 1914." *Journal of the Association of Military Surgeons* (May 1914): 441–46.

"A Picture of Mexico." *World's Work* (June 1913): 513–16.

"The President and Mexico." *North American Review* (December 1913): 737–44.

"President Wilson and Mexico." *American Review of Reviews* (September 1913): 280–83.

"President Wilson and the Mexican Embargo." *The Outlook*, February 14, 1914, 330.

Reed, John. *Insurgent Mexico*. New York: Penguin Books, 1983. First published in 1914.

Reynolds, S. W. "The Mexican Situation." *Journal of Race Development* (January 1914): 280–92.

Rowell, Chester H. "The Japanese in California." *World's Work* (June 1913): 195–201.

Russell, Thomas H. *Mexico in Peace and War*. Chicago: Reilly and Britton, 1914.

Sala, Antenor. *Emiliano Zapata y el problema agrario de la república mexicana*. Mexico City: Imprenta Franco-Mexicana, 1919.

Scheutte, Oswald F. "What Watchful Waiting Has Cost." *Leslie's Weekly*, April 9, 1914, 342–43.

Scott, James B., ed. *President Wilson's Foreign Policy*. New York: Oxford University Press, 1918.

Simonds, Louis C. "Mexico As It Is." *Atlantic Monthly*, October 1913, 564–74.

Smith, Randolph W. *Benighted Mexico*. New York: John Lind, 1916.

Starr, Frederick. *Mexico and the United States: A Story of Revolution Intervention and War*. Chicago: Bible House, 1914.

Taft, William H. *Our Chief Magistrate and His Powers*. New York: Columbia University Press, 1916.

———. "The Powers of the President." *Yale Review* (August 1914): 25–42.

Thomson, Arthur. *The Conspiracy against Mexico*. N.p., 1919.

"The Tragic Ten Days of Madero." *Scribner's Magazine*, January 1914, pp. 97–111.

Tweedle, Alec [Ethel]. *Mexico: From Díaz to the Kaiser*. New York: George H. Doran, 1919.

Twentieth Century History of Southwest Texas. 2 vols. Chicago: Lewis Publishing, 1907.

"The Vergara and Benton Case." *Independent*, March 27, 1914, 400–401.

"Victoriano Huerta: A Sketch in Life." *Atlantic Monthly*, June 1914, 721–32.

Williams, Mary W. *Anglo-American Isthmian Diplomacy, 1815–1915*. Washington, DC: American Historical Association, 1916.

Wriston, Henry M. "Presidential Special Agents in Diplomacy." *American Political Science Review* (August, 1916): 481–99.

Zayas Enríquez, Rafael de. *The Case of Mexico and the Policy of President Wilson.* New York: Albert and Charles Boni, 1914.

Books and Articles

Adams, John A., Jr. *Bordering the Future: The Impact of Mexico on the United States.* Westport, CT: Praeger, 2006.

———. *Conflict and Commerce on the Rio Grande: Laredo, 1755–1955.* College Station: Texas A&M University Press, 2008.

———. *Mexican Banking and Investment in Transition.* Westport, CT: Quorum Books, 1997.

"An Exciting Border Incident," *Frontier Times*, August 1929, 441–43.

Anaya Ibarra, Pedro Maria. *Precursores de la Revolución Mexicana.* Mexico City: Secretaria de Educación Pública, 1955.

Anders, Evan. *Boss Rule in South Texas: The Progressive Era.* Austin: University of Texas Press, 1982.

Anderson, Adrian. "President Wilson's Politician: Albert Sidney Burleson of Texas." *Southwestern Historical Quarterly* (January 1974): 339–54.

Angle, Paul M. *Crossroads: 1913.* Chicago: Rand McNally, 1963.

Arriojo Vizcaíno, Adolfo. *El sueco que se fue con Pancho Villa.* Mexico City: Editorial Oceano, 2000.

Atkin, Ronald. *Revolution! Mexico, 1910–1920.* New York: John Day, 1970.

Ayers, Edward L. *The Promise of the New South.* Oxford: Oxford University Press, 2007.

Baecker, *Die Deutsche Mexikopolitik, 1913–14.* Berlin: Colloquium Verlag, 1971.

———. "Los intereses militares del imperio Aleman en Mexico, 1913–14." *Historia Mexicana* 29 (1972): 347–62.

Baker, Ray S. *Woodrow Wilson: Life and Letters—1913–1914.* 8 vols. New York: Greenwood Press, 1968.

Baldwin, Deborah J. *Protestants and the Mexican Revolution: Missionaries, Ministers, and Social Change.* Urbana: University of Illinois Press, 1990.

Beatty, Edward. "The Impact of Foreign Trade on the Mexican Economy: Terms of Trade and the Rise of Industry, 1880–1923." *Journal of Latin American Studies* (May 2000): 399–433.

Beesly, Patrick. *Room 40: British Naval Intelligence, 1914–18.* London: Hamish Hamilton, 1982.

Beman, Lamar. *Intervention in Latin America.* New York: H. W. Wilson, 1928.

Bemis, Samuel F. *The Latin American Policy of the United States: An Historical Interpretation.* New York: W. W. Norton, 1967.

Benavides Hinojosa, Artemio. *El General Bernardo Reyes: Vida de un Liberal Porfirista.* Monterrey: Ediciones Castillo, 1998.

Benjamin, Thomas, and Mark Wasserman, eds. *Provinces of the Revolution.* Albuquerque: University of New Mexico Press, 1990.

Berbusse, Edward J. "Neutrality-Diplomacy of the United States and Mexico, 1910–1911." *Americas* (January 1956): 265–83.

Berdahl, Clarence A. *War Powers of the Executive in the United States.* Urbana: University of Illinois Press, 1921.

Berg, Scott A. *Wilson*. New York: G. P. Putnam Sons, 2013.

Bernstein, Marvin D. *The Mexican Mining Industry, 1890–1950*. Albany: State University of New York, 1964.

Blaisdell, Lowell L. "Henry Lane Wilson and the Overthrow of Madero." *Southwestern Social Science Quarterly* (September 1962): 126–35.

Bourne, Kenneth. British Documents on Foreign Affairs: Reports and Papers from the Foreign Office Confidential Print. Part 1, Series C, Vol. 15. n.p.: University Publications of America, 1987.

Brands, H. W. *The Reckless Decade*. Chicago: University of Chicago Press, 1995.

Breceda, Alfredo. *Mexico Revolucionario, 1913–1917*. Madrid: Tipografia Artistica, 1920.

Brenner, Anita. *The Wind That Swept Mexico: A History of the Mexican Revolution, 1910–1942*. Austin: University of Texas Press, 1976.

Brown, Jonathan C. *Oil and Revolution in Mexico*. Berkeley: University of California Press, 1993.

Bruner, Robert F., and Sean D. Carr. *The Panic of 1907*. Hoboken, NJ: Wiley and Sons, 2007.

Burr, Anna R. B. *The Portrait of a Banker: James Stillman, 1850–1918*. New York: Duffield, 1927.

Burton, David H. *Cecil Spring Rice: A Diplomat's Life*. Rutherford, NJ: Fairleigh Dickinson University Press, 1990.

Calderon, Roberto R. *Mexican Coal Mining Labor in Texas and Coahuila, 1880–1930*. College Station: Texas A&M University Press, 2000.

Calhoun, Frederick S. *Power and Principle: Armed Intervention in Wilsonian Foreign Policy*. Kent, OH: Kent State University Press, 1986.

Callahan, James M. *American Foreign Policy in Mexican Relations*. New York: Macmillan, 1932 and 1967.

Callcott, Wilfrid H. *Liberalism in Mexico, 1857–1929*. Hamden, CT: Archon Books, 1965.

Calvert, Peter. *The Mexican Revolution, 1910–1914: The Diplomacy of Anglo-American Conflict*. Cambridge: Cambridge University Press, 1968.

Carlson, Adolf. *Joint Army-Navy War Planning on the Eve of the First World War: Its Origins and Legacy*. Carlisle, PA: Army War College, 1998.

Carmen, Michael D. *U.S. Customs and Mexico Revolution*. El Paso: Texas Western Press, 1976.

Chamberlain, George A. *Is Mexico Worth Saving*. Indianapolis: Bobbs-Merrill, 1920.

Chamberlin, Eugene K. "The Japanese Scare at Magdalena Bay." *Pacific Historical Review* (November 1955): 345–59.

Chastain, James G. *Thirty Years War*. El Paso: Baptist Publishing House, 1927.

Churchill, Winston L. S. *The World Crisis, 1911–1918*. London, 1931.

Clements, Kendrick A. "Emissary from a Revolution: Luis Cabrera and Woodrow Wilson." *Americas* (January 1979): 353–71.

———. "Woodrow Wilson's Mexican Policy, 1913–15." *Journal of Diplomatic History* (Spring 1980): 113–36.

Clenenden, Clarence C. *Blood on the Border: The United States Army and the Mexican Irregulars*. New York: Macmillan, 1969.

Cline, Howard F. *The United States and Mexico*. Cambridge, MA: Harvard University Press, 1963.

Coatsworth, John. *Growth against Development: The Economic Impact of Railroads in Porfirian Mexico*. DeKalb: Northern Illinois University Press, 1981.
Coerver, Don M., and Linda B. Hall. *Revolution on the Rio Grande: Governor Colquitt of Texas and the Mexican Revolution, 1911–1915*. San Antonio: Trinity Border Research Institute, 1981.
———. *Texas and the Mexican Revolution: A Study in State and National Border Policy, 1910–1920*. San Antonio: Trinity University Press, 1984.
Coker, William S. "The Panama Tolls Controversy: A Different Perspective." *Journal of American History* (December 1968): 555–64.
Contreras Delgado, Camilo, and Moisés Gámez, eds. *Procesos y espacios mineros: Fundición y minería en el centro y noreste de México durante el porfiriato*. Tijuana: El Colegio de la Frontera Norte, 2004.
Cooper, John M. *Walter Hines Page: The Southerner as American, 1855–1918*. Chapel Hill: University of North Carolina Press, 1977.
———. *The Warrior and the Priest: Woodrow Wilson and Theodore Roosevelt*. Cambridge, MA: Harvard University Press, 1983.
———, and Charles E. Neu, eds. *The Wilson Era: Essays in Honor of Arthur S. Link*. Arlington Heights, IL: Harlan Davidson, 1991.
Cox, Patrick L. "'An Enemy Closer to Us Than Any European Power': The Impact of Mexico on Texas Public Opinion before World War I." *Southwestern Historical Quarterly* (July 2001): 40–80.
Cronon, E. David, ed. *The Cabinet Diaries of Josephus Daniels, 1913–1921*. Lincoln: University of Nebraska Press, 1963.
Cumberland, Charles C. "Border Raids in the Lower Rio Grande Valley—1915." *Southwestern Historical Quarterly* (January 1954): 285–311.
———. *Mexican Revolution: The Constitutionalist Years*. Austin: University of Texas, 1972.
———. "Mexican Revolutionary Movements from Texas, 1906–1912." *Southwestern Historical Quarterly* (July 1948): 285–303.
Da Camara, Kathleen. *Laredo on the Rio Grande*. San Antonio: Naylor, 1949.
Daniell, L. E. *Personnel of the Texas State Government with Sketches of Representative Men of Texas*. San Antonio: Maverick Printing House, 1892.
Daniels, Josephus. *The Wilson Era: Years of Peace—1910–1917*. Chapel Hill: University of North Carolina Press, 1944.
Davids, Jules. *American Political and Economic Penetration of Mexico, 1877–1920*. New York: Arno Press, 1976.
De la Garza, Beatriz. *A Law for the Lion: A Tale of Crime and Injustice in the Borderlands*. Austin: University of Texas Press, 2003.
De León, Arnoldo, ed., *War along the Border: The Mexican Revolution and Tejano Communities*. College Station: Texas A&M University Press, 2012.
Dewey, Alicia M. *Pesos and Dollars: Entrepreneurs in Texas-Mexico Borderlands, 1880–1940*. College Station: Texas A&M University Press, 2014.
Diamond, William. *The Economic Thought of Woodrow Wilson*. Baltimore: Johns Hopkins Press, 1943.
Díaz, George T. *Border Contraband: A History of Smuggling across the Rio Grande*. Austin: University of Texas Press, 2015.
Dulles, John W. F. *Yesterday in Mexico: A Chronicle of the Revolution, 1919–1936*. New York: Arno Press, 1952.

Eisenhower, John S. D. *Intervention!: The United States and the Mexican Revolution, 1913–1917*. New York: W. W. Norton, 1993.

Emmerson, Charles. *1913: In Search of the World before the Great War*. New York: Public Affairs, 2014.

Fabela, Isidro, ed. *Documentos historicos de la revolucion mexicana*. 28 vols. Mexico City, 1960–76.

Fenwick, Charles G. *The Neutrality Laws of the United States*. Washington, DC: Carnegie Endowment for International Peace, 1913.

Fehrenbach, T. R. *Fire and Blood*. New York: Bonanza Books, 1985.

———. *Lone Star: A History of Texas and the Texans*. New York: American Legacy Press, 1968.

Fenberg, Steven. *Unprecedented Power: Jesse Jones, Capitalism, and the Common Good*. College Station: Texas A&M University Press, 2011.

Fernández, Roberto D. *Los gobernantes de México*. Sabinas, Coahuila: Editorial Cuahtemoc, 1931.

Ficker, Sandra K., and Paola Riguzzi. *Ferrocarriles y vida economica en Mexico, 1850–1950*. Mexico City: UNAM, 1996.

Fowler, W. B. *British-American Relations, 1917–1918*. Princeton, NJ: Princeton University Press, 1969.

Frantz, Joe B. *Texas*. New York: W. W. Norton, 1976.

Fuller, John O. *The Movement for the Acquisition of All Mexico*. New York: DaCapo Press, 1969.

Garner, Alan. *Porfirio Diaz*. Harlow, UK: Pearson Education, 2001.

Garner, Paul. *British Lions and Mexican Eagles: Business, Politics, and Empire in the Career of Weetman Pearson in Mexico, 1889–1919*. Stanford, CA: Stanford University Press, 2011.

George, Alexander L., and Juliett L. George. *Woodrow Wilson and Colonel House: A Personality Study*. New York: John Day, 1956.

Gilderhus, Mark T. *Diplomacy and Revolution: U.S.-Mexican Relations under Wilson and Carranza*. Tucson: University of Arizona Press, 1977.

———. "Senator Albert B. Fall and the 'Plot against Mexico.'" *New Mexico Historical Review* (October 1973): 299–311.

Glasrud, Bruce A., and Harold J. Weiss, eds. *Tracking the Texas Rangers: The Twentieth Century*. Denton: University of North Texas Press, 2013.

Goldsmith, Raymond W. *The Financial Development of* Mexico. Paris: OECD, 1966.

Gole, Henry G. *The Road to Rainbow: Army Planning for Global War, 1934–1940*. Annapolis, MD: Naval Institute Press, 2003.

Gonzales, Michael J. "Imaging Mexico in 1910: Visions of the Patria in the Centennial Celebration in Mexico City." *Journal of Latin American Studies* (2007).

———. *The Mexican Revolution, 1910–1940*. Albuquerque: University of New Mexico Press, 2002.

Gould, Lewis L. *Progressives and Prohibitionists: Texas Democrats in the Wilson Era*. Austin: University of Texas Press, 1973.

Grayson, Cary T. *Woodrow Wilson: An Intimate Memoir*. New York: Holt, Rinehart, and Winston, 1959.

Gregg, Robert D. *The Influence of Border Troubles on Relations between the United States and Mexico*. Baltimore, 1937.

Grey of Fallodon, Edward Grey, Viscount. *Twenty-Five Years, 1892–1916*. 2 vols. New York: Frederick A. Stokes, 1925.

Grieb, Kenneth J. "El Caso Benton y la Diplomacia de la Revolucion." *Historia Mexicana* (October 1969): 282–301.

———. "The Lind Mission to Mexico." *Caribbean Studies* (January 1968): 25–43.

———. "Reginald del Valle: A California Diplomat's Sojourn in Mexico." *California Historical Society Quarterly* (December 1968): 315–28.

———. "Standard Oil and the Financing of the Mexican Revolution." *California Historical Society Quarterly* (1971): 59–71.

———. *The United States and Huerta*. Lincoln: University of Nebraska Press, 1969.

Guzman, Martin Luis. *Memoirs of Pancho Villa*. Austin: University of Texas Press, 1965.

Gwynn, Stephen, ed. *The Letters and Friendships of Sir Cecil Spring Rice*. 2 vols., Boston: Houghton Mifflin, 1929.

Haley, P. Edward. *Revolution and Intervention: The Diplomacy of Taft and Wilson with Mexico, 1910–1917*. Cambridge, MA: MIT Press, 1970.

Hall, Linda. *Alvaro Obregon, Power and Revolution in Mexico, 1911–1920*. College Station: Texas A&M University Press, 1981.

Hanrahan, Gene Z. *The Bad Yankee: American Entrepreneurs and Finances in Mexico*. 2 vols. Chapel Hill: Documentary Publications, 1985.

———. *The Madero Revolution: The Origins of the Revolution in Texas, Arizona, New Mexico, and California, 1910–11*. London, 1976.

———. *The Murder of Madero and the Role Played by U.S. Ambassador Henry Lane Wilson*. Salisbury: Documentary Publications, 1981.

———, ed. *Documents on the Mexican Revolution*. 4 vols. Salisbury: Documentary Publications, 1981.

Hardy, Osgood. "The Revolution and the Railroad of Mexico." *Pacific Historical Review* (September 1934): 249–69.

Harris, Charles H., and Louis R. Sadler. "The 1911 Reyes Conspiracy: The Texas Side." *Southwestern Historical Quarterly* (April 1980): 325–48.

———. *The Texas Rangers and the Mexican Revolution*. Albuquerque: University of New Mexico Press, 2004.

———. "The 'Underside' of the Mexican Revolution: El Paso, 1912." *Americas* (July 1982): 69–83.

Hart, John M. *Empire and Revolution: The American in Mexico since the Civil War*. Berkeley: University of California Press, 2002.

———. *Revolutionary Mexico: The Coming and Process of the Mexican Revolution*. Berkeley: University of California Press, 1989.

Heckscher, August. *Woodrow Wilson*. New York: Charles Scribner's Sons, 1991.

Heindel, Richard H. *The American Impact on Great Britain, 1898–1914*. New York: Octagon Books, 1968.

Henderson, Peter V. N. *Félix Díaz, the Porfirians, and the Mexican Revolution*. Lincoln: University of Nebraska Press, 1981.

———. *Mexican Exiles in the Borderlands, 1910–1913*. El Paso: Texas Western Press, 1979.

Hendrick, Burton J. *Life and Letters of Walter H. Page*. 2 vols. New York: Doubleday, Page, 1921.

Hendrickson, Kenneth E., Michael L. Collins, and Patrick K. Cox, eds. *Profiles in Power: Twentieth-Century Texans in Washington*. Austin: University of Texas Press, 2004.

Hernández Sáenz, Luz María. "Smuggling for the Revolution: Illegal Traffic of Arms on the Arizona-Sonora Border, 1912–1914." *Journal of the Southwest* (Winter 1986): 357–77.

Herwig, Holger H., and Christon I. Archer. "Global Gambit: A German General Staff Assessment of Mexico Affairs." *Estudios Mexicanos* 1, no. 2 (1985): 303–27.

Hilderbrand, Robert C. *Power and the People: Executive Management of Public Opinion in Foreign Affairs, 1897–1921*. Chapel Hill: University of North Carolina Press, 1881.

Hill, Larry D. *Emissaries to a Revolution: Woodrow Wilson's Executive Agents in Mexico*. Baton Rouge: Louisiana State University Press, 1973.

———. "The Progressive Politician as a Diplomat: The Case of John Lind in Mexico." *Americas* 27 (April 1971): 355–72.

Hodgson, Godfrey. *Woodrow Wilson's Right Hand: The Life of Colonel Edward M. House*. New Haven, CT: Yale University Press, 2006.

Horgan, Paul. *Great River: The Rio Grande*. 2 vols. New York: Rinehart, 1954.

Houston, David F. *Eight Years with Wilson's Cabinet*. New York: Doubleday, Page, 1926.

Hovey, Tamara. *John Reed: Witness to Revolution*. New York: Crown Publishers, 1975.

Huber, Stephen H. *Industry and Underdevelopment: The Industrialization of Mexico, 1890–1940*. Stanford, CA: Stanford University Press, 1989.

Fabela, Isidro. *Historia diplomatica de la revolucion mexicana*. 2 vols., Mexico City, 1958.

Inman, Samuel G. *Intervention in Mexico*. New York: Association Press, 1919.

James, Marquis. *Mr. Garner of Texas*. New York: Bobbs-Merrill, 1939.

Johnson, David N. *Madero In Texas*. San Antonio: Corona Publishing, 2001.

Johnson, William Weber. *Heroic Mexico*. New York: Harcourt Brace, 1984.

Joyce, Davis D. "Senator Albert B. Fall and U.S. Relations with Mexico, 1912–1921." *International Review of History and Political Science* (1973): 53–76.

Justice, Glenn. *Revolution on the Rio Grande*. El Paso: Texas Western Press, 1992.

Kandell, Jonathan. *La Capital: The Biography of Mexico City*. New York: Henry Holt, 1988.

Katz, Friedrich. "Alemania y Francisco Villa." *Historia Mexicana* (September 1962): 88–102.

———. *The Life and Times of Pancho Villa*. Stanford, CA: Stanford University Press, 1998.

———. *The Secret War in Mexico: Europe, the United States, and the Mexican Revolution*. Chicago: University of Chicago Press, 1981.

Kemmerer, Edwin W. *Inflation and Revolution: Mexico's Experience of 1912–1917*. Princeton, NJ: Princeton University Press, 1940.

Kerig, Dorothy P. *Luther T. Ellsworth: U.S. Consul on the Border during the Mexican Revolution*. El Paso: Texas Western Press, 1975.

Klein, Maury. *The Life and Legend of Jay Gould*. Baltimore: Johns Hopkins University Press, 1997.

Knight, Alan. *The Mexican Revolution: Porfirians, Liberals, and Peasants*. 2 vols. Cambridge: Cambridge University Press, 1986.

Krauze, Enrique. *Mexico: Biography of Power*. New York: Harper Collins, 1997.

Lane, Anne W., and Louise H. Wall, eds. *The Letters of Franklin K. Lane*. Boston: Houghton Mifflin, 1922.

Lara Pardo, Luis. *Matchs de Dictadores*, Mexico City, 1942.

Lea, Tom. *The King Ranch*. 2 vols., Boston: Little Brown, 1957.

Levario, Miguel A. *Militarizing the Border: When Mexicans Became the Enemy*. College Station: Texas A&M University Press, 2012.

Licéaga, Luis. *Félix Díaz*. Mexico City: Editorial Jus, 1958.

Lim, Julian. "Chinos and Paisanos: Chinese Mexican Relations in the Borderlands." *Pacific Historical Review* (February 2010): 50–85.

Link, Arthur D. "The Wilson Movement in Texas, 1910–1912." *Southwestern Historical Quarterly* 48 (October 1944): 169–85.

Link, Arthur S. *Wilson: The New Freedom*. Princeton, NJ: Princeton University Press, 1956.

———. *Wilson and the Progressive Era, 1910–1917*. New York: Harper, 1954.

———. *Wilson: Confessions and Crises, 1912–1915*. Princeton, NJ: Princeton University Press, 1964.

———. *Wilson the Diplomatist: A Look at the Major Foreign Policies*. Baltimore: Johns Hopkins Press, 1957.

———. *Wilson: The Struggle for Neutrality, 1914–1915*. Princeton, NJ: Princeton University Press, 1960.

———, ed. *Woodrow Wilson and a Revolutionary World, 1913–1921*. Chapel Hill: University of North Carolina Press, 1982.

Lowe, Alan C. *The Development of War Plan Green: The U.S. Army and Mexico*. Carlisle, PA: Army War College, n.d.

Lyon, Jessie S. "Huerta and Adachi: An Interpretation of Japanese-Mexican Relations, 1913–1914." *Americas* (April 1978): 476–89.

Martinez, Oscar. *Fragments of the Mexican Revolution: Personal Accounts from the Border*. Albuquerque: University of New Mexico Press, 1983.

Massie, Robert K. *Castles of Steel*. New York: Ballantine Books, 2003.

Maurer, Noel. *The Power and the Money: The Mexican Financial System, 1876–1932*. Stanford, CA: Stanford University Press, 2002.

McCaleb, Walter F. *The Public Finances of Mexico*. New York: Harper and Brothers, 1921.

McLynn, Frank. *Villa and Zapata: A History of the Mexican Revolution*. New York: Basic Books, 2000.

Mena Brito, Bernardino. *Carranza sus amigos sus enemigos*. Mexico City: Ediciones Botas, 1935.

Meyer, Lorenzo. *Mexico and the United States in the Oil Controversy, 1917–1942*. Austin: University of Texas Press, 1972.

Meyer, Michael C. *Huerta: A Political Portrait*. Lincoln: University of Nebraska Press, 1972.

———. "The Mexican-German Conspiracy of 1915." *Americas* (July 1966): 76–89.

———. *Mexican Rebel: Pascual Orozco and the Mexican Revolution, 1910–1915*. Lincoln: University of Nebraska Press, 1967.

———. "The Militarization of Mexico, 1913–1914." *Americas* (January 1971): 293–306.

Miller, Thomas L. *The Public Lands of Texas: 1519–1970*. Norman: University of Oklahoma Press, 1972.

Milne, David. *Worldmaking: The Art and Science of American Diplomacy*. New York: Farrar, Straus and Giroux, 2015.

Mount, Houston F. *Oilfield Revolutionary: The Career of Everette Lee DeGolyer.* College Station: Texas A&M University Press, 2014.

Nadelmann, Ethan A. *Cops across Borders: The Internationalization of U.S. Criminal Law Enforcement.* University Park: Pennsylvania State University Press, 1993.

Neu, Charles E. "In Search of Colonel Edward M. House: The Texas Years, 1858–1912." *Southwestern Historical Quarterly* (July 1989): 20–23.

Niemeyer, Vic. "Frustrated Invasion: The Revolutionary Attempt of General Bernardo Reyes from San Antonio in 1911." *Southwestern Historical Quarterly* 67 (October 1963): 213–25.

Notter, Harley. *The Origins of the Foreign Policy of Woodrow Wilson.* Baltimore: Johns Hopkins Press, 1937.

Parkes, Henry B. *A History of Mexico.* Boston: Houghton Mifflin, 1950.

Pletcher, David M. "Mexico Opens the Door to American Capital, 1877–1880." *Americas* (July 1959): 1–14.

———. *Rails, Mines, and Progress: Seven American Promoters in Mexico, 1867–1922.* Ithaca, NY: Cornell University Press, 1958.

Portales, Marco. *Why Pancho Villa and Emiliano Zapata Wore* Cananas. Bryan, TX: Insite Printing, 2010.

Powell, Fred Wilbur. *The Railroads of Mexico.* Boston: Stanford, 1921.

Prucha, Francis P. *The Sword of the Republic: The United States Army on the Frontier, 1793–1846.* Bloomington: Indiana University Press, 1977.

Quezada, J. Gilberto. *Border Boss: Manuel B. Bravo and Zapata County.* College Station: Texas A&M University Press, 1999.

Quirk, Robert E. *An Affair of Honor.* New York: W. W. Norton, 1967.

———. *The Mexican Revolution: 1914–1915.* Bloomington: Indiana University Press, 1960.

Raat, W. Dirk. *Revoltosos: Mexico's Rebels in the United States, 1903–1923.* College Station: Texas A&M University Press, 1981.

———, and William H. Beezley. *Twentieth-Century Mexico.* Lincoln: University of Nebraska Press, 1986.

Rausch, George J. "The Exile and Death of Victoriano Huerta." *Hispanic American Historical Review* (May 1962): 131–51.

Reed, S. G. A. *A History of the Land Grants and Other Aids to the Texas Railroads by the State of Texas.* Kingsport, TN: Kingsport Press, 1942.

———. *A History of the Texas Railroads.* Houston: St. Clair Publishing, 1941.

Richardson, Rupert N. *Colonel Edward M. House: The Texas Years, 1858–1912.* Abilene, TX: Hardin Simmons University Press, 1964.

Richmond, Douglas W. "Confrontation and Reconciliation: Mexicans and Spaniards during the Mexican Revolution, 1910–1920." *Americas* (October 1984): 215–28.

———. *Venustiano Carranza's Nationalist Struggle, 1893–1920.* Lincoln: University of Nebraska Press, 1983.

Rippy, Fred J. *British Investments in Latin America, 1822–1949.* Minneapolis: University of Minnesota Press, 1959.

———. *Latin America in World Politics.* New York: Alfred A. Knopf, 1928.

Rodríguez O., Jaime E., and Kathryn Vincent. *Myths, Misdeeds, and Misunderstandings: The Roots of Conflict in U.S-Mexican Relations.* Wilmington, DE: Scholarly Resources, 1997.

Romero, Robert Chao. *The Chinese in Mexico, 1882–1940.* Tucson: University of Arizona Press, 2010.

Ross, Stanley R. *Francisco I. Madero: Apostle of Mexican Democracy*. New York: Columbia University Press, 1955.

Ruiz, Ramon E. *The Great Rebellion, Mexico 1905–1924*. New York: W. W. Norton, 1980.

Saragoza, Alex M. *The Monterrey Elite and the Mexican State, 1880–1940*. Austin: University of Texas Press, 1988.

Schiff, Warren. "German Military Penetration into Mexico during the Late Díaz Period." *Hispanic American Historical Review* (November 1959): 568–79.

Schmidt, Arthur. *The Social and Economic Effect of the Railroad in Puebla and Veracruz Mexico, 1867–1911*. New York: Garland, 1987.

Schmidt, Hans. *Maverick Marine: General Smedley D. Butler*. Lexington: University Press of Kentucky, 1998.

Schuler, Friedrich E. *Murder and Counterrevolution: The Eyewitness Account of German Ambassador Paul von Hintze, 1912–1914*. Lincoln: University of Nebraska Press, 2015.

———. *Secret Wars and Secret Policies in the Americas*. Albuquerque: University of New Mexico Press, 2010.

Scholes, Walter V., and Marie V. Scholes, "Wilson, Grey, and Huerta." *Pacific Historical Review* (May 1968): 151–58.

Scott, Florence J. *Royal Land Grants North of the Rio Grande, 1777–1821*. Rio Grande City: Texian Press, 1969.

Seymour, Charles. *The Intimate Papers of Colonel House*. 4 vols. New York: Houghton Mifflin, 1926.

Simpson, Lesley B. *Many Mexicos*. Berkeley: University of California Press, 1967.

Smith, Arthur D. Howden. *Mr. House of Texas*. New York: Funk and Wagnalls, 1940.

Smith, Michael M. "Carrancista Propaganda and the Print Media in the United States." *Americas* (October 1995): 155–74.

Smith, Robert S. *The United States and Revolutionary Nationalism in Mexico, 1916–1932*. Chicago: University of Chicago Press, 1972.

Smith, Tony. *The Pattern of Imperialism: The United States, Great Britain, and the Late-Industrializing World since 1815*. Cambridge: Cambridge University Press, 1981.

St. John, Rachel. *Line in the Sand: A History of the Western U.S.-Mexico Border*. Princeton, NJ: Princeton University Press, 2011.

Stephenson, George M. *John Lind of Minnesota*. Minneapolis: Associated Faculty Press, 1935.

Sweetman, Jack. *The Landing at Veracruz: 1914*. Annapolis, MD: Naval Institute Press, 1968.

Teitelbaum, Louis M. *Woodrow Wilson and the Mexican Revolution, 1913–1916*. New York: Exposition Press, 1967.

Thompson, Jerry. *Laredo: A Pictorial History*. Norfolk, VA: Donning, 1986.

Tischendorf, Alfred. *Great Britain and Mexico in the Era of Porfirio Díaz*. Durham, NC: Duke University Press, 1961.

Torre Villar, Ernesto de la., et al. *Historia documental de Mexico*. Mexico City: UNAM, 1964.

Trow, Clifford W. "Woodrow Wilson and the Mexican Interventionist Movement in 1919." *Journal of American History* (January 1971): 46–72.

Truett, Samuel. *Fugitive Landscapes: The Forgotten History of the U.S-Mexico Borderlands*. New Haven, CT: Yale University Press, 2006.

Tuchman, Barbara. *The Zimmerman Telegram*. New York: Viking Press, 1958.

Turlington, Edgar. *Mexico and Her Foreign Creditors*. New York: Columbia University Press, 1930.

Turner, Frederick C. "Anti-Americanism in Mexico, 1910–1913." *Hispanic American Historical Review* (November 1967): 502–18.

Turner, John K. *Barbarous Mexico*. Austin: University of Texas Press, 1984.

Ulloa Ortiz, Berta. "Carranza y el armamento norteamericano." *Historia Mexicana* 17, no. 2 (1967): 253–62.

———. *La revolucion intervenida: Relaciones diplomáticas entre México y Estados Unidos, 1910–1914*. Mexico City, 1976.

Vanderwood, Paul J. *Disorder and Progress: Bandits, Police, and Mexican Development*. Lincoln: University of Nebraska Press, 1981.

Vanderwood, Paul J., and Frank N. Samponaro. *Border Fury: A Picture Postcard Record of Mexico's Revolution and U.S. War Preparedness, 1910–1917*. Albuquerque: University of New Mexico Press, 1988.

Vandiver, Frank E. *Black Jack: The Life and Times of John J. Pershing*. 2 vols. College Station: Texas A&M University Press, 1977.

Vera Estañol, Jorge. *Al margen de la constitución de 1917*. Los Angeles: Wayside Press, 1920.

Viereck, George S. *The Strangest Friendship in History: Woodrow Wilson and Colonel House*. New York: Liveright Publishers, 1932.

Walworth, Arthur. *Woodrow Wilson*. New York: Norton, 1978.

Webb, Walter Prescott. *The Texas Rangers: A Century of Frontier Defense*. Boston: Houghton Mifflin, 1935.

Weinstein, Edwin A. "Woodrow Wilson's Neurological Illness." *Journal of American History* (September 1970): 324–51.

Werstein, Irving. *Land and Liberty: The Mexican Revolution, 1910–1919*. New York: Cowles, 1971.

Wilkinson, J. B. *Laredo and the Rio Grande Frontier*. Austin: Jenkins Publishing, 1975.

Williams, Joyce G. *Colonel House and Sir Edward Grey: A Study in Anglo-American Diplomacy*. Lanham, MD: University Press of America, 1984.

Wilson, Henry Lane. *Diplomatic Episodes in Mexico, Belgium, and Chile*. Port Washington, NY: Kennikat, 1971. Reprint of 1927 edition.

Winkler, John K. *The First Billion: The Stillman and the National City Bank*. New York: Vanguard, 1934.

Winkler, Max. *Investments of United States Capital in Latin America*. Boston: World Peace Foundation, 1929.

Womack, John. *Zapata and the Mexican Revolution*. New York: Vintage Books, 1968.

Young, Elliott. "Red Men, Princess Pocahontas, and George Washington: Harmonizing Race Relations in Laredo at the Turn of the Century." *Western History Association* (Spring 1998): 48–85.

Zelden, Charles I. *Justice Lies in the District: The U.S. District Court, Southern District of Texas, 1902–1960*. College Station: Texas A&M University Press, 1993.

Zoraida Vazquez, Josefina, and Lorenzo Meyer. *The United States and Mexico*. Chicago: University of Chicago Press, 1985.

Dissertations, Reports, and Unpublished Manuscripts

Anderson, William W. "The Nature of the Mexican Revolution as Viewed from the United States, 1910–1917." PhD diss., University of Texas at Austin, 1967.

Balmaseda-Napoles, Francisco A. "Mexico and the United States, 1912–1917: A Study of Selected Writings of Isidro Fabela." PhD diss., Case Western Reserve University, 1974.

Bryan, Anthony T. "Mexican Politics in Transition, 1910–1913: The Role of General Bernardo Reyes." PhD diss., University of Nebraska, 1969.

Coker, William S. "United States–British Diplomacy over Mexico, 1913." PhD diss., University of Oklahoma, 1965.

Cuellar, Carlos E. "The House of Armengol: Doing Business on the Rio Grande Border, 1881–1939." Master's thesis, Texas A&M International University, 1990.

Elliott, Claude. "The Building of the Southern Pacific Railroad through Texas." Thesis, University of Texas at Austin, 1928.

Garza, James A. "On the Edge of a Storm: Laredo and the Mexican Revolution, 1910–1917." Master's thesis, Texas A&M International University, 1996.

Gilderhus, Mark T. "The United States and the Mexican Revolution, 1915–1920: A Study of Policy and Interest." PhD diss., University of Nebraska, 1968.

Godley, Andrew. "Weetman Pearson in Mexico and the Emergence of a British Oil Major, 1901–1919." Henley Business School, University of Reading, 2007.

Holcombe, Harold E. "United States Arms Control and the Mexican Revolution, 1910–1924." PhD diss., University of Alabama, 1968.

Huckaby, George P. "Oscar Branch Colquitt: A Political Biography." PhD diss., University of Texas at Austin, 1946.

Kunimoto, Iimura. "Japan and Mexico, 1886–1917." PhD diss., University of Texas at Austin, 1975.

Lowry, Philip H. "The Mexican Policy of Woodrow Wilson." PhD diss., Yale University, 1949.

Nolan, Mary Lee. "The Refugees: Flight from the Mexican Revolution, 1910–1914." N.d., Oregon State University as seen in Mexico Revolution Collection at Texas A&M.

Robertson, O. Zeller. "Mexico and Non-intervention, 1910–1919: The Policy, the Practice, and the Law." PhD diss., University of California, 1969.

Rocha, Rodolfo. "The Influence of the Mexican Revolution on the Mexico-Texas Border, 1910–1916." PhD diss., Texas Tech University, 1981.

Sandos, James A. "The Mexican Revolution and the United States, 1915–1917." PhD diss., University of California at Berkeley, 1978.

Smith, Cecil B. "Diplomatic Relations between the United States and Mexico concerning Border Disturbances during the Díaz Regime, 1876–1910." Thesis, University of Texas at Austin, 1928.

Tanner, Eric C. "The Texas Border and the Mexican Revolution." Master's thesis, Texas Tech University, 1970.

Index

Other Books in the Elma Dill Russell Spencer Series in the West and Southwest

Aspects of the American West Three Essays
Joe B. Frantz and W. E. Hollon

Trader on the American Frontier: Myth's Victim
Howard R. Lamar and Kristin E. Parsons

America's Frontier Culture: Three Essays
Ray A. Billington and W. T. Jackson

How Did Davy Die?
Dan Kilgore

Grave of John W. Hardin: Three Essays on Grassroots History
C. L. Sonnichsen

Juan Davis Bradburn: A Reappraisal of the Mexican Commander of Anahuac
Margaret S. Henson

Civil War Recollections of James Lemuel Clark
L. D. Clark

Texas Longhorn: Relic of the Past, Asset for the Future
Donald E. Worcester

Red Hole in Time
Muriel Marshall

Travels in Mexico and California
A. B. Clarke

Mexican War Journal and Letters of Ralph K. Kirkham
Robert R. Miller

Regional Studies: The Interplay of Land and People
Glen E. Lich

Immigrant Soldier in the Mexican War
Frederick Zeh and William J. Orr

Where Rivers Meet: Lore from the Colorado Frontier
Muriel Marshall

Massacre on the Lordsburg Road: A Tragedy of the Apache Wars
Marc Simmons

Geronimo's Kids: A Teacher's Lessons on the Apache Reservation
Robert S. Ove and H. Henrietta Stockel

Defiant Peacemaker: Nicholas Trist in the Mexican War
Wallace L. Ohrt

Life among the Texas Indians: The WPA Narratives
David La Vere

Plains Indians
Paul H. Carlson

Conquest of the Karankawas and the Tonkawas, 1821-1859
Kelly F. Himmel

Chiricahua Apache Women and Children: Safekeepers of the Heritage
H. H. Stockel

Hispanics in the Mormon Zion, 1912-1999
Jorge Iber

Comanche Society: Before the Reservation
Gerald Betty

True Women and Westward Expansion
Adrienne Caughfield

Robertsons, the Sutherlands, and the Making of Texas
Anne H. Sutherland

Life Along the Border: A Landmark Tejana Thesis
Jovita González and Maria E. Cotera

Lone Star Pasts: Memory and History in Texas
Gregg Cantrell and Elizabeth H. Turner

Secret War for Texas
Stuart Reid

Colonial Natchitoches: A Creole Community on the Louisiana-Texas Frontier
H. S. Burton and F. Todd Smith

Yeomen, Sharecroppers, and Socialists: Plain Folk Protest in Texas, 1870-1914
Kyle G. Wilkison

More Zeal Than Discretion: The Westward Adventures of Walter P. Lane
Jimmy L. Bryan

On the Move: A Black Family's Western Saga
S. R. Martin

Texas That Might Have Been: Sam Houston's Foes Write to Albert Sidney Johnston
Margaret S. Henson

Tejano Leadership in Mexican and Revolutionary Texas
Jesús F. De la Teja

Texas Left: The Radical Roots of Lone Star Liberalism
David O. Cullen

How Did Davy Die? And Why Do We Care So Much?
James E. Crisp and Dan Kilgore

Drumbeats from Mescalero: Conversations with Apache Elders, Warriors, and Horseholders
H. H. Stockel

Turmoil on the Rio Grande: History of the Mesilla Valley, 1846-1865
William S. Kiser

Texas Right: The Radical Roots of Lone Star Conservatism
David O' Donald Cullen and Kyle G. Wilkison

We Never Retreat: Filibustering Expeditions into Spanish Texas, 1812–1822
Ed Bradley

General Alonso de León's Expeditions into Texas, 1686–1690
Lola Orellana Norris

Comanches and Germans on the Texas Frontier: The Ethnology of Heinrich Berghaus
Daniel J. Gelo and Christopher J. Wickham,
with contributions by Heide Castañeda

CPSIA information can be obtained
at www.ICGtesting.com
Printed in the USA
BVHW080806070219
539571BV00015B/213/P

9 781623 495848